Ordinary Lifestyles

Ordinary Lifestyles

Popular Media, Consumption and Taste

Edited by
David Bell & Joanne Hollows

Open University Press

Open University Press
McGraw-Hill Education
McGraw-Hill House
Shoppenhangers Road
Maidenhead
Berkshire
England
SL6 2QL

email: enquiries@openup.co.uk
world wide web: www.openup.co.uk

and Two Penn Plaza, New York, NY 10121-2289, USA

First published 2005

A catalogue record of this book is available from the British Library

ISBN-10: 0 335 21550 5 (pb) 0 335 21551 3 (hb)
ISBN-13: 978 0335 21550 8 (pb) 978 0335 21551 5 (hb)

Library of Congress Cataloguing-in-Publication Data
CIP data applied for

Typeset by BookEns Ltd, Royston, Herts.
Printed in the UK by Bell & Bain Ltd, Glasgow

Contents

Notes on contributors

David Bell, Cultural Studies, Manchester Metropolitan University, UK.

Frances Bonner, English, Media Studies & Art History, University of Queensland, Australia.

Steven Brown, Psychology, Loughborough University, UK.

Elizabeth Bullen, Literary Studies, Deakin University, Australia.

Fan Carter, Media and Cultural Studies, Kingston University, UK.

Stephen Duncombe, Gallatin School, New York University, USA.

David Dunn, television producer/director and independent scholar, UK.

Johannah Fahey, Education, Monash University, Australia.

Robert Fish, Human Geography, University of Exeter, UK.

Danielle Gallegos, Centre for Social and Community Research, Murdoch University, Australia.

Mark Gibson, Centre for Everyday Life, Murdoch University, Australia.

David B. Goldstein, English, University of Tulsa, USA.

Ruth Holliday, Interdisciplinary Gender Studies, University of Leeds, UK.

Joanne Hollows, Media and Cultural Studies, Nottingham Trent University, UK.

Jane Kenway, Education, Monash University, Australia.

Felicity Newman, Communications and Cultural Studies, Murdoch University, Australia.

Tim O'Sullivan, Faculty of Humanities, De Montfort University, Leicester, UK.

Elspeth Probyn, Gender Studies, University of Sydney, Australia.

Rachel Russell, Sociology, Glasgow Caledonian University, UK.

Lisa Taylor, Media and Cultural Studies, Wolverhampton University, UK.

Melissa Tyler, Business School, Loughborough University, UK.

Gregory Woods, Gay and Lesbian Studies, Nottingham Trent University, UK.

Acknowledgements

We would like to thank all the contributors for their hard work, patience and good humour along the long road to completing this book. Chris Cudmore and Hannah Cooper at the Open University Press have similarly smoothed the process of publication.

David would like to thank his new colleagues at MMU for making him feel at home, and for giving him space to finish putting the book together. More importantly, he would like to thank his former colleagues and students in Cultural Studies at Staffordshire University, especially those who took part in his module 'Writing Lifestyles', for endless chats about *What Not to Wear* and *Heat* magazine. That the department has been forced to close due to falling student numbers truly breaks his heart. Finally, thanks as ever to Ruth, Mark, Daisy and Jon, and to Joanne for being a perfect co-editor.

Joanne would like to thank colleagues at Nottingham Trent University. In particular she'd like to thank Steve and Ben for sharing ideas in team teaching that helped inform this book, and Roger and Dave for their roles in giving me some temporary respite from admin that made the completion of this book possible. As usual, thanks to Mark for maintaining the 'ordinary' bits of life while I was at the computer, and to David for being an equally perfect co-editor!

1 Making sense of ordinary lifestyles

David Bell and Joanne Hollows

The aim of this collection is to critically interrogate the role and function of lifestyle media in the formation of contemporary taste cultures and everyday practices. Lifestyle media's recent rapid expansion on television schedules and their dominance at the top of publishing's bestseller lists has not been matched by sustained academic scrutiny, perhaps, as Frances Bonner (2003) recently argued, because they are seen as just too ordinary. One of the key aims of this book is to take lifestyle media seriously, and to show that watching makeover television or cooking from a celebrity chef's book are significant social and cultural practices, through which we work on our ideas about taste, status and identity. In opening up the complex processes which shape taste formations and forge individual and collective identities in consumer culture, lifestyle media demand our serious attention, as well as our viewing, reading and listening pleasure.

In making sense of lifestyle media and the cultural importance of the idea of lifestyle, the chapters in this book address a series of key issues. First, the contributors consider continuities and discontinuities in terms of conceptions of and about the role of lifestyle; areas of life subject to lifestylization; media formats employed; and audiences addressed. Second, the book explores the relationship between abstract theorizing about lifestyle in relation, for example, to debates about post-Fordism and postmodernity, and the analysis of specific ways in which ideas about lifestyle have been mediated at particular moments and in particular places. Third, the chapters examine the impact of the growth of the 'discourse of lifestyle' on media production, formats, genres and markets. Fourth, *Ordinary Lifestyles* examines the extent to which lifestyle media produce, reproduce, reformulate or dissolve social and cultural identities and identifications, and the relations between them. Fifth, chapters analyse the role of cultural intermediaries in the production and reproduction of taste cultures. Finally, the book explores the ways in which ideas of the 'ordinary' and of 'ordinary people' permeate not only lifestyle media, but also the ways in which people understand their own lived practices.

The contributors to this volume primarily concentrate on questions about lifestyle and lifestyle media in the UK, USA and Australia. While we think it is crucial to understand how questions of lifestyle are articulated within distinctive national formations, we also believe that the debates this book raises will resonate in other national contexts. Likewise, while most contributors concentrate on developments from the 1980s onwards, some of the chapters also place these changes within a wider history of lifestyle media and lifestylization.

In this opening chapter, we seek to offer an introduction to how the concept of lifestyle has been used in social and cultural theory, as these ideas form a framework that the later chapters draw on. We also seek to map some of the main characteristics of lifestyle media, examining their significance for media institutions, identifying key formats, and analysing how they intersect with wider consumer cultures and everyday practices.

Making sense of lifestyle

The term lifestyle has not only become part of contemporary common sense but is also central to contemporary consumer culture. The concept is employed in different ways across a range of academic and professional discourses. For example, in politics, marketing and advertising, people are often organized into particular lifestyle categories, while health professionals may associate lifestyles with specific forms of 'healthy' or 'risky' behaviours such as low-fat or high-fat eating (Jagose 2003). Indeed, some of the chapters that follow examine the cultural significance of these constructions of lifestyle categories (see for example Woods, this volume; Brown, this volume). However, these wider conceptions of lifestyle often presume that lifestyles, and the consumer goods, services and practices through which they are constructed, are freely chosen by individuals. The idea of freedom of choice has been questioned by sociologists who have focused on the 'forces, mechanisms and institutional arrangements' that limit our ability to choose (Warde and Martens 1998: 129). In fact, the opposition between freedom and constraint structures many debates about the significance of lifestyle in sociology and cultural studies.

While we would argue that the importance of lifestyle to the way in which identities are mediated, produced and lived has a longer history stretching back towards the early twentieth century at least (see Bell and Hollows forthcoming), the *theoretical* significance of lifestyle as a sociological or cultural concept is frequently related to social, economic and cultural changes that are associated with the 1960s and/or 1970s onwards. These are usually explained in terms of a shift from modernity to postmodernity (or late capitalism) and/or a shift from Fordist to post-Fordist methods of production, both of which are associated with distinctive consumer cultures. At the heart of these debates is a concern with whether or not these transformations have eroded traditional social structures which form the basis for identity and replaced them with an imperative to choose how we construct our identities through lifestyle practices.

Fordism is commonly understood as a new way of organizing production that emerged in the early twentieth century related to a wider set of social, cultural, political and economic changes. Fordism is associated with the principles of Taylorism that sought to rationalize the production process to increase efficiency and productivity to enable mass production. However, in order to sustain mass production and stabilize the economic basis of Fordism, there was also a need for mass consumption. Therefore, after a crisis caused by overproduction and industrial action in the late 1920s and the 1930s, Fordism was stabilized through a relative increase in workers' wages and state intervention (which co-ordinated welfare provision). This enabled the conditions for mass consumption. Fordist consumer culture was organized around the family as the key unit of consumption (and thereby positioned women's economic role around a responsibility for consumption). The principle of rationality that under-pinned production was also applied to design, distribution, retailing and consumption (Lee 1993; Slater 1997; Winship 2000). While Henry Ford's famous claim that 'You can have any colour as long as it's black' certainly overemphasizes the degree of standardization of consumer goods in this period, Fordism has nonetheless been predominantly characterized in terms of mass consumption in which middle-class modes of consumption operated as a norm. Although such a portrait undoubtedly oversimplifies the case (see Bell and Hollows forthcoming), the dominant view of Fordism is one of an age where the importance of using consumer goods to construct lifestyles began to be accentuated, but where there was little scope for lifestyle *differentiation* through consumption.

By the early 1970s, the infrastructural costs and inflexibility of mass production methods appeared to signal the end for Fordism. Further-more, this inflexibility was a growing problem in the face of 'increasingly saturated consumer markets and of ever faster turnover of fashions, tastes, trends (itself the result of decades of Fordist mass-marketing)' (Slater 1997: 189). The shift to post-Fordism is understood in terms of a change from mass production, mass markets and mass consumption to the pursuit of niche markets enabled in part by the flexibility afforded by new manufacturing technologies which afford 'just-in-time' production that can better respond to the accelerating pace of shifts in fashion (Lee 1993; Lury 1995; Slater 1997).

The pursuit of niche markets means that goods are no longer produced for an undifferentiated mass, but instead aimed at particular lifestyle groupings. In identifying goods with specific lifestyles, post-Fordist consumer culture heightens the importance of 'market research, packaging and promotion' (Hebdige 1990: 89). The proliferation of goods is also characterized by 'aesthetic obsolescence', where an increasing number of commodities are distinguished only by aesthetic differences, and where things are increasingly disposed of because they are 'out of fashion' rather than being used up, worn out or broken (Lee 1993: 136). These changes in consumer culture accentuated the importance of continually making choices. This involved revising 'what in the 1960s and 1970s were solid market blocs – the working class, youth, the housewife, etc ... *Campaign* makes the point that: "Lifestyle advertising is about differentiating oneself from the Joneses", not as in previous decades, keeping up with them' (Mort 1988: 208–9). For some critics, the increased emphasis on making a choice between consumer goods, which gives us freedom to construct lifestyles, marks the end of traditional social structures and divisions associated with production, leaving us free to play with identity through consumption. For such critics, lifestyle is no longer associated with traditional groupings such as class and gender, but rather 'connotes individuality, self-expression and a stylistic self-consciousness' (Featherstone 1991a: 83)

Many of the features associated with the rise of post-Fordist consumer culture are also linked to a wider set of social and cultural transformations associated with the shift to postmodernity (see Harvey 1989). There is considerable debate and confusion surrounding this term, although there is broader agreement that there was a significant shift in our experience of the world from the 1960s onwards. Many critics share a concern with an alleged breakdown of the social hierarchies and structures that produced and sustained modern life. For some this leads to a 'death of the social' (and, in the process, the death of political life): a feeling of belonging to society, and living within structured social relations, is replaced by a world in which, it is claimed, experience is no longer collective but individualized. This destabilizes traditional hierarchies so, for example, distinctions between high and low cultures become blurred (see Connor 1989). A concurrent process is identified by Baudrillard (Poster 1988), in which consumption also becomes individualized as we come to inhabit a world in which consumer goods no longer have any use value and instead only have sign value. From such a perspective, we are encouraged to play with these signs to construct our identity in a world that has lost any 'real' meaning. The stylization of goods as signs contributes to a wider process in which there is what Featherstone (1991a) calls an 'aestheticization of everyday life'. These changes can be seen to signal a change in consumer culture:

> Rather than unreflexively adopting a lifestyle, through tradition or habit, the new heroes of consumer culture make lifestyle a life project and display their individuality and sense of style in the particularity of the assemblage of goods, clothes, practices, experiences, appearance and bodily dispositions they design together into a lifestyle.
>
> (Featherstone 1991a: 86)

Like some of the changes associated with post-Fordism, Featherstone's discussion of the way in which theories of postmodernity characterize consumer culture once again accentuates the idea that individuals have increasing freedom to construct lifestyles through stylized consumer goods, and are no longer constrained by traditional social hierarchies (while implicitly reinscribing hierarchies though his gendering of the 'heroic' consumer). Chaney (2001) calls these new consumers 'postmodern standalone subjects' – precisely the subjects of lifestyle.

Whether these changes are epochal shifts associated with the move from modernity to postmodernity is open to debate. For some critics, contemporary experience is marked by an intensification as much as by a transformation of modernity. Giddens (1991), for example, prefers to call our current age 'late modernity'. Setting aside this debate over terms, however, Giddens also concurs that there have been significant shifts in our experiences of everyday life, and of identity. Identity has become, he suggests, a 'project of the self': something we are all knowingly engaged in, endlessly working to refine our sense of who we are. Lifestyle can be seen as a particularly important aid in this work, especially given its flexible accommodation of not just consumer products but also products and practices of self-knowledge and self-improvement, such as therapy (though we should note that these too are increasingly commodified, see Furedi 2003). As Giddens reinforces, lifestyle implies choice, making it part of the broader 'detraditionalization' of life today: in place of 'handed down', fixed identity positions based on tradition, lifestyle places emphasis on choice, change and reflexivity. 'The more post-traditional the settings in which an individual moves', Giddens (1991: 81) adds, 'the more lifestyle concerns the very core of self-identity, its making and remaking.'

While few critics dispute the importance of the idea that contemporary consumer culture encourages us to play with lifestyle, there is considerable debate about whether this indicates the end of traditional social divisions such as class, or rather a transformation in class relations

(Featherstone 1991a). For example, Skeggs (2004: 49) argues that the individualized pursuit of lifestyle choices described by theorists such as Giddens simply 'describes what exists for a privileged few and then suggests that this is a perspective that applies to many others'. Rather than analysing contemporary consumer culture, she argues, these critics reproduce the obligation to pursue individuality constructed in 'consumer market rhetoric' (p. 57). Therefore, we need to consider how an investment in lifestyle, far from being about individual choice, may still be closely related to class relations and positions.

Lifestyle, class and distinction

The key influence on many critics who argue that lifestyle is still closely related to class differences is the French sociologist Pierre Bourdieu, who conducted extensive research into the tastes and preferences of different social groups in France in the 1960s, most famously in his book *Distinction: A Social Critique of the Judgement of Taste* (Bourdieu 1984). While our ability to play with lifestyle is clearly related to the amount of economic capital we have at our disposal, for Bourdieu the distinctive ways in which classes consume cannot simply be explained by economic inequalities. He argues that our class position is not just shaped by the amount of economic capital we possess, but also by the amount of cultural capital. Cultural capital refers to the dispositions we bring to our consumption practices, demonstrated, for example, by the goods we choose to consume. Those who are rich in cultural capital not only legitimate their own dispositions as *the* legitimate dispositions (they have the power to do so because they possess symbolic capital), but also pass on these cultural resources to their children. Our reserves of cultural capital are largely inherited as through our upbringing in our families we learn to discriminate, classify and make sense of the world through what Bourdieu calls the habitus, a 'system of dispositions' through which we distinguish between what is, and isn't, our kind of thing. Cultural capital is also legitimated through the education system: qualifications are the reward for demonstrating the 'right' kind of cultural dispositions.

If we take the example of food consumption, we can see how economic capital and cultural capital are articulated in the food practices of different classes. For example, Bourdieu argues that the tastes and dispositions of the working class (in 1960s France) were shaped by their position as manual labour and by the scarcity of their economic resources. Their food practices can be seen as a cultural response to this: the working class in his study show a preference for cheap cuts of meat (due to their lack of economic capital) and substantial portions (to sustain manual labour) but they also celebrate the importance of putting food on the table through generous and abundant quantities of food eaten in an informal and convivial atmosphere. In contrast, the bourgeoisie, who are rich in both economic and cultural capital, have radically different dispositions towards food. As Miller (1994: 150) explains: 'a person who has been brought up with the abstractions of education and capital, and who is certain of obtaining daily necessities, cultivates a distance from these needs, and affects a taste based in the respect and desire for the abstract, distanced and formal'. Therefore, the bourgeoisie forsake the immediate satisfactions of eating, preferring food categorized as 'light' and 'refined'. The style and presentation of food is privileged, alongside a restrained and formal style of eating. While both working-class and bourgeois food practices demonstrate a specific cultural logic, it is bourgeois food tastes that are seen as legitimate and that can therefore generate 'a profit in distinction'. While the working class may see bourgeois food practices as sterile and pretentious, they lack the symbolic capital to displace the legitimacy of bourgeois taste. In Bourdieu's theory, consumption is a site of class struggle, where those classes that can, pursue strategies for gaining distinction and, in the process, 'do' class dominance. Those unable to compete find themselves subject to symbolic violence by being positioned as vulgar or common, and thus illegitimate in their tastes.

Not only does Bourdieu's work suggest that 'some are more equal than others' in their freedom to make individualized lifestyle choices (Dittmar 1992), it also shows how the importance of the idea of lifestyle in post-Fordist consumer culture coincides with the rise of new middle-classes, who are perfectly positioned to capitalize on the new emphasis on lifestyle. Based in new service industries and white-collar jobs that have grown from the 1960s onwards, these new middle-classes transformed the social space of class relations. However, at the same time, these new classes 'take their lifestyles more seriously than their careers' (Binkley 2004: 72). The new bourgeoisie (new middle-class) are 'the new taste-makers', who reject the sobriety and abstinence of the old bourgeoisie 'in favour of a hedonistic morality of consumption, based on credit, spending and enjoyment', where people are judged by 'their capacity for consumption, their "standard of living", their lifestyle as much as their capacity for production' (Bourdieu 1984: 310). The new petit bourgeoisie, who tend to work at lower levels of the same industries, also invest in consumption and 'the art of living', and have an approach to life based on 'a morality of pleasure as duty' (pp. 366–7) which values the 'amusing, refined, stylish, artistic [and] imaginative' (p. 359). Less secure in their class position than the new bourgeoisie, the new petit bourgeoisie's consumption is also characterized by a sense of anxiety: they are never sure that they have got things quite right, so they consciously seek to educate themselves in the art of lifestyle (Ashley et al. 2004). In a post-Fordist economy which demands we make choices between a plethora of consumer goods, 'knowledge becomes crucial: knowledge of new goods, their social and cultural value, and how to use them appropriately' (Skeggs 2004: 136).

From such a perspective, the new petit bourgeoisie are not only the 'natural' audience for an expanding lifestyle media but also, as many of the chapters that follow make clear, lifestyle media and manuals frequently legitimate the tastes of the new middle-classes (see, for example, Holliday, this volume; Taylor, this volume). Indeed, Bourdieu characterizes sections of these new middle-classes as 'cultural inter-mediaries' because their occupational positions give them 'a certain amount of cultural authority as shapers of taste and inculcators of new consumerist dispositions' (Nixon and Du Gay 2002: 497). Workers in media and cultural production, including the consumer-oriented advertising, PR and promotion industries, cultural intermediaries act as 'interpreters', disseminating knowledge about taste and status to particular target markets or lifestyle groups. From such a perspective, the expansion of lifestyle media is not about the rise of lifestyle as a move beyond class, but rather an emphasis on lifestyle as an attempt to gain authority by new middle-classes whose cultural capital affords them considerable 'riches' in this area of life.

Bourdieu's work has proved an invaluable way of understanding how certain classes use lifestyle to distinguish themselves and make themselves 'out of the ordinary'. However, Alan Warde's (1997) research on food tastes in the UK questions whether class differences are understood in terms of distinction or might be better seen as 'undistinguished difference'. Furthermore, Warde argues that the emphasis on the use of symbolic goods in the construction of lifestyle ignores 'the mundane, routine, inconspicuous elements of consumption practice', things that are 'largely impervious to mechanisms like status-enhancement or the pursuit of fashion'. (Warde 2002: 19). Indeed, Daniel Miller's (1998) ethnographic research suggests that everyday shopping practices are far more about demonstrating care and love for others than the hedonistic pursuit of distinguished identities. Further-more, taking a 'heroic' disposition towards everyday life is problematic for women, as they have traditionally been associated with a conception of 'everyday life' as 'mundane' and 'non-heroic' (Felski 2000; Probyn, this volume).

The literature on lifestyle, whether concentrating on individuals or classes seeking distinction or status through consumption, tends to underplay the value of 'being ordinary' in many people's everyday practices (see Taylor, this volume). Savage et al.'s (2001: 889) research in the UK, for example, found that most of their respondents 'chose to play down any cultural distinction they may be able to make claim to in order to play up their ordinariness'. Rather than seeing ordinariness as 'beyond' class, this research demonstrates that the appeal of 'being ordinary' lies in people's attempts to resist being classified and identified as a specific class. As we go on to discuss in the next sections, ordinariness is not simply a way in which people understand their own lifestyles and identities, but is also a central feature of the forms and concerns of lifestyle media.

Lifestyling media and mediating lifestyle

A key focus of *Ordinary Lifestyles* is the role of lifestyle media in producing, circulating and promoting ideas about taste and lifestyle. But arriving at an adequately succinct yet all-encompassing definition of what constitutes 'lifestyle media' is in itself a tricky task. First, it demands an accommodation of the different media *products* that are centred on ideas of taste and lifestyle. Such a list includes, not exhaustively, radio and television programmes, plus spin-off videos and DVDs; print media (books, magazines, newspaper columns and supplements, again including spin-offs); web-based media, both author-ized and unofficial (see Goldstein, this volume); advertising and promotional materials (print, broadcast and web); live performance and personal appearance (PA), and so on – not to mention the dense intertextuality and extra-textuality between these platforms, or the 'micro-media' produced to circulate 'subcultural capital' (Thornton 1995; Duncombe, this volume).

Next we need to factor in the focus of this media content: the *topics* of lifestyle media. Again without claiming exhaustivity, these include cookery and other food and drink topics; fashion, style and grooming; home improvement, including DIY, gardening, interiors and property development; self-improvement (bodily, financially, spiritually, and so on); travel; shopping and consumer issues – including cultural consumption. At the edges of this attempt at hazy definition lurk grey areas and questions, about where lifestyle media end, or blend into other genres and formats (such as reality television, 'celebrity media', infommercial, etc.). In fact, one of the key – and most remarked upon – features of lifestyle media is its intense proliferation and hybridization, as well as increasing genre bending and blending. While some forms have been apparently stable for a long time – women's magazines or cookbooks, for example – more careful historical reading shows a

volume) once bemoaned, the over-democratization of taste as a result of the penetration of lifestyle media into all our lives results in a lifestyled sameness, radically devaluing the cultural capital that has been so carefully cultivated. Of course, this isn't the whole story. Lifestyle media are differentiated in terms of taste and class, as well as in terms of format, genre and content. As media producers understand audiences to be composed of fractions distinguished by a host of socio-economic variables, so it is inevitable that programming and publishing will seek to address particular audience groups. In one sense this sets up a battle between media outputs, with particular magazines, shows or websites gaining allegience precisely by distancing themselves and their imagined audience from their competitors, achieved through the deployment of increasingly differentiated variations of cultural capital. So *Elle Deco* isn't really noting the death of taste or style, otherwise that would also mean the death of *Elle Deco*. It is performing a more subtle act of distance and distinction: now more and more people know the rules of 'good taste', those rules are declared 'bland', and something new is picked out (or something old is refashioned) in order to separate *Elle Deco* and its readers from the blandscapes of mass-consumed taste (even mass-consumed 'good taste'). This in part accounts for the restless hybridizing of lifestyle media: the search for novelty extends to media products about taste, as more and more aspects of our lives and our selves are rendered 'lifestyle-able'. Moreover, the ways in which lifestyle can be mediated also shifts, similarly reflecting status-based differentiations in media output.

Furthermore, as David Giles (2002) shows, the democratization of taste through lifestyle television is often a far from complete process, especially in terms of how shows reinforce a distinction between what Palmer (2004: 184) calls the seemingly 'effortless middle-class taste' of presenter-experts and the rather more fragile or precarious class performances by 'ordinary people' participating in programmes. While similar processes are less discernible in print media, where the address is more one-way (except in letters pages), we can nonetheless argue that the central role of the 'expert' and the discourse of expertise is at the heart of lifestyle media, even if pretence is made to render the presenter a non-expert, even an incompetent: the UK show *TV Dinners*, for example, depicted ex-chef Hugh Fearnley-Whittingstall in a subservient role to the 'ordinary person' hosting a dinner party, and Hugh often performed *faux-naïveté* or incompetence in their kitchen, rather than flexing his considerable culinary cultural capital (see also Smith and Wilson 2004 on television chefs' attempts to invisibilize 'the discourse of credentialed professionalism' through the performance of 'amateurism', and Bruns-don 2004 on changing modalities of presenting and 'expertise' in British lifestyle television).

While other experts practise a more bullish address to their 'victims' – including, on British television screens, *What Not to Wear*'s Trinny Woodall and Susannah Constantine and *You Are What You Eat*'s Gillian McKeith – the expert plays a crucial role in both distinction and democratization. After all, even the narrative of shows like *What Not to Wear* and *You Are What You Eat* is *successful* personal transformation, highlighting precisely that taste *can* be acquired. This reminds viewers that even experts have to work at taste. So, while Giles (2002: 626) is right to argue that 'ordinary' participants in lifestyle television shows 'need to work up entitlement to participate on an equal footing to the host', and that such entitlement is 'related to notions of aesthetic taste', which he suggests means disempowerment for some participants, the successful 'reveal' – the hallmark of contemporary lifestyle television – reminds us that anyone can be a kind-of expert. Expertise is thus performed and simultaneously undermined through the very act of performance.

Mobile schedules and format fatigue

One of the surprise successes of factual programming on terrestrial British television at the time this book was being assembled was *Tribe*, a series in which 'explorer and ex-Marine' Bruce Parry visited and lived with a succession of tribal peoples, participating in their everyday lives and their rituals. While it is stretching the definition a little to suggest that *Tribe* is a lifestyle television programme in the commonly used sense of the term (although some critics accused Parry of lifestyling anthropology), it nevertheless points towards the subtle shifts of topic, tone and emphasis within the genre as a whole. *Tribe* follows on from the success of other 'anthropological lifestyle shows' such as the BBC's *Ray Mears' Bushcraft*, which focused on 'bush craft' traditions as practised by different peoples past and present (and, intertextually, Parry's own breakthrough televisual role in the children's eco-Tour-Ed. reality television series *Serious Jungle*, *Serious Desert* and *Serious Arctic*). Clearly, lifestyle media is not a static thing, but one that changes over time (and the same is true, of course, of other branches of lifestyle media, though these have been less commented on). As the Midlands Television Group's 8–9 Slot project has mapped, the development of lifestyle (and other 'factual entertainment') programming on British terrestrial television can be understood as the product of changes both within the broadcast industry and within British society (Brunsdon et al. 2001). Included in their analysis is the 'daytime-ization' of prime time scheduling, with the migration of formats, including lifestyle programming, from day to night (see also Medhurst 1999; Moseley 2000). This daytime-ization also marked the disappearance from terrestrial schedules of 'serious' documentary and current affairs, as well as quizzes, light entertainment shows and sitcoms. The coming of non-terrestrial television, patterns of home ownership, changing leisure practices, and a host of other factors are convincingly offered by the group's researchers in order to explain how our television screens got filled up with cooking, wallpapering, botox, water features, and colonic irrigation. That is what makes the BBC's *Tribe* closer to lifestyle television than to other instances of anthropological documentary: the shape of the narrative, the style of filming, the experiential, confessional storying. It might be that this kind of 'Tour-Ed.' makeover also confirms Brunsdon's (2001) claim that lifestyle television offers more inclusive and diverse images and ideas about ordinary people and everyday life than a great deal of media output. These shows teach us openness, and suggest the transformative potential of experience; even if we cannot participate in the precise experiences shown – this is not didactic television in any literal sense – we can nonetheless learn to approach our own life experiences, however mundane, with that same sense of willingness to try new things, or what Moseley (2001: 39) calls the 'discourse of accessibility and achievability' at the heart of much contemporary lifestyle media.

Of course, not everyone has such an upbeat position on the lifestyling of the media or of society. Sidestepping the singularly unproductive 'dumbing down' debate, critics have bemoaned the saturation of schedules and bestseller lists with makeover shows and books-of-the-series, bemoaned the serial reproduction of limited formats (see, for example, Anthony 2004) and the cult of celebrity, bemoaned the trivial pursuit of lifestylization as a neoliberal privatization of the public sphere and marketization of citizenship (see Brunsdon et al. 2001). But the task of academics must be to take these issues, and these criticisms, seriously; to refuse to dismiss lifestyle media as trivial, to seek to understand the cultural work of lifestylization, to provide analyses that enable us to contextualize lifestyle media, in all their diversity, to see commonalities and differences. This does not, as Charlotte Brunsdon (2003) also insists, mean a relativistic take that refuses to make evaluative judgements. But it does mean interrogating those judgements at the same time. So, while Brunsdon is right to conclude that 'lifestyle programmes are replete with implicit and explicit aesthetic judgement' (2003: 19), we must also acknowledge, paraphrasing Bourdieu (1984), that lifestyle media classify, but they classify the classifier.

Making lifestyles ordinary

> Television, these days, is said to be more ordinary than it used to
> be.
>
> (Taylor 2002: 479)

At the heart of many discussions of lifestyle media is the notion of ordinariness. This seemingly commonsensical term is revealed to be complexly articulated in lifestyle (and other related) media, and is seen to be manifest in a number of ways. These include, first, the *voice* of lifestyle media, both in terms of the mode of address to the audience – chatting to rather than talking at, or what Frances Bonner (2003: 50) refers to as 'conversationalization' – and in terms of the diversity of regional accents, uses of slang, ways of talking and writing that de-emphasize authority and play on chattiness and matiness, perhaps best epitomized in the UK by television chef Jamie Oliver's much maligned 'mockney' (Hollows 2003b). Second, ordinariness is conferred, as already noted, through a transformation in the status of the expert and of expertise. Lisa Taylor (2002) borrows Bauman's (1987) notion of the shifting role of intellectuals from legislators to interpreters in order to usefully flesh this out: lifestyle experts function like personal shoppers rather than schoolteachers, advising us on consumer choices – *interpreting* the lifestyle landscape for us rather than dictating how to live (even if, for example in *What Not to Wear* or *You Are What You Eat*, the tone is seen to be somewhat dictatorial). Voice and manner are important here, too, in making expertise ordinary, which also means making it accessible and inclusive.

Third, ordinari-ization means that more ordinary people are on television (Moseley 2000) and in other lifestyle media – as both 'ordinari-ization' experts and as participants of the assorted makeovers on offer – and that simultaneously, people in the media are seen to be more ordinary. For example, *Heat* magazine also includes heavy use of paparazzi shots of celebs doing ordinary things, like shopping, arguing, getting drunk, falling in and out of love, showing, as Felski (2000) notes, that everyone has an everyday life, made up of repetition, home and habit. Television shows like *Celebrity Big Brother* reveal that celebrities also fart and bicker, while *Pop Idol* shows the achievability (and arbitrariness) of celebrity. So ordinari-ization, Taylor continues:

> describes how lifestyle programmes fasten onto the sense that
> we are all, insofar as we connect to the backdrop of everyday life,
> ordinary; we are all somehow anchored to routine, to a place
> called home and to the mundanity of everyday habit.
>
> (Taylor 2002: 482)

Frances Bonner (2003) notes that watching television, including lifestyle television, is itself profoundly ordinary, making consumption of lifestyle media part and parcel of its ordinari-ization (even 'watercooler TV' is ordinari-ized in this way). The threading of media into everyday life, through practices of watching, listening or reading, but also through extratextual practices such as chatting, have of course been discussed in terms of genre like soap opera (Geraghty 1991). In the sense that lifestyle television draws on the conventions of the docu-soap, we can make a connection through to the ways in which lifestyle media texts assume an everydayness, making their consumption, as well as their focus, firmly in what Bonner (2003: 45) names the realm of the 'domestic mundane'. The 'soapification' of lifestyle is reflected in the narrative arcs of lifestyle television, with the cliffhanger of the 'reveal' and the focus on emotional response to the makeover, while 'extratextual soapification' can be found both in media coverage of the lives and lifestyles of lifestyle 'experts' and in 'true life exposés' of participants' experiences of being lifestyled (see, for example, Robinson 2003).

While coming to terms with the complexity of lifestyle media – its forms, formats and histories, its place in the economies of the media, its consumption and its cultural significance – is beyond the scope of a single volume, this book aims to build on existing research in order to advance debates and set agendas for future study. As this opening chapter has made clear, making sense of lifestyle media demands an interdisciplinary approach in order to understand how lifestyle is both mediated and incorporated into our everyday lives.

Reading ordinary lifestyles

Part I, **Media form and industry**, offers ways of contextualizing lifestyle media in terms of wider debates about media industries, forms and audiences. Tim O'Sullivan's chapter not only considers how television mediates ideas about lifestyle, but also highlights the role of television as *part of* our lifestyles. O'Sullivan shares common concerns with Frances Bonner, and both their chapters demonstrate how lifestyle media have *a history* and are not simply a contemporary phenomenon. Bonner's chapter focuses on lifestyle television shows. By examining how different formats work in specific national contexts, she shows the importance of maintaining a sense of genre and subgenre specificity. Bonner also shares with David Goldstein an emphasis on the economic dimensions of lifestyle media. Goldstein demonstrates how Martha Stewart operates as an entertainment package across different media forms. He analyses the changing star image of Martha Stewart and how she invites us to 'work' at lifestyle in specific ways.

In Part II, **Home front**, the contributors examine how the home is often a privileged site in lifestyle media. Ruth Holliday's chapter focuses on television home improvement programmes. Linking the shows to a wider history of 'rational recreation', she analyses how they invite us to 'improve' ourselves as well as our homes and, in the process, legitimate particular classed and gendered aesthetics. The importance of class distinctions in the ways lifestyles are mediated is also a feature of Mark Gibson and Felicity Newman's discussion of food in Australia. Their chapter concentrates on Australian television cookery shows and on the ways in which class and lifestyle are articulated within ideas of nation. The final chapter in this section, by Danielle Gallegos, shares Newman and Gibson's interest in the relationship between food, nation and lifestyle, and examines changing constructions of Australian food and multiculturalism from the 1930s to the present.

The chapters in Part III, **The great outdoors**, take us out of the house or away from home. Through an analysis of British popular gardening media, Lisa Taylor depicts a series of class wars, or battles over class-inflected taste and aesthetics, played out through gardening shows and columns. David Dunn moves further afield, exploring British holiday television programmes. He notes their increasing co-option into the lifestyle and reality formats, showing how these programmes construct the holiday as an escape from 'ordinary life'. Gregory Woods' chapter centres on lesbian and gay tourism, especially on how it is represented in promotional brochures which construct a niche market by effectively lifestyling and also ordinari-izing homosexuality. Robert Fish explores the rural as a lifestyled space. Like Taylor in the garden, Fish shows how the countryside – as it is mediated through 'style' magazines and television drama – becomes a battleground around issues of class and taste.

Part IV focuses on **Learning lifesyles** – specifically on how young people have become increasingly recruited into taste and lifestyle formations. The chapters focus on the construction of 'youth' and the possibilities and problems of enrolling young people into the project of lifestyle. Carter tracks how one UK girls' magazine, *Sugar*, created a market position through the idea of 'learning femininity' in readiness for becoming a woman: teen magazines in the 1990s became saturated by lifestyle talk, with their traditional concerns made over as elements of lifestyle, often mediated by commodities. Tyler and Russell's chapter focuses on a chain of UK shops, Girl Heaven, which also mediate youthful femininity through consumption. Girl Heaven provide a 'retail environment' – a place to learn the makeover and the reveal. Fahey,

Bullen and Kenway focus on the problem of young people's lack of engagement with science. In Australia, popular science has found the lifestyle media a youth friendly platform on which to stage science's re-enchantment. Their chapter explores this through a discussion of *Sleek Geeks*, a science radio show that knowingly addresses its implied audience to produce 'ordinary science'.

Lifestyle is often equated with leisure and consumption, but Part V, **Work/life balancing**, shows how work is variously implicated in lifestyling. Focusing on US zines, Stephen Duncombe explores their critique of alienated labour, and their lifestyle strategies to reject conventional work. A more common way of expressing the experience of alienated labour today is through the language of stress, and Steven Brown surveys the development of checklists to measure or calculate levels of stress. The answer to the problem of 'stress' today seems to be recalibrating the work/life balance – a lifestyle answer. Elspeth Probyn offers a very different take on work/life balancing, writing about academic multitasking, and about thinking things through. She counter-poses Peirce's ideas about habit with Bourdieu's notion of the habitus, coming to favour Peirce's version of habit as 'moments when thought relaxes' – ending the book with a framing of ordinary lifestyles as the productive site of new thinking.

PART 1
Media form and industry

2 From television lifestyle to lifestyle television

Tim O'Sullivan

'Rearrange television around *your* life!' proclaims one of the current slogans of satellite and digital television broadcaster Sky, advertising its Sky+ Box in the UK. With a seductive swirl of visuals and music, the advert foregrounds and idealizes the power of the modern, 'state-of-the-art' television viewer, free to watch just *what* they want, just *when* they want to. Advertising, it would seem, remains the 'magic system' (Williams 1980), continuing to deal in the alchemy of turning abstract objects into desirable things, the 'must haves' of contemporary lifestyle culture. In what is a magically reversed panoptic environment, itself epitomizing an appeal to a particular lifestyle with its fashionably minimalist, 'loft living' and 'discerning' cosmopolitan vista and contemporary aesthetic, two dimensions are significant. First, in the flat plasma screen 'on the wall', television as a material, designed object or apparatus appears to contradict history and to defy established technical and domestic convention: the 'box in the corner', replaced by 'the window on the wall' (if not 'the world'). Second, this transformation is reinforced by the image of the viewer/consumer's apparent ability and power to construct and navigate their own schedule, at a time of massively expanded menus of television 'choice', across terrestrial and digital systems, channels and programmes. Thus the advert doubly marks and celebrates a watershed, the passing of an era, whereby the historically established technical and cultural relationships, the 'one-way' constraints between the producers and viewers of television have tilted, are now confounded, 'thrown off' and made to look obsolete. To paraphrase Berman (1988), 'all that *was* solid now melts into air'.

In the world of this ad, 'keeping up with television' is posed as a matter of the utmost importance and urgency. This involves investment in new aspirational hardware. The return from this is entry into a world of ultimate television control, one that reverses the historical logic of the institutionally scheduled, national menu; this is redefined according to the priorities of your own lifestyle and taste culture. With a hard-drive recorder and access across the full range of analogue and digital channels, the conditions are ripe for you to assert/navigate your own *lifestyle* and its particular requirements. What you select as live or recorded, niche or mainstream, is now simply a button (and standing order/credit card number) away.[1] As a result of this brief opening analysis, I want to suggest that we might usefully recognize and work with a distinction between 'television lifestyle' and 'lifestyle television'.

Television lifestyle

> Television may well still be understood as a symbolic and partly (if not mainly – *pace* McLuhan) visual medium – but it is also one with a physical materiality all of its own, and a wide range of material effects in and on its primary physical setting, in the home, all of which, I would suggest, must be given a far more central place in the study of the medium than they have, thus far, been granted.
>
> (Morley 1995: 187)

As Morley suggests perceptively, a concern with television lifestyle starts with the materiality of how television appears and is indexed, prioritized and used in the actual domestic culture; how it occupies a space (or in fact multiple 'spaces') in the private situation and related household settings, within that mesh of inherited physical and symbolic arrangements that Bourdieu (1984) called the 'habitus'; and what the 'television' looks like, where it is positioned, and how it is used, regarded and assimilated into particular everyday routines and relationships, connecting and interfacing private territories and the dynamics of lifestyles, with public and mediated forms of cultural circulation, the advanced and ever-advancing epitome of what Williams (1974) once called 'mobile privatization'. The work of researchers like James Lull (1988) in China and worldwide, or Ondina Leal (1990) in Brazil, for example, provides an important kind of modern television anthropology, mapping the appearance of television sets across dispersed global locations and lifestyles (see also Ang 1996; Tufte 2000).[2]

A television set may not be as highly charged or powered as a motorbike – nor is it a stylish and celebrated icon like an Italian scooter or even a Citroen DS – but like these machines, the television set, as a designed apparatus, has what Morley calls a 'physics' of material and symbolic presence in modern lifestyle cultures.[3] However, television is not a simple object or sign. Once domesticated, the actual appearance of the household television set tends to merge into familiar 'invisibility', part of the taken for granted background to everyday life and the recurrent practices of what Scannell (1996) has called 'dailiness'. Television is part and parcel of most lifestyle cultures in these terms, but – when turned on – it is much more regarded as a *source* of symbolic, mediated culture, culture which has been 'televized', organized into 'flows' and competitive rhythms of daily, weekly and seasonal programming, diverse forms of 'intimacy at a distance'.

Paul Willis (1978b) once outlined a suggestive model for the analysis of objects and cultural forms and the ways in which they function and can be analytically 'traced' within specific subcultures – what we might now regard as lifestyle milieux and their repertoires and networks. He suggested three interrelated levels of analysis, from the material object itself, to its dynamic and symbolic presence in identity, time and generation. First, he argued there is a basic or *indexical* level of relationship: 'assessing how the artefact is "indexed" to the life style' (p. 10). Crudely, for our purposes here: where is television watched? What does it 'look like'? How does it 'fit in'? How important or 'planned' is it? When and for how long? How does television viewing compare with other non-work, non-sleep, 'discretionary' forms of leisure activity both in the home, out of the home and in sociable or solo modes? What of other media usage, 'around' television, in a converging and fragmenting world? (see Livingstone 2002; Ofcom 2004)

Second, Willis argued that the *homological* level of analysis needs to go beyond pure 'quantitative frequencies of appearance' to ask questions of a *synchronic* and interpretative nature concerning the resonance of the object or form at a particular moment in time:

It investigates what are the correspondences, the similarities of internal relation, between a style of life and an artefact or object ... The essential base of a homological culture relation is that an artefact or object has the ability to reflect, resonate and sum up crucial values, states, and attitudes for the social group involved with it.

(Willis 1978b: 11)

This is a snapshot of television, frozen in lifestyle. How does the orientation towards and use of television at a given point in time indicate either a 'belonging' to, or identification with, dominant, emergent, residual or alternative forms of lifestyle and their 'own' 'distinctions'?

Finally, Willis suggested a shift of gear, into the *integral* level of consideration. This is *diachronic* and interpretative and tries to grasp, in this case, the shifting dynamics of television in lifestyle over generational and historical time. As a result, the focus encompasses the 'unravelling' relationships between objects and their symbolic significance in lifetime and lifestyle. From the appearance of television, to the

social (re)negotiation of television, across these three levels of relationship, there remains much to be documented and learned about
television *in* lifestyle, now more than ever, subordinate to viewer choice
and within the determined, inherited and creative conditions, contexts
and possibilities of contemporary lifestyle. Like the advert discussed at
the beginning of this chapter, these are constantly represented and
imaged, as part of the 'magical', ever-changing technical and consumerist 'communicopia' of modern times, defined by an excess of 'choices'.
As Featherstone has noted in this respect:

> In contrast to the designation of the 1950s as an era of grey
> conformism, a time of mass consumption, changes in produc-
> tion techniques, market segmentation and consumer demand
> for a wider range of products, are often regarded as making
> possible greater choice (the management of which becomes an
> art form) not only for the youth of the post 1960s generation,
> but increasingly for the middle aged and the elderly.
>
> (1987: 55)

Television itself has been deeply implicated in these shifts and
transformations, fundamental to the growth and acceptance of
consumer culture. Recent research in the UK tends to indicate that
television viewing and 'television time' continues to be a significant
part of the household 'hub' of media use. The average household
continues to spend in excess of 24 hours – the equivalent of one full day
per week – in rooms with televisions on (although this is undoubtedly
inflected differently across the myriad lifestyles which result from
fragmentations of class, gender, generation, ethnicity, occupation and
so on, and the proliferation of television channels and programmes in
recent years). For Gauntlett and Hill (1999), in their detailed study of
television and everyday life, the presence of television has implications
not only for domestic geography, but is perhaps most significant in
terms of temporality. In particular, they highlight its contribution to
the organization and mesh of household schedules and routines, which
give order to, and a focus for 'free', 'spare' and 'discretionary' forms of
time (see also Scannell 1996). Although different lifestyles are in part
defined and distinguished by particular orientations to leisure in and/
or out of the home,[4] in the home, television is an omnipresent
background and resource for both the expression and assertion of
distinction and distanciation in terms of lifestyle, and also for the
negotiation of commonality and identification.[5] What we regularly
choose to watch on television, where, how, with whom and when,
provides a significant set of indicators concerning our position with

regard to lifestyle culture. Are we simply 'what we watch'? How do lifestyles exist outside of television?

It is claimed that averages of television viewing, radio listening, mobile telephony and broadband communications continue to increase in the UK in recent years (Ofcom 2004). These have to be mapped against the 'lean back/lean forward' dimensions and tugs of contemporary lifestyle configurations and their respective developments. There are converging dimensions to the current transformations taking place in the domestic mediascape, and these are also fragmenting the notion of a central household 'lifestyle hub' around the television. Media consumption and activity in the home does not now always take place in shared rooms or singular sociable settings. Recent consumer research, for instance, indicates:

> Whereas the living room used to be the hub of the home, now more and more 11–14 year olds prefer to be alone in their technology filled bedrooms, communicating with friends via mobile phone, texting or e-mail. And, as Britons become more obsessed with technology, the strong sense of family is likely to diminish further ... Seventy-seven per cent of children aged between 11 and 14 have a television in their bedroom, and 64 per cent have their own DVD player or video recorder ... One in four also has a computer in his or her room.
>
> (*Daily Telegraph* 2004: 3)

Television lifestyle: snapshots from the past

In the UK, television has been a vital agent in the growth, mobilization and expansion of lifestyle culture in a number of direct and also complex ways, although studies of the early phases of the 'domestication' of television – and its associated 'imaging' and entry into its taken for granted place in domestic lifestyle – have been more developed in the USA than in Britain.[6]

When the BBC restarted the Television Service in June 1946, the size of the British viewing audience was very small. Silvey, for instance, notes that nine months after the resumption of the service there were still less than 15,000 homes possessing a 'combined sound and television licence', the great majority concentrated in the London area, 'limited to the range of the Alexandra Palace transmitter' (Silvey 1974: 153). As Ellis (2000) has observed, these were conditions of television 'scarcity', when the ownership of a television set capable of receiving the limited, black and white, single channel service was in itself an unstable technical and cultural novelty. At this stage, the 'place' of television in the home was as yet unfixed and unfamiliar, as were its contents, with the scheduled 'flow' of the BBC Television Service programming yet to really develop from the wartime base of radio (Williams 1974; see also Laing 1991). However, television in the immediate post-war period in the UK rapidly came to symbolize the new modernity, as radio homes became television homes: 'You could tell from the aerials who had and who hadn't got sets. I remember that we were one of the first three in the road to get one. If you had a car and a television set, you'd really arrived' (respondent in O'Sullivan 1991: 166).

This was not an overnight event, although it is often depicted as such. The development of a national technical transmission system was a considerable undertaking, and it was not until 1960 that over 80 per cent of the British population could receive, never mind see, television. The Coronation in 1953 is often singled out as the key milestone, when it is claimed that more people watched the ceremony on television than listened on radio. From 1946 to the late 1950s, television sets were expensive, initially scarce commodities, often unreliable, with poor quality black and white vision, and to begin with extremely limited programming. However, reflecting on the adverse conditions facing the expansion of television in Britain in the late 1940s, Maurice Gorham, the first Head of Television Services at the BBC, later remarked:

> [It] was not because people did not want television after the war but because they could not get it. There were no sets. There was no such thing as 'sales resistance' in those early years; every dealer had waiting-lists and every set that left the manufacturers found its way into a home, but supply fell far short of demand.
> (Gorham 1952: 237)

As a result, for hardy enthusiasts, building your own television became one means of dealing with post-war austerity, harnessing wartime expertise and developing the thrifty, 'make-do-and-mend' wartime ethic for new home and nascent lifestyle aspirations, from which a full-blown, domestic DIY culture was yet to emerge (Figure 2.1).

Although for many at that time television lifestyle was a relatively restricted and novel experience, questions about how to deal with the new intrusive technology, and how to 'fit' and accommodate it appropriately into the particular lifestyle of the home, were being asked, albeit in distinctly gendered fashion. Television lifestyle was in itself news. In the English Midlands, local newspaper *The Leicester Mercury*, for instance, regularly began to feature television stories in the late 1940s and early 1950s, and in its report on the 1951 Radio and Television Show

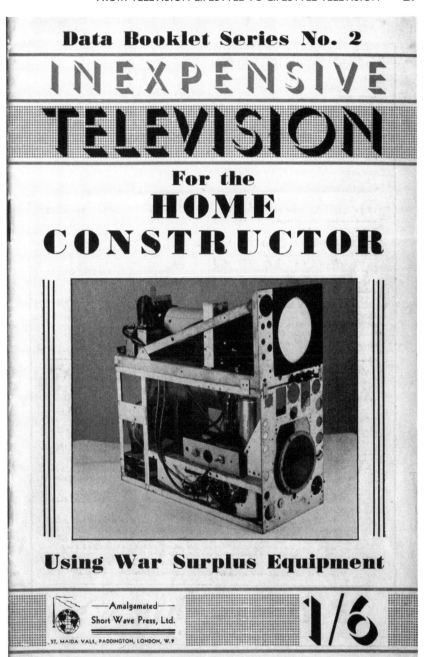

Figure 2.1 Pamphlet: *Inexpensive Television – For the Home Constructor (Using War Surplus Equipment)*, published by Amalgamated Short Wave Press Ltd

from Earls Court, television 'almost without interference' was hailed as a major technical breakthrough (*Leicester Mercury* 1951: 6). Alongside this, in her report from the show, Kate Almey added the following commentary:

> The eye-catching part of the show this year is undoubtedly television. It was the camouflage around the actual receivers that interested me as a woman. Salesman after salesman agreed that if a woman has anything to do with choosing television for her home, the deciding factor is nearly always its appearance.
>
> Which explains why the television receiver of the future will nearly always be found behind closed cabinet doors.
>
> Just for the moment, with television quite a thing to be proud of owning, housewives don't object to a receiver with a staring blank screen face in their lounge. The 1951 Radio Show points surely to the fact that unconcealed screens may soon be regarded as a sign of ostentation.
>
> Doors are undoubtedly the thing. The vogue for concealment reaches its £700 pinnacle in a handsome reproduction antique oak chest with bookshelves at each side. Until its doors are unlatched you would never guess that behind them lay a large television screen and a radio.
>
> No one need pay £700, however, to buy a shut-up television set. Manufacturers with famous names are displaying cabinet consoles in walnut or mahogany that would do credit to any drawing room for under £100. Doors are so hinged as to enable them to be swung right back when viewing time comes.
>
> Several firms have studied the housewife to this further extent. They have fitted cabinets with castors, knowing full well that a movable piece of furniture finds favour with the woman whose job it is to clean under and around it.
>
> (*Leicester Mercury* 1951: 6)

In contrast, by the early 1960s television was much less a novelty feature or alien invader in the British home. As an index of this, images of 'typical' domestic interiors used in advertising and magazines began to depict the television set as an integral, almost taken for granted component of home settings – part of the 'hub' of the home and household. In the case, for instance, of *Homemaker: The Practical How-to-Do-It Monthly* for February 1960 (itself an indicator of the developing post-war, DIY self-improvement, lifestyle culture, with its features on 'Stone fireplaces for the small home', 'Do up your door', 'Brighter bed linen' and 'A three year plan for vegetables'), the very idea of disguising the television apparatus with cabinet-type doors had already become an anathema. Instead, at least in some homes, the television set required its own dedicated space, the 'ideal television corner', replete with 'bench seating piled with gay cushions' ('from Hamptons, in felt about 30/s'). (See Figure 2.2).

Examples like these can help to begin to develop the historical understanding of the place of television *in* lifestyle. As I have suggested, its changing appearance and forms of design and consumption during the past 60 years are a relatively hidden but not insignificant part of the relationships that have constituted and developed lifestyle cultures. In order to develop and supplement such analysis, however, a related focus presents itself – lifestyle television.

Figure 2.2 The 'ideal television corner' (*Homemaker* 1960)

Lifestyle television

> On Tuesday night, if you couldn't face the bowel movements on *You Are What You Eat*, there was *Wife Swap*, in which two women hurled abuse at each other's lifestyles, or *Location, Location, Location*, where the camera lingered on Kirstie Allsopp's breasts in between images of a couple bickering over the bidets. ... This summer there are more than 70 reality and lifestyle programmes a week on terrestrial television. Most are couched as real-life learning experiences, professing to help turn their subjects into happier people, when all they are really doing is exploiting their misery – shaming, chastening and humbling them in front of an audience of millions.
>
> (Thomson 2004: 18)

The sheer amount of lifestyle programming – together with its close hybrid relation, reality television – is one of the most significant controversies currently facing the BBC as it prepares for Licence Review in 2006. Has the television success story of the 1990s run its course and lost its audience power already? In addition to a range of dedicated 'lifestyle channels' available on digital television systems, most daytime and evening schedules on terrestrial television offer programmes that deal in an ever-widening menu and array of lifestyle concerns and preoccupations for viewers to choose from (see Brunsdon et al. 2001). In an earlier discussion of lifestyle and consumer culture, Featherstone noted:

> The term 'lifestyle' ... connotes individuality, self-expression, and a stylistic self-consciousness. One's body, clothes, speech, leisure pastimes, eating and drinking preferences, home, car, choice of holidays, etc. are to be regarded as indicators of the individuality of taste and sense of style of the owner/consumer.
>
> (1987: 55)

As a result, it is not surprising that it is difficult to navigate through current television schedules without encountering programmes, series and segments that are preoccupied with these and related indicators. In hybridized modes that draw on and interweave semi-documentary, entertainment and promotional formats, lifestyle television now encompasses (and reveals) the body, the home and the wider world. In this mediated, selected and stratified universe, lifestyle television continues to offer recurrent lessons and advice in the ever-more effective stylistic management and transformation of the body, health, fashion, cookery, gardening, house and home, DIY, cars, travel and holidays, and property. These updated and proliferating 'how-to-do-it' guides coexist uneasily within the increasingly hybridized formats that emerged to achieve dominance in the 1990s. A first phase of programmes like *Changing Rooms* or *Ground Force* adapted and reinstated the magazine fashion formula of personalized makeover and reveal, with (ordinary) tales and images of 'before-and-after', compressed and often competitive transformation (Moseley 2000). In the process, the experts were displaced or changed status ('ordinari-ized'), giving way to celebrity presenters/participants. If these formats continue to retain some claim to an instructional or self-empowering enterprise, they have also been subsequently the dynamic and platform for a second phase of more recent lifestyle television, which more or less abandons pretensions to the practical and instead thrives on showing lifestyles 'in collision'. In programmes like *Wife Swap*, *Holiday Swap*, or *House Doctor* (see Holliday, this volume), viewing is solicited more by the apparently 'unmediated', unpredictable, but at the same time, knowingly contrived, *clashes* of lifestyle, class and forms of difference, than it is by any therapeutic or transformative discourse. You witness the slices and clashes of lifestyle, and in the process, you judge, compare (and position) yourself.

The scale and changing dynamics of lifestyle programmes and their ability to mobilize audiences as they do in current times might be thought to be a defining characteristic of contemporary British television. There is, however, a *history* of lifestyle television and its development. It is tempting to identify its roots in that relatively restricted but nonetheless staple part of the British post-war television schedule, that inherited and carried forward from pre-war radio and magazines a (wartime?) preoccupation with gardening, cookery and matters related to the home. This tended to be instructional and focused around an acknowledged expert. In the late 1940s, for instance, the BBC broadcast *Television Garden* (presented by Fred Streeter 1946–51) and *Cookery* (with Philip Harben, the 'television chef', 1946–51).[7] A number of related programmes and formats were also developed in these early stages, catering for implied/assumed feminine viewers with their interests in fashion, or the lifestyles of celebrities and 'gracious living'.[8] For implied masculine viewers, in addition to gardens, throughout the 1950s and 1960s the growth of domestic DIY culture became synon- ymous with the name and television personality of Barry Bucknell, television's first 'do-it-yourself' expert: *Do It Yourself* (1954), *About the House* (1957), *Bucknell's House* (1962) and *The ABC of Do-It-Yourself* (1966).

It may be accurate to suggest that programmes like these and their origins represent the fundamental bedrock and hence the generic foundations for all subsequent transformations in lifestyle television. In the search for audiences, British television responded to and latched onto the all-consuming cultural shifts of the time. In the 1960s and 1970s, for instance, holiday programmes and popular music formats appeared alongside new developments in lifestyle movements. From 1955 onwards, with the development of commercial programming, television 'mined' lifestyles and acted to selectively relay and promote them. In the era of television advertising, small promotional lifestyle segments began to routinely appear in the 'commercial breaks'.[9] From the 'exotic' Martini Set to the more domestic preoccupations of Katy and Philip (the Oxo couple/family), appeals to an overall sense of lifestyle emerged as one of the key advertising discourses of the modern period.

In this context, general studies of advertising have pointed to the shifts in underlying strategy which have characterized historical developments in the twentieth century (see, for example, Leiss et al. 1986). Utilitarian or informational appeals, itemizing and extolling the technical virtues of the product, have been largely superseded by transformational modes, where what is at stake concerns much more the symbolic lifestyle or 'totemic' value of the particular commodity rather than its functional use or application. We need to know more about the ways in which, in the UK, television advertising and television in general contributed to the growth of 'lifestyle culture' and its associated (trans)formations.

Lifestyle television now requires a focus and mode of analysis that is less concerned with matters contextual and more engaged with the ways in which television has provided an historical conduit for the mediation of images of lifestyle, providing and mediating spaces which allow various and increasing forms of 'intimacy at a distance', across and between private and public spheres. Programmes which began by instructing and mobilizing particular and restricted lifestyle aspirations, providing relatively simple televisual lessons in how to choose, make and attain the burgeoning ideals of modern consumption – status, style, distinction, and identity – have, in order to recruit audiences and viewers in times of greatly increasing competition, worked around and transformed this didactic instructional enterprise with a number of differing and developing aims, devices and appeals. In the pursuit of viewers, lifestyle television now allows us to inspect how 'ordinary people' live their lives (Brunsdon et al. 2001); to witness and experience 'their' lifestyles under contrived conditions of crisis or transformation, competition, makeover or just 'raw' revelation. In the process, inevitably, one is drawn to speculate or make comparative moral judgements about how one might live, how one shouldn't live, and so on. As Lisa Taylor (this volume) has noted with some understatement in this respect, '[t]he ways in which lifestyle knowledges are presented have undergone changes since the early 1970s: the authoritative tone of public service has been replaced with what Ellis has called "popular public service"'.

To conclude by borrowing from the work of Basil Bernstein (1990), the whole system of the classification and framing of lifestyle on television appears to have shifted quite dramatically since the early days in the 1940s and 1950s. As Medhurst has observed, lifestyle television now refuses easy or accurate generic labelling:

> Lifestyle TV is, I confess, a limp and baggy label, but its very looseness points to one important fact. These are programmes that hover between genres – they're not exactly fact, but never quite fiction; they flirt with game-show codes, yet have a mildly pedagogic agenda; they tell stories, but in the context of real people's lives. That woolly word 'lifestyle' also indicates that this kind of television is not content to stay hemmed inside the box that transmits it: these are programmes designed to leak out into the living rooms, the kitchens, and the gardens beyond. Don't just watch us, copy us – this is their cajoling message.
>
> (1999: 27)

If the classification of lifestyle television has become steadily more problematic, more hybrid and parasitic, so too has the framing at play in these programmes. The conventional mode of lifestyle instruction, with the secure expert solving the viewers' problems, has given way to accommodate lifestyle-as-entertainment formats, orchestrated by celebrity presenters, and in turn these have been overtaken by 'reality lifestyle' programmes. From our particular position in television lifestyle, we continue to watch our choice of lifestyle television.

Notes

1. Systems like this allow for 'live', 'instant' replay and programmable recording functions. They supersede video formats at a time when DVD has emerged as the current platform for replay and recording. They also offer subscription online cinema and exclusive access to live sporting spectaculars, etc., at a price.
2. Television was legalized and introduced into Bhutan, the last nation to 'let TV in', in 1999 (see http://www.pbs.org/frontlineworld/stories/bhutan/whatson.html).
3. See Willis (1978a), Hebdige (1989), Barthes (1973). Some televisions, have, of

course, achieved 'retro' iconic status – for example, the 1960s spherical/ hanging television.

4. Much television consumption takes place on a regular basis in domestic/ private spaces, or what Moores (2000) called 'staying/going places'. However, as McCarthy (2001) has indicated, 'ambient' television screens increasingly address us in the public spaces of social life: in shopping malls, pubs and bars, airports, etc.

5. While television in the home is generally assumed to be universal, some households and families live without television. This (sometimes temporary) statement is itself often an indicator of a key lifestyle commitment (see, for example, the White Dot society, http://www.whitedot.org).

6. Perhaps as a result of the earlier 'take-off' of television in the USA. See, for example, Boddy (1985, 2004), Spigel (1992, 2001), Marling (1994).

7. Harben became a cooking celebrity and worked in television until 1969. *Kitchen Magic*, featuring Fanny and Johnny Craddock, appeared on the BBC in 1955. *Gardening Club* with Percy Thrower (later developed into the still running *Gardener's World*) ran on the BBC from 1955 to 1967.

8. See, for example, on the BBC, *About the Home* (1953), *Family Affairs* (1955), *Your Own Time* (1958).

9. In addition to spot television adverts per hour, 'ad-mags' became part of the early ITV schedules. Each 15-minute advertising magazine programme was regionally focused, and consisted of a series of adverts featuring stories about products in major shops, car showrooms or related sites of consumption. *What's in Store in the Midlands*, for example, ran until these sponsored shows were closed down in 1963, when regulators decided that the viewer might find endorsements of products within programmes confusing.

3 Whose lifestyle is it anyway?

Frances Bonner

This chapter starts from an observation about lifestyle programming – that in Australia, in addition to locally originating shows, house and garden makeover programmes like *Changing Rooms* and *Ground Force* are made locally from imported formats, while cooking shows are bought outright and screened as imported programmes – and investigates what this can tell us about the subgenres themselves and about the international trade in programmes and their formats. Australia is not alone in importing cooking shows. Most if not all systems import at least a few, even the notoriously parochial USA, though there they are not screened on the networks, only on cable. *Two Fat Ladies* was an international hit and Nigella Lawson and Jamie Oliver have followers almost as widely. Nor is Australia alone in formatting programmes, though game shows (including reality ones) rather than makeovers are more commonly studied as the examples.

It might be thought that the similarities between the UK and Australia were no greater (or no less) for interior design than for cooking. Furthermore, the social changes in the UK detailed by Charlotte Brunsdon (2003) in her discussion of the televisual transformation which has seen the 8 to 9 pm slot heavily marked by lifestyle shows – the increase of home ownership and of associated discourses of value and investment; increased female participation in the paid workforce; and the postponement of childbearing by ABC class women – are notable in Australia too (though home ownership itself was high before the 1990s). Yet no DIY or makeover shows are imported into Australia and no cooking shows formatted here.

Television and our use of it is so much a part of our everyday life that it is not difficult to see some aspects of it as natural or inevitable, rather than their being highly conventional. Looking at how different systems operate, even though the principal systems considered – the Australian and the British – are very similar (or perhaps precisely because they are), enables fresh insights to be generated by denaturalizing the situation to some extent. This chapter seeks to examine what it is about the genres which means that in Australia makeover shows are sold as formats while food shows are traded 'as is' and also the reverse of this, what the fact of direct sales or formatting can tell us about the genres.

Formatting and the Australian situation

The international trade in television formats is a substantial one and unlike the trade in programmes themselves is not structured by language, nor dominated by the export power of the United States. Both fiction and non-fiction programmes are formatted and while earlier studies concentrated on game shows and various forms of drama (Cunningham and Jacka 1996; Moran 1998), more recent work looks at lifestyle and reality game shows (Johnston-Woods 2002; Bonner 2003). Although the trade is extensive, Moran makes it clear that the legal basis on which format sales is predicated (that there can be intellectual property in the formats of television programmes) is shaky. Despite very frequent talk of legal challenges over copyright infringement and the existence of relevant and 'elaborate legal machinery', no case has ever been successfully prosecuted (Moran 1998: 15–17). The Australian producers of one of the formatted programmes discussed here, *Ground Force*, threatened to sue the makers of a similar, locally originating garden makeover programme, *Backyard Blitz*, but no case eventuated and both have continued to screen. Formats nonetheless continue to be bought since doing so gives access to the commercial experience of the originators; for example, their understandings of the key elements and the precise character of the demographic appeal. Even so, the extent to which formats produce similar shows varies considerably. Some formats like *Who Wants to Be a Millionaire?* are very tightly policed, others are much looser. The British and Australian versions of *Hot Property* appear to share a title and a concern with real estate, but the game show element so central to the British show is absent from the Australian one.

The Australian broadcast television system consists of two public broadcasting networks, the Australian Broadcasting Commission (ABC) and the Special Broadcasting Service (SBS), which has a multicultural remit, together with three commercial networks. Pay-TV developed late and slowly in Australia and still has less than 25 per cent penetration. Digital broadcasting is only just beginning to have an impact. In part because of the smaller population, imported programming is of much greater significance to Australian television than it is to British. The amount of imported programming is regulated by law with a little over 50 per cent required to be 'local content' (i.e. Australian made). An Australian version of an imported format counts as local content and I have argued previously that significant localization is possible even with quite strictly policed formats (Bonner 2003). The most frequently imported genres are fictional shows of all types, closely followed by documentaries.

A much smaller proportion of imported programming comes from the category that I have elsewhere called 'ordinary television', that is television which concerns itself with mundane issues, usually involves the participation of ordinary people and which addresses viewers in their everydayness (Bonner 2003). Lifestyle programmes form part of this category. While a varied range of both British and American ordinary television is screened in Australia in the summer out-of-ratings-period, if one looks at terrestrial broadcast television in the core times of the year, imported American ordinary television is almost entirely talk shows and reality game shows, while imported British ordinary television is limited primarily to cooking shows. Otherwise, imported lifestyle programmes can only be found on pay-TV where the calls for cheap content and the lack of requirements for local content mean that it is worthwhile even to screen imported version of shows which are also locally formatted.

Lifestyle programming is a category even more popular in Australia than it is elsewhere. It has been customary for the last seven to eight years for the top ten programmes of any month to include more (up to four) lifestyle than drama programmes. The most popular lifestyle programmes included both locally made shows (*Burke's Backyard*, now in its 17th year, is held to have been the first recognizable lifestyle show in the world) and formatted ones like *Changing Rooms*. The most popular of the regular lifestyle shows is *Backyard Blitz*, already mentioned as similar to *Ground Force*, the Australian version of which rates less well.

The two principal formatted makeover shows in Australia are *Ground Force* and *Changing Rooms*. The former operates close to the format with a team of gardeners visiting the home of a deserving person to transform their garden. The recipient will have been nominated by a friend or relative and sent away on a holiday, so that each programme builds towards the climactic 'reveal' when the transformation can be presented as a surprise gift and the week's narrative concluded.

Initial changes in the format of *Changing Rooms* in Australia reveal a degree of uncertainty about its reception on the part of the local producers. It started at 30 minutes following the shorter British version and even in its later extended version was only 40 minutes. It also screens in very short runs of six to eight episodes, as opposed to *Ground Force*'s occupation of the schedule for the majority of the year. Regardless of length, the structure and narrative are the same: two couples under the direction of 'experts' make over a room in each other's houses. Both versions exhibit the same tendency to produce colourful, even theatrical, rooms which look arresting on television, even if this means disregarding the owner's requests. Unlike *Ground Force*, there is a much greater likelihood of recipients disliking the makeover and feeling the pressure to disguise this for the camera. For this show, then, part of the appeal of the format lies in a rather malicious pleasure of trying to detect whether the recipients are telling the truth when they say how much they like their new room (or indeed waiting for someone who would not be inhibited about behaving properly towards a gift giver). No Australian designer employed on the show has received an equivalent public profile to that managed by Laurence Llewellyn-Bowen from the British version, but then no subordinate Australian *Ground Force* team member has risen to the heights that Charlie Dimmock has managed either.

The edge of malice – or what Charlotte Brunsdon (2001), focusing on the recipients, refers to as the risk of humiliation – that can be found in *Changing Rooms* and also in some other British makeover shows, is generally absent from lifestyle programmes originated in Australia. The picture instead is one of nice people giving and receiving useful advice in a consumer friendly climate. *The Block*, an Australian originating programme whose first series final was one of the highest rating Australian programmes ever, combined elements of the makeover with a reality game show. It thus had access to a ready source of less pleasant behaviour. But even this show, in which four couples renovated the four flats of the eponymous Bondi block, took care to ensure that any snide comments came from fellow participants, not from the presenters or (in any obvious way) from the programme's design. The format has been sold internationally, although the British version was not a success.

Forerunners of the current programmes

The immediate difference between the two types of lifestyle programme being examined here are that cooking shows are built around the personality presenter, while makeover shows, regardless of the national prominences that presenters and team members may be able to achieve, are built around a narrative of transformation and disclosure which can readily be replicated with different casts. Cooking shows have a longer televisual history, predating the appearance of lifestyle television, and the form appears remarkably resilient and adaptable to changing televisual times.

It is possible to find programmes from before the 1990s which gesture towards lifestyle programming. House and garden shows including sections in which certain parts of a property were transformed have long been regular elements of television schedules, but examination of them reveals how new the 'lifestyle' approach is. Charlotte Brunsdon (2001) has argued that instructional and enthusiast programmes like dressmaking and gardening shows are specific but very different British forerunners (and gardening shows operated similarly in

Australia). She pays particular attention to a changed 'grammar of the close-up': where in the 1970s the close-up was on the task being performed, it now focuses far more on the face of the people involved to track their feelings. Ordinary people were far less involved in the earlier programmes and the fundamental principal of lifestyle programmes – that one's possessions reveal one's self and that the self can be transformed by updating the possessions (see Bonner 2003) – was nowhere articulated.

The continuity between cooking shows of the past and those of today is much more substantial. Shows organized around the personality of a presenting cook or chef have been screening since soon after the start of television. One of the most famous of British celebrity cooks, Fanny Cradock, started appearing on British screens in 1955 with *Fanny's Kitchen*. The presence of her 'husband' Johnnie also gestured to the inclusion of family members we think of as a recent trend. Graham Kerr, whose *Galloping Gourmet* series was made by the Canadian Broadcasting Commission between 1969 and 1971 and recently repeated as part of the BBC's *Saturday Kitchen*, was the best known internationally of all early celebrity chefs. British-born, Kerr had emigrated to New Zealand in his twenties, so he sounded British, which combined with the non-specific studio location to enable the foreign origins of his programmes (some were also made in Australia and the USA) to be played down at a time when little foreign-originating material of any kind, and very little non-fiction, was being played on British screens. Certainly he is the only one of six television cooks featured in the 2002 BBC history of cooks on British television, *The Way We Cooked*, not to have been British-based. He operated from a flamboyant, over-the-top personality, drawing on the image of the bachelor playboy. His manner can easily be traced through Keith Floyd to Jamie Oliver.

Although there are and have been cooking shows that do not focus on the personality of the presenter (the segments of daytime shows which present recipes and food hints, and prime time programming like the UK's *Masterchef or Foodlover's Guide to Australia*), the programmes which are most likely to be exportable are those organized around the personality, even celebrity, of the presenting cook. Niki Strange's (1998) categorization of the tendencies of cooking shows involves three educative aspects (Cook-Ed., Tour-Ed. and Raw-Ed.) and a separate personality category, although she stresses that most programmes involve the operation of several of these. Of the presenters she discusses (Delia Smith, Keith Floyd, Madhur Jaffrey and Gary Rhodes), Floyd is the person who most obviously demonstrates the organization of the programme around his public persona. The shows which were exported all had his name in the title, beginning with *Floyd on Food* in 1986. His fondness for a glass of wine, games with the cameraman and the casualness with which he approached cooking made the programmes more entertaining than a staid presentation would have been, but it was with the additional travelling component (Strange's Tour-Ed.) that his exportability as prime time programming really flourished, starting with *Floyd on France* in 1987. Obviously when he made series set in countries to which the shows were exported, like 1991's *Floyd on Oz*, the links were intensified (although Australian viewers watched more critically). Rick Stein has more recently followed this practice.

Makeover shows have not had historical precedents involving personalities in the same way, though the Llewellyn-Bowen and Dimmock examples mentioned earlier, not to mention Trinny Woodall and Susannah Constantine from *What Not to Wear*, indicate that there is nothing about the shows to preclude this developing. But the personalities are constrained by the structure of the show; indeed by its format. The important aspects of the garden makeover lie in the gift, the before-and-after shots, the reaction to the reveal and the opportunity for significant quantities of product placement. All but the last of these involves ordinary people and it is here that a major difference from the cooking shows is demonstrated.

Ordinary people in lifestyle shows

Makeover shows are performed on the bodies and possessions of ordinary people. The analogy, and it can be taken a long way, for the cooking shows is with the ingredients. In both cases there is a transformation, but in makeovers the raw materials speak, react and provide a focus for viewer identification in parallel to the presenters and other members of the team. In cooking shows the main person speaking, reacting and providing a focus for the viewer (if not necessarily an identificatory one) is the cook.

Ordinary people can appear on cooking shows. *Ready Steady Cook* regularly involves them cooking in tandem with professional chefs, though with the lengthening of the programme and the switch of presenter from Fern Britton to Ainsley Harriott (as well as an increase in the presence of celebrities from other television programmes), the proportion of the show in which ordinary people can be seen has diminished. In considering why cooking show formats are not sold to Australian producers, this programme provides an eminently formatt-able example.[1] Indeed Endemol, who now own the format, have sold it to ten countries and *Can't Cook, Won't Cook* to nine. An American programme I have read about but not seen, called *Plate Date,* sounds as if it operates to the same format as *Dishes*, the 1999 Channel 4 cooking-based dating show. That I have been unable to find Australian instances of formatted cooking shows indicates that while cooking programmes can be formattable if they involve ordinary people, the Australian system sees the subgenre as involving only importation or local origination, without the intermediary form.

One needs to be careful, however, about just how strongly one makes the point that it is the presence of ordinary people that makes programmes amenable to formatting. Many of the celebrity television cooks do involve ordinary people in their programmes. The Galloping Gourmet cooked in front of a studio audience, one (female) member of which sampled the food cooked at the end of each programme. The Two Fat Ladies cooked for targeted groups of varying degrees of ordinariness while Nigella, Jamie and Australian chef Kylie Kwong (of *Kylie Kwong – Heart and Soul*) serve their food to groups of friends. Leaving aside the question of how much Nigella's friends could be presented as 'ordinary', these people are not central to the format. In all instances, the dishes could be cooked whether or not the friends were present to eat them (the tendency of Nigella's friends to be filmed out of focus, especially in the rarely in focus *Forever Summer* series, indicates how peripheral they really are).

It would also be possible to argue that the suppliers of produce so often featured in food or cooking shows (what Strange would refer to as the Raw-Ed. component) is another way in which ordinary people can be found in cooking programmes. While this is true, they are almost always presented as other than ordinary – as evidenced by the title of the Rick Stein show celebrating suppliers: *Food Heroes*. The people Stein or Jamie or the Two Fat Ladies visit are chosen precisely because they provide exceptional products, they were or are the best greengrocers or apiarists or cheesemakers, they breed the best organic pigs. It was their extraordinariness that was celebrated. *Food Heroes* could readily be replicated in other countries, but it is not really formattable; Rick Stein is what makes it special and there is more than one equivalent Australian programme. Stephanie Alexander's *A Shared Table* is closest in similarly celebrating regional producers and drawing on Alexander's own non-televisual fame as a chef and cookbook writer. Suppliers are also featured in the much longer running *A Food Lover's Guide to Australia*, though that has two less prominent presenters, who did not even appear on screen until the third series.

Product placement and the national in food programmes

Television cooks provide viewers with their expertise not only in terms of their skills and recipe knowledge but also in their knowledge about sourcing the best or the most suitable ingredients. While on the one hand it can lead to celebrations, like Stein's and Alexander's, of artisanal producers, it can also lead to more explicitly commercial relationships like Delia's and then Jamie's with Sainsbury's. Both the information about the artisanal producers and the promotion of supermarket chains are flattened when the programmes are exported. When Jamie forgets his Sainsbury's bag of produce as he bounds back onto the stage during *Happy Days Live with Jamie Oliver*, it draws extra attention to his endorsement of a particular supplier, but not for Australian viewers, who can neither buy the goods nor for the most part recognize the bag or the name. It is a reminder that programmes viewed in countries other than those in which they originate are not the same programmes. The context and local knowledge change what they say. The accents and speech patterns which convey so much about class and region in the UK pass blithely by Australian listeners who on a good day can just about tell a Scot from a non-Scot, but are reliant on visual cues and publicity stories to 'place' Nigella.

The products that do travel with the programmes are the more explicitly connected ones – the cookbooks, videos and DVDs and the celebrity-named culinary equipment, like Jamie's line for Royal Worcester. Such spin-off merchandise is available from makeover programmes too, of course. The advantage of being made locally to a purchased format is that the products embedded in makeover shows are always readable by the audience and available to buy. When programmes are imported across more substantial language barriers, they are even less readable or useful for product placement. Overwhelmingly, programmes imported by English-speaking countries are made in English, and in Australia such few alternatives as exist screen on the multicultural broadcaster. The French documentary about particular French dishes, *Terres de Gout*, has screened intermittently on SBS since 2002 as *Question of Taste*. The emphasis on regionality makes it useless for product placement except for intending tourists. A better known example is the Japanese *Iron Chef* which has circulated internationally since being adapted into a (largely) dubbed American version, but highly localized key ingredients like natto as well as the chefs' predilection for expensive ingredients like foie gras render its operation as a cooking programme with any connection to its viewers' lives (or lifestyles) slight.

It might be thought that it is the linkage of these two programmes with the national that produces the problem, but this is not the case. Cooking programmes are one of the major ways in which television is able to talk about other people's national. What is needed, however, is a local interpreter. Madhur Jaffrey has long spoken to the British about India and Indian food. Korma Dasa spoke to Australians about Indian vegetarian food in programmes like *Cooking with Korma*, which were widely exported. Lorenza di Medici spoke of Italian cooking to English speaking viewers in an American-made programme (*The Medici Kitchen*), authenticated by her illustrious connections. A number of English-speaking cooks of Chinese background speak of Asian food – Ken Hom, Kylie Kwong, and Martin Yan (of *Yan Can Cook*) have all been seen on Australian and many other screens. Dorinda Hafner provides a particularly interesting example of the 'local interpreter'. Ghanaian-born, she emigrated first to the UK and then to Australia from where she presented *A Taste of Africa*, which was the first of several series, including *A Taste of America*, co-produced by SBS and Channel 4 and exported widely. Co-production instances like this and the more recent *Surfing the Menu* (using Australian-born London resident chef Ben O'Donoghue, from *The Best*, and co-produced by the ABC and UKTV) reduce the clarity with which one can talk about importing, exporting and localizing through formatting, but they maintain their international appeal by continuing to be organized around the personality of the presenters.

Presenters as cultural intermediaries

These examples provide a particularly clear way in which we could talk of cooking presenters being cultural intermediaries: Hafner is an intermediary in that she brings Australian and British viewers information about African food. This, however, is not quite what the term refers to. 'Cultural intermediaries', as Pierre Bourdieu conceived them (although he mainly used the term 'new petite bourgeoisie'), are people 'engaged in presentation and representation … and in all the institutions providing symbolic goods and services' (1984: 359). Bourdieu explicitly mentions television presenters among his examples. The particular relevance of lifestyle presenters is revealed by a later comment, that '[s]eeking its occupational and personal salvation in the imposition of new doctrines of ethical salvation, the new petite bourgeoisie is predisposed to play a vanguard role in the struggles over everything concerned with the art of living, in particular domestic life and consumption' (Bourdieu 1984: 366).

The 'art of living' is precisely the concern of lifestyle programmes and the blandishments of presenters about the importance of transformations, of constantly looking up-to-date in one's clothing and surroundings, present this as an ethical concern, especially in terms of Bourdieu's explanation of the ethical position of the new petite bourgeoisie, that it involves the duty to 'have fun' (1984: 367). Makeovers are all about pleasure, the pleasure of the gift and of its giving, the pleasure of turning a drab garden into something fresh and bright that features an 'entertainment area' and the pleasures for both those making the show and its viewers of watching the recipient's face. The same applies to the cooking programmes. Food preparation must be fun; it is never presented as work. This is most clearly demonstrated in Jamie's separation of his being a cook on television from the serious business of being a professional chef, as examined at length by Hollows (2003b). He does not, however, sustain this disavowal in *Jamie's Kitchen*, which screened in the UK late in 2002 and in Australia the next year, and which followed Jamie's attempts to make a group of unemployed people into apprentices able to be employed in his own restaurant. Despite the presence of the celebrity chef and the programme's concern with food preparation, this was not a lifestyle show, but a docu-soap, and thus the concern with work and the dramas of the workplace, together with the integral presence of ordinary people, was completely appropriate. Yet looking more broadly at cooking programmes, because many of the presenters (indeed almost all of the male ones) are chefs, work does enter the programmes. Filming may take place inside a presenter's restaurant, as it did notoriously for the hot-tempered Gordon Ramsay. *Friends for Dinner*, which called on the services of most of the stable of BBC food presenters to help ordinary members of the public with their dinner parties, regularly showed the particular episode's chef at work in his restaurant being interrupted by a phone call from the dinner party hostess. In this way it stressed the gap between home cook and professional, while maintaining the fiction that, within the home, cooking is fun.

The gender differences between male and female presenters are worth emphasizing. Although both men and women work professionally with food, very few of the women run restaurants (Kylie Kwong is the only one to do so of those in programmes screening for the first time in Australia during 2003–4) and very few of the men have as their principal professional activity the range of other food activities – food writing, catering and food consultancy – that sustain the women (Ainsley Harriott is an exception here). The privileging of the term 'chef' over 'cook' reveals a continuing hierarchy here – especially since the men also work as food writers and consultants, although as I have pointed out previously (Bonner 1994) usually only after they get television exposure, while for the women it is what qualifies them for presenting. Note that it is the more recent women presenters who are likely to have restaurant experience, like Silvana Franco and Kylie, although Stephanie Alexander also did.

According to Keith Negus (2002), it is the role of cultural intermediaries to explain both the use value and exchange value of new commodities. It is hard to imagine a clearer instance of this than that provided by lifestyle presenters displaying something like a new model glue gun which will speed the transformation of a living room into a space to impress one's friends. Each programme, whether makeover or food show, introduces products and tells us how to incorporate them into our lives. Considering this reveals another way in which it is the cooking programmes rather than the makeovers which are amenable to importation. As mentioned earlier the products that pervade makeovers are able to be localized within the format so the hardware stores can be tailored to fit what viewers are expected to want to buy. Despite the supermarket names being meaningless to the viewer of imported food shows, the ingredients sold are far more likely to be non-branded (especially now that the emphasis for middle-class food – and most prime time food programming targets middle-class viewers – is on fresh unprocessed ingredients). Whether for Australian or British viewers, slicing fennel for a gratin involves no specific product promotion. The programme remains readable and the shifting trends in fashionable foods move more readily around the world than do the styles of interior design or particular plants whose suitability has climatic nuances. In all instances, the advice about how the commodity discussed will enhance (or perhaps more precisely, better exhibit) one's lifestyle (its exchange value) is consistent.

Conclusion

We need to extend our conception of the domination of lifestyle programming by the celebrity presenter. Looking at the international trade in programmes and formats demonstrates how much more significant this is in distinguishing food programmes from other lifestyle ones. Celebrity chefs can move internationally in a way neither the garden nor the makeover celebrities can. Food itself, which can speak so clearly of nation, region and ethnicity, can also through an attachment to a personality transcend this linkage. Dorinda Hafner can speak to both British and Australian audiences about American food despite having no attachment to the country. Neil Perry's Australian programme *Food Source*, screening as part of the BBC's *Saturday Kitchen*, can take British viewers on an Australian gastronomic journey that speaks both of

Australia and of the culinary traditions of many of its migrant communities.

But whose lifestyle is it that these cultural intermediaries are showing us? For the most part it is a highly segmented and artificial one. Celebrity chefs alighting in a foreign country and displaying moments of culinary exoticism are only showing us a lifestyle inasmuch as they are offering fragments for us to appropriate into our own existing ones. Cooking programmes speak first of the presenter and her or his lifestyle, and we may emulate this a little through following their recipes, purchasing their products or even, to use Hollows's (2003a) example, Nigella's solutions for time poverty. Makeovers present a different picture whether they are formatted or locally originating. The lifestyles they depict are both more hybrid and more accessible. Ostensibly, the lifestyle depicted is that of the recipients, though what we are shown is a version of their lifestyle 'enhanced' by those producing the programme. Inasmuch as those chosen to be made over are similar to the viewers, then the result, though aspirational, should not be impossible. The whole point is to demonstrate desired consumption patterns. They are also more thoroughgoing, in that one or more rooms of a house or a large section if not all of the garden and the ways in which they mesh with a person's domestic life are revealed, while the cooking programmes focus much more tightly on food preparation and consumption. Only a few of the cooking presenters, most notably Nigella, Jamie and Kylie, take us into their domestic lives. More usually we are shown a version of their working lives rendered domestic to inform our 'art of living'.

Notes

1. In 2005 Channel 10 announced it would begin screening a local daytime version of *Ready Steady Cook*, entirely paid for by advertisers. It was the latter aspect that was regarded as an innovation. Prime time remains free of formatted cooking programmes.

4   Recipes for living
Martha Stewart and the new American subject

David B. Goldstein

Entertaining, by its nature, is an expansive gesture, and demands an expansive state of mind in charge.

(Martha Stewart, *Entertaining*, 1982)

There is nothing innocuous left.

(Theodor Adorno, *Minima Moralia*, 1974)

Georgic and American culture

Since its inception, georgic poetry (from the Greek 'to work earth') has blended moral and political concerns in a didactic framework. The classic example of this tradition remains Virgil's *Georgics*, a four-part poem about farming and animal husbandry, written between 37 and 30 BCE. The poem presents itself as a meditation on simplicity:

What makes the crops joyous, beneath what star, Maecenas, it is well to turn the soil, and wed vines to elms, what tending the kine need, what care the herd in breeding, what skill the thrifty bees – hence shall I begin my song.

(Virgil 1986 I, II: 1–5)

An urban dweller with limited farming experience, Virgil points his thoughts toward the city from rural retirement. 'The poem's public urgency,' writes one critic, 'strikes us long before its practical advice on tilling the soil' (O'Loughlin 1978: 59). While the poem does provide farming advice, the instructions serve primarily as allegories for the labour of human relationships: cultivation teaches culture. For example, in the final book, concerned with beekeeping, the character of bees is described in emphatically anthropomorphic terms:

They alone have children in common, hold the dwellings of their city jointly, and pass their life under the majesty of law. They alone know a fatherland and fixed home, and in summer, mindful of the winter to come, spend toilsome days and garner their gains into a common store.

(IV: 153–7)

Passages like this paint a double vision of an ideal society, in which all animals conduct themselves nobly in the context of a peaceful, agrarian existence. Agricultural labour is romanticized as an antidote both to the strife of the politically corrupt urban space and to human immorality. The georgic becomes a way of envisioning an exterior landscape that teaches the interior landscape how to be.

The dark side of Virgil's agrarian vision resides in the inescapability of labour itself. The upright husbandman oscillates between idyllic leisure and '*labor effusus*', empty or poured out labour, which will never fill up the task of living:

I have seen seeds, though picked long and tested with much pains, yet degenerate, if human toil, year after year, culled not the largest by hand. Thus by the law of fate all things speed towards the worst, and slipping away fall back; even as if one, whose oars can scarce force his skiff against the stream, should by chance slacken his arms, and lo! headlong down the current the channel sweeps it away.

(I: 197–203)

The struggle of the oarsman against an implacable stream severs the georgic from the pastoral world. Romanticization of labour does not efface labour itself. Rather, labour constitutes the instrument that must endlessly reinvent utopia.

The georgic tradition in Britain reached its zenith in the neoclassical poetry of the eighteenth century (see Chalker 1969; Low 1985). In America, however, georgic concerns dispersed themselves widely across literary forms, stepping into the role of a national mythology. Its twin messages of the vaunting of agricultural labour and the endless reality of hard work found intense sympathy with a fledgling nation negotiating between an agrarian heritage and an increasingly industrialized economy. These two messages often diverged in the early literature of the United States, making the georgic elements of texts at times hard to identify. I will suggest elsewhere that the first strand of georgic, in which agricultural labour becomes a civic religion, is epitomized in the writings of Thomas Jefferson. Here we concern ourselves with the dark side of georgic, the trope of endless labour. While it may rely on the metaphorics of agriculture, this strain ultimately proves less interested in the actual tillage of the soil than in the interior of the individual mind, the soil upon which humans endlessly refashion a utopia of lived experience. This strain emerges most clearly in the writings of another founding father, Benjamin Franklin.

In his *Autobiography*, first published in 1793, Franklin (1986) fuses the georgic with a quintessentially American ideology of self-improvement through hard work. Although Franklin tends to disparage agricultural labour, his emphasis on the self-improving nature of toil combines georgic metaphor with Protestant sensibility.[1] Franklin half-ironically explains his 'bold and arduous Project of arriving at moral Perfection' (p. 66) in terms of a man tending the fields of his mind:

> And like him who having a Garden to weed, does not attempt to eradicate all the bad Herbs at once, which would exceed his Reach and his Strength, but works on one of the Beds at a time, and having accomplish'd the first proceeds to a second; so I should have, (I hoped) the encouraging Pleasure of seeing on my Pages the Progress I made in Virtue, by clearing successively my Lines of their Spots, till in the end by a Number of Courses, I should be happy in viewing a clean Book after a thirteen Weeks' daily Examination.
>
> (Franklin 1986: 70)

Franklin in turn paraphrases and extends the English philosopher Francis Bacon (1974: 147), who in 1605 wrote: 'These Georgics of the mind, concerning the husbandry and tillage thereof, are no less worthy than the heroical descriptions of virtue, duty, and felicity.' Franklin, who had little use for country living, employed the georgic for its ability to teach a proper moral relation to daily life through sheer effort.

The Franklinian georgic has influenced American culture in a variety of ways, reframing in modern terms the mode of instruction that Virgil and Hesiod propound as an explicit set of rules regarding how to farm. For Franklin, overt lecturing may fade in the face of lessons on how to live one's life with metaphoric or literal reference to the rural world. Over the past three centuries didactic and non-didactic writers alike have responded to Franklinian georgic: Emerson, Thoreau, Longfellow, Frost and Wendell Berry, to name a few, have integrated georgic concerns into their poetry, exploring the tensions between a romanticized vision of agricultural labour and the moral meanings of hard work. This legacy continues to make itself felt in American political life too, from farm subsidies to global isolationism.

The increasing power of the commodity in late twentieth-century American life has brought the georgic into crisis. 'What the philosophers once knew of life,' lamented Theodor Adorno (1974: 15), 'has become the sphere of private existence and now of mere consumption'. Yet 'the teaching of the good life', the task Adorno calls the province of philosophy, is also the charge of the georgic. If the sphere of 'mere consumption' redefines philosophy, it also transforms the meanings of georgic. The heir of Franklinian georgic in contemporary America, I will suggest here, is Martha Stewart. Rather than teaching the possibility that georgic can offer a template for resistance against the reign of the commodity, Stewart explores the possibility that georgic rhetoric and commodification can interpenetrate to the point that they can no longer be disengaged. Following in the footsteps of Franklin, who used the printing press to transform the American relationship to industry in all senses of the term, Stewart has built a communications empire based on the close relations between consumerism and interiority. 'Mere' consumption in Stewart operates with the full moral strength of Franklin's work ethic, positing an apparently harmonious, but always in fact conflicted, relation between the personal and domestic, and between the domestic and public realms. Self-sufficiency is the constantly shifting landscape on which Stewart's battle for a national ethos is played out. In teaching her readers and viewers how to live, Martha Stewart proposes a georgic of the commodified American subject.

Martha Stewart Living Omnimedia (MSLO) continues to have a tremendous and – until Stewart's trial for insider trading (in which she was not convicted of insider trading, but only of lying about a particular trade) placed the company under extraordinary scrutiny – largely undocumented influence upon American conceptions of interiority, domesticity and consumption. Using an approach broadly indebted to Adorno's theories of Western culture and aesthetics, I describe the assumptions and processes that Stewart employs in her programme for the reinvention of American labour. I focus upon the rhetoric of Stewart's recipes and on the role that food plays in her approach to the domestic sphere.

Martha *improbus*

Martha Stewart enacts the Franklinian georgic. We might understand this strain as the impulse that refigures work as the driving force behind all aesthetics, that effaces agricultural work not by idealizing it or its products, but by consuming it under a massive, all-encompassing grid of labour of which agriculture plays but a small part. This side of georgic is highly attuned to its own transience in the face of outside pressure. In Virgil's case, the pressure is of civil war; the idyllic poem ends with a heavily ironic paean to Caesar Augustus, who 'gave a victor's laws unto willing nations' (1986 IV: 561–2). For Stewart the domestic space itself exerts this pressure: her battle plan is the calendar. Her labours are Herculean in scope and variety, but thoroughly modern and middle-class in conception. 'We all have so much work to do,' she reiterates, 'and so very little time to do it' (Stewart 1999: 14). We must struggle against the current of life, but must also keep in mind that *labor omnia vicit improbus* (Virgil 1986 I: 145-6) – labour unrelenting has conquered, and shall conquer, all. This is the meaning of life, or rather, of living.

Martha's georgic originates in nostalgia for a lived experience of food.[2] *Entertaining* (1982), her first volume, begins with a chapter called 'Of Kitchens and Learning', which describes in detail the three kitchens where the author spent her youth, and which self-consciously locates antecedents for Martha's mania for entertaining and love of food. 'With six children' in her mother's kitchen, she tells us, 'quantity was the rule'. 'My earliest memories were bound up with mushroom soup and pierogi'. There are pictures of objects used in those kitchens – a butcher block, a mixing bowl – that Martha now owns and calls 'legacies of my childhood'. The narrative continues through Martha's first trip to Europe and her deepening interest in growing her own food: 'I realize now that I had moved to the country long before we actually left West 101st Street'. The pictures accompanying the chapter mostly show Martha in her gardens, engaged in typically georgic activities – hoeing cabbages, picking sunflowers, feeding the chickens, and, in the ur-gesture of Virgil's *Georgics*, tending to her bees. The photo that begins the chapter shows Martha in her rustic kitchen with its wood-burning stove, standing amidst a utopian bounty of produce from her garden and ovens (Stewart 1982: 1-9). Throughout *Entertaining*, she quotes the literature of Scott, Wharton, Tolstoy and the great journalist and food writer A.J. Liebling, thus situating her own writing in a continuum of literary representations of personal relationships to food.

But a glance at Martha Stewart a quarter-century later painted a different picture. While parodies of Martha's rhetoric of self-sufficient farming habits abound, the emphasis in *Martha Stewart Living* is no longer on food. Most of the recipes in the flagship magazine are shunted to the back, while the spin-off magazines, such as *Martha Stewart Weddings*, *Good Things*, and *Kids* emphasize craft and entertainment. (The recently launched *Everyday Food*, which is now both a magazine and a television programme, focuses upon the utilitarian side of food, or as its tag line explains, 'fast family-friendly ideas', thus downplaying either labour or food's connection to the land.) On her eponymous television show, recipes and gardening advice compete for airtime with arts and crafts, field trips and interior decoration projects. The Internet site – until its 2004 redesign – exhibited a studio kitchen display where one could click on and buy various kitchen appliances and furniture. Her line of home products, cross-marketed through K-Mart, extends beyond the kitchen into every other room of the house. The idea of growing one's own food has been incorporated into a larger programme that embraces the full range of domestic labour, or 'home living'. Yet Martha's labour of living exhibits a curious, seemingly paradoxical quality: in a society in which people, especially women, seem to have less time and inclination to engage in household chores, and in which 'time-saving devices' are marketed with ever-increasing fervour to a salivating public, Martha's approach to domestic labour is to create more work. She shows you how to soak birch bark overnight in order to glue and nail it onto picture frames, giving them rustic, expressive flair. This is a process that takes hours – instead one could buy a wood picture frame for a nominal sum. This sort of work, which one finds at every turn of Martha's oeuvre, is presented as a way of letting you be 'yourself'. This is where Living and Entertaining intertwine: you express your personality by spending time and effort on craft, construction and cooking projects, which your visitors and family will perceive and appreciate as manifestations of you. Martha's georgic is a georgic of selfhood (both her own and her readers').

The process by which the georgic sensibility of the company has developed is rooted, to a degree perhaps unsurpassed in consumerism, in the persona of Martha Stewart herself. In order to analyse the power that Stewart's image has exerted upon the ontological development of her company, it will be useful to divide this development into its pre-trial and post-trial emanations. This is because Stewart's trial, and its apparent unmasking of the corrupt businesswoman behind the perfect housewife, seemed to mount a grave challenge to the wisdom of placing Martha's face at the forefront of her products. Whether this challenge ever actually materialized is a question I will take up in the next section, but here I wish to address the ways in which the origins of MSLO lie in a powerful and brilliant fusion of image and message – a company whose authenticity derives from and reciprocally ratifies its founder.

Unlike a company such as AOL Time Warner or Disney, whose massive networks are dispersed under countless guises, Martha's pre-trial empire had but one face: Martha. The enterprise is founded upon the appealing illusion that the company displays Martha's life to our personal viewing pleasure (an illusion that the trial rendered an ironic reality). Martha's website allowed any visitor to navigate through the studios (mock-ups of the ground floors of two of her houses), clicking on interesting details for more information and viewing rooms from different angles. Being constantly reminded that what is on view is a close copy of Martha's 'actual' houses gives a distinctly voyeuristic feel to the process. But of course her 'home' is a studio, with the heavy fresnels and ellipsoidals clearly in evidence. The relentless marketing of Martha Stewart's bodily presence has the contradictory effect of rendering her ethereal: she has become a corporate entity, no longer an actual person. She simply does too much, is in too many places at once, has too tight a grip on perfection to be believable as an individual. Her vast squadron of assistants helps make possible this multiplicity without rendering it any less disorienting. Her body has been rendered corporate in both a capitalistic and quasi-religious sense – Martha's body is diffused throughout culture, everywhere and nowhere, in houses and gardens, draped on bodies and placed inside mouths.

Martha's voyeuristic presentation of her domestic interiors corre-sponds to an aggressive refashioning of the surfaces of those interiors, a process that points to a curious re-envisioning of the American concept of work. Martha changes her hairstyle, her look, and her kitchen approximately once every 18 months, as a glance through back issues of the magazine illustrates. Yet she makes little effort to efface her mistakes or her prior images; instead, she revels in the change by juxtaposing new and old whenever she can. New episodes of her pre-trial television show were often followed by reruns from prior years, in which a differently coifed but equally styled Martha smiles at you from the suspended time of now. The 1998 reissue of *Entertaining* comes with a new updated cover (no more long hair or white lace frock), but the rest of the book's pictures proudly display their early 1980s vintage. Her two studio kitchens, whose facades change regularly, are explicitly based on those of Martha's two main houses, in Westport, Connecticut, and East Hampton, Long Island. Upon renovation, one of the studio kitchens was made supermodern, but the counters installed were soapstone, a surface that according to the website 'oxidizes with time and use, deepening in color and aquiring [sic] an attractive patina of age. You can speed up this process by oiling the stone once a month for the first year after it is installed'.[3] The All-Clad pots were old-style copper – although spanking new. That the kitchen studios negotiate between old and new reflects a rethinking of the meaning and function of kitchen space. Watching these constant transformations can be exhausting, but that process of continual change constitutes the most fundamental work that goes on at MSLO: Martha markets Martha, and Martha is a moving target.

In her self-transformations, Martha echoes Bacon's and Franklin's visions of self-husbandry. The continual tillage of the mind, Bacon and Franklin both argue, prepares one for private study and public activity. Only by constantly turning and ploughing the soil of one's character can one succeed in the just life. But Franklin takes this idea several steps further, articulating a georgic philosophy predicated upon the impor-tance of presenting the proper appearance to the outer world. As he describes in detail his method of self-improvement, it becomes clear that this improvement is motivated more by the wish to 'seem' than the wish to 'be'. Informed by 'a Quaker friend' that he has left humility off a list of his attributes of moral perfection, he promptly adds it, 'giving an extensive Meaning to the Word. I cannot boast of much Success in acquiring the *Reality* of this Virtue; but I had a good deal with regard to the *Appearance* of it' (Franklin 1986: 75). Even moral perfection itself worries him from the standpoint of how he will look to others. '[A] benevolent Man,' he jokes, 'should allow a few Faults in himself, to keep his Friends in Countenance' (p. 73).

For Franklin, the appearance of self-transformation works just as well as its reality. For Martha, the appearance *is* the reality. Martha engages the idea of self-cultivation on the level of performative image, constantly reproducing herself as commodity. The idea of morality itself resurfaces in its most banal form, as a tag: 'It's a good thing'. What remains of the moral register has been put in the service of a kind of commodified version of individual expression. It's a good thing because it saves time, or because it looks pretty, or because it makes you feel good. It is the good neither of Plato, nor of Augustine, but of General Electric's 'We bring good things to life'. It is also a tautological good. In naming all aspects of her empire after herself, in making all aspects of goodness self-referential, Martha reminds us that her product is precisely Martha. Selfhood is the totalizing feature of MSLO, the unity of definition and purpose behind it. At the core is no actual self, but a series of mirrors between the conglomerate's captivated audience and the corporate stage. Adorno (1974: 50) writes: 'In many people it is already an impertinence to say "I"'. 'Martha Stewart' is the self we have always never had. It enters from outside to invent us from within.

For Martha the concept of family, perhaps the central icon of unique experience in American life, presents itself as another route by which the public world inverts and abolishes the private. The cover of the December 1998/January 1999 issue of *Martha Stewart Living* features an angelic tow-headed child sleeping on a long leather chair before a Christmas tree adorned with burning candles. We later find out that the boy is Charlie, Martha's 'real' nephew; the house is Martha's retreat in Seal Harbor, Maine. The consummately nostalgic advertisement for Christmas-present is thus revealed to be a 'genuine' private family moment. We are even told in a PPS in the issue's opening 'Letter from Martha' that 'the candles on the cover were lit only for the photograph, then quickly extinguished' (Stewart 1998/9: 16). Presumably this was done to let Charlie sleep on undisturbed, without fear of the house burning down. But the revealing power of this moment in turn exposes a greater obfuscation: when the family member is used as a model, any division between the private and public personae of that family member is compromised. Is Charlie an individual or a construct? For his parents, one assumes, he is his own reality. But for the reader of the magazine he has become commodified image. To speak of there being a slim division between Martha's private and public lives is to miss the point: Martha Stewart Living constitutes an abolition of the private sphere. Pressed into the service of commodification, the intimacy of private space – that quality conjured in the naive curve of Charlie's apparently oblivious sleeping form – becomes itself a commodity. As the US government and media continue their agonistic and hyperbolized savaging of the boundary between private and public life, Martha reminds us every day that it is possible the boundary is irrelevant.

The georgic unchained

But that was before March 2004, when Stewart was convicted of lying to government investigators about the reasons for her sale of nearly 4000 shares of ImClone Systems, a biotechnology company then run by her friend Samuel D. Waksal. In the wake of the trial, MSLO had to scramble to develop a strategy to address the problem that its greatest asset was now its most serious liability. Once 'exposed' as a greedy businesswoman rather than as the genuine über-housewife, Martha's plight elicited disdain and anger, along with an outpouring of sympathy. Whatever the reasons behind this myriad of reactions (of which a full analysis must await another venue), the company responded by literally edging her off the page.[4] Since Martha Stewart's prosecution began in 2003, Martha's name has dwindled on her magazines as if on a prison diet of instant potatoes. It once stood out on a field of solid colour in the upper left-hand corner of each cover, but now is tucked above the 'ng' of 'Living', and appears nowhere on the cover of recent magazine launches such as *Everyday Food* and *Good Things*, replaced by proximate phrases such as 'from the editors [or kitchens] of *Martha Stewart Living*'. The hallmark pages of her flagship magazine, 'Martha's Calendar' and 'A Letter from Martha', have been excised, the former replaced by the self-effacing 'Gentle reminders' (a pared down calendar that eschews the sense its predecessor cultivated of actually being Martha's to-do list), while the latter, with her trademark reproduced signature, has vanished. She has been demoted from 'Chairman, Chief Executive Officer, and Editorial Director', to 'Founding Editorial Director'. Numerous other changes, both cosmetic and structural, have taken place, all of them seeking to dissociate Martha from the conglomerate that bears her name. Like the God of

Paradise Lost, Martha appears to have withdrawn her presence from her own creation in order to create it anew.

Countless journalists and business pundits have wondered openly whether this is possible, and at first the answer appeared to be 'no'. Between 2002, when concerns about Stewart's stock trades surfaced, and 2004, *Martha Stewart Living* magazine lost 70 per cent of its advertising revenue and 22 per cent of its rate base (Grigoriadis 2005). Martha's television shows were cancelled or temporarily suspended, and the radio call-in show 'Ask Martha' was taken off the air. The company laid off more than 100 employees and posted a US$15 million loss in the third quarter of 2004 alone (Hays 2004b). Merchandise sales through K-Mart, with whom Martha had brokered a deal that at least one critic thought 'had tilted heavily in Martha's favor' from its start in 1987 (Byron 2002: 260), were declining. MSLO's attempts to develop product lines untainted by its founder have either failed, as in the purchase of theweddinglist.com, which ended in a US$6 million write-down, or have yet to demonstrate success, as with the launch of the *Everyday Food* magazine and its attendant public television show (Hays 2004a).

Yet as of this writing (February 2005), the trends are reversing: MSLO's stock price has climbed steadily since Martha started serving her sentence, and rose almost to its pre-trial peak recently in the wake of the announcement that Stewart would star in the sequel to the wildly popular *The Apprentice*, a reality show in which several young business-men and women attempted to secure an internship with real estate mogul Donald Trump (Kennedy 2005). The new show will feature Stewart auditioning a similar cadre of aspirants in the lifestyle business, and its licensing fees are said to be 'trending significantly higher' than for Stewart's earlier show (Hays 2005). This rejuvenation of Martha's image and, by extension, her company, is due, I would suggest, to two factors. First, the attempt to separate Martha Stewart's life from *Martha Stewart Living* has in fact been pursued less drastically than it seemed. Second, Stewart's time in jail has accomplished what the most eloquent trial defence could not hope to do: paradoxically, it has re-established her georgic credentials. It has authenticized her.

The first point is made in the recent *New York* article 'The Return of Martha Stewart' (Grigoriadis 2005), whose cover sports a glowing, airbrushed close-up of Martha's face, her ears adorned with pink pearls, against a light blue background: half angel, half senior class portrait for 'most likely to succeed'. Vanessa Grigoriadis points out in the article that the three major figures involved in the running of MSLO during and after Stewart's trial – current CEO Susan Lyne, publicist Susan Magrino and co-founder Sharon Patrick – all bear at least a passing physical resemblance to Martha. In fact, MSLO is packed with echoes and mirrors of Martha herself; most of the company's techniques for distancing itself from Martha also have the disconcerting effect of diffusing Martha throughout MSLO's structure. The enigmatic phrase 'from the editors of *Martha Stewart Living*', for example, suggests syntactically what was always true visually: that Martha Stewart's life is the subject from which her editors draw for their content. Sometimes the visual alterations themselves actually increase the name's presence in its context. While her name has dwindled on the *cover* of the flagship magazine, for instance, it has grown on the magazine's *spine*, where 'Martha Stewart LIVING' has been replaced by the more uniform and unifying 'MARTHA STEWART LIVING'. Meanwhile she has operated a kind of shadow website, marthatalks.com, which goes unmentioned on the corporate site but which provides a kind of online stand-in for the letters and calendars that used to populate the magazine. Instead of advice about gardening and decorating, marthatalks.com displays supportive emails from fans, links to newspaper articles that place her case in a favourable light, and provides a chronology – a legal calendar of sorts – of documents relating to the trial.

On the other hand, after assiduously withdrawing from the public eye for most of her trial, Stewart has found her public again by entering prison. Encouraged by Sharon Patrick, her co-founder, former president, and former COO (who then left the company), Martha chose to serve her term immediately, which was strictly unnecessary since her appeal was pending. The result has been a spectacular public relations coup, 'a roots thing ... where the poor girl from Nutley ... triumphs once again over adversity' (Grigoriadis 2005: 22). As one brand consultant put it, 'If she gets back to running the basics of the business and has this added patina, if you will, of having suffered and moved ahead in her life – well, Americans love that' (quoted in Hays 2005). While it is certainly true that the fable of the powerful public figure who falls from grace and finds new humility seems to hold limitless appeal for the American public, there is another phenomenon at work that has gone unexamined in the media. Almost every mention of Stewart's prison experience includes a detail about her zeal for lifestyle tasks even in the Big House: according to various sources, she gathers wild onions and dandelions in the prison yard, avidly waxes the warden's floors, concocts flans and Vietnamese dishes in the microwave, has learned to crochet, sorts Scrabble pieces, and entered a holiday decorating contest with a flock of paper cranes (she lost to a crèche). Rather than dim her focus on 'living' as she conceives of it, her prison experience seems only to intensify it. Her abiding interest in transforming her environment, however hostile, through the lifestyle skills her company teaches, ratifies her relation to those skills and the philosophy that underpins them. She works very hard, according to the georgic principle that *labor omnia vicit improbus*: unrelenting labour conquers all. Her austere tillage of the cracks in the prison yard matches the austere tillage of the mind that Franklin counsels. In returning to her 'roots thing', she returns to the foundations of her georgic message: leisure is a form of endless work. This endless work is that of the body as well as the mind, a constant project of self-improvement. The clearest possible setting for such a message may well be the correctional facility.

One might ask whether the obsessive relationship to the domestic arts that Stewart has displayed in prison is genuine, or a public relations stunt, or a psychic reaction to a difficult situation – but such questions miss the point. Rather, Martha's prison experiences demonstrate the complete coalescence of domesticity and interiority, of commodity and self, through the *labor improbus* of georgic lifestyle. In prison, Martha becomes re-authenticized, playing out the drama of her company's mission in circumstances stripped to bare essentials. There is no way to separate business calculations from heartfelt actions because Martha is co-extensive with her business: when she picks dandelions, her company's stock rises, and she makes money. (Over the course of her term, the value of her personal stake in the company has risen to an estimated US$827 million from US$318 million; see Hays 2005.) That a founder's fortunes might rise and fall with those of her company is not in itself rare. But that a founder's fortunes might rise and fall with her microwaved flan illustrates the total fusion between Martha Stewart the person and Martha Stewart the lifestyle, and in turn, between the lifestyle she teaches and the conception of self that lifestyle dictates.

Recipes for living

The georgic, as Hesiod and Virgil remind us, is a poetics of instruction. So too the consummate form of knowledge transmission regarding food: the recipe. Recipe and georgic have much in common, but function according to radically different paradigms. Georgic, eminently and imminently allegorical, is always verging into metaphor and symbol. In georgic, the author's self-positing is crucial to the text's reception. A recipe presents itself as fully realized in its practicality, and seeks no other rhetorical sphere than that of process analysis. Its author is seen as ancillary to a larger historical progression, usually encapsulated in the phrase 'handing down'. Yet a recipe is also a performance, by both the writer and the reader-participant. Thus it seems appropriate to evaluate it in terms of its performative aspects. How does Martha Stewart, to whom performing is a central element of the construction of the individual, treat the genre of the recipe?

If the MSLO paradigm is a performance paradigm (Stewart's friends apparently refer to the prison term as 'the intermission' – see Hays 2005), its script is the recipe. And none of the changes wrought by Stewart's trial and sentence have altered the rhetoric of the recipes in *Martha Stewart Living*. In order to examine the recipes, we must consider them from the point of view of their two broadest functions – as a formal genre and as a lesson in how to do something. The recipe form gives structure to *MSL*: the television show is divided into individual recipe performances, the magazine ordered by event-appropriate recipes, the internet site (through hyperlinks) blends recipes seamlessly with a shopping list of *MSL* merchandise. And on the macro-level, the MSLO empire presents a consistent recipe for living, made up of recipes for every aspect of domestic life. They are recipes imbued with the author function – Martha's recipes – though they are generally written by committee, tested and refined through a kind of communal, if not terribly reliable, process.

Recipe generally distinguishes between the writer and the reader-performer, with emphasis falling on the second category. Martha's concept of recipe, especially on her television show, elides the distinction – she both authors and performs. Ostensibly she does this to show her readers and viewers 'how to do it', an idea long embraced by home improvement and gardening shows and the US TV Food Network. The use value of such a recipe displayed on television without accompanying text is variable at best. The exchange value is all, an invitation to a voyeurism in which one sees the inside of one's own kitchen as a potentially utopian space, perennially new and full of elegant devices; one sees oneself as a consummate performer with time on one's hands. Martha extrapolates this to all areas of the house – the bedroom, the library, the mudroom you never had. What she teaches in these laboratories of domestic decorousness is how to watch her teach. The 'light music' (as Adorno 1978 would call it) that punctuates the show's segments has a Pavlovian aspect: it acts as a mood lightener, ushering its viewers into a pleasant space in which the minutiae of domestic habitation become the sylphs and sprites that catalyse the battle of bourgeois self-making.

The culinary recipes in *Martha Stewart Living* exhibit a uniform corporate persona. All extraneous words are trimmed, and explanations are standardized and contracted into the smallest space possible. This is certainly a function of magazine editing, which puts a premium on space and line length. Yet it is ironic that a magazine which presents itself as the emanation of a single self sounds so interchangeable with the recipe language of other magazines. Even the recipe headnotes, an obvious place in which an authorial voice might find expression, tend to strike a tone both tyrannical and vacuous. 'Buy the very freshest produce, and cook just until tender for the best flavor', starts a recipe for 'Summer Black-Eyed Pea Salad' (*MSL* 1999: 192). Couched as a helpful hint, it is a phrase whose adverbs announce its annihilation: 'very' empties 'freshest', and 'just' hollows out 'tender'. It may be true that inexperienced cooks need to be told to buy fresh and cook briefly. But while freshness for an actual farmer might involve a precise network of associations, in this case it stakes out a feeble relevance as 'a good thing'.

Martha's recipes teach us how to accept the corporation into our daily lives. We the readers are spoon-fed blandness in place of even the illusion of interaction with another self. The most redemptive quality of recipe – that its reader performs, expresses, and therefore transforms it – is compromised by Martha's rubric of entertainment. These recipes are to be produced for the pleasure of others, which in turn means they are meant to conform to a simulation of what pleasure might consist in.[5] The recipes of *MSL*, like its lessons about interior decoration, teach you to substitute self-expression with its corporate simulation: how to replace you with 'you'.

Where Martha's authorial 'voice' did come across, and presumably will again, in issue after issue of *Martha Stewart Living* magazine, was on the opening page (after the calendar), 'A Letter from Martha'. Stamped with a facsimile of Martha's signature, this 'letter' constitutes the recipe that the magazine's nominal 'recipes' fail to deliver: it instructs the reader in how to live. In the June 1999 'Letter', Martha takes on the subject of labour itself:

> While reading [Bill Gates' new book] (using my newly reinvigo-rated speed-reading skills, because my reading time has become increasingly scarce), it occurred to me that not only business but life in general is proceeding seemingly at the speed of light.
> (Stewart 1999: 14)

The parentheses inject a supposed interpolation of selfhood within an already personal narrative: we catch a glimpse of Martha's daily life, beyond the public self. That the parentheses in fact enclose an instance of Franklinian self-advertising is what we have come to expect. 'We all have so much work to do,' she continues, 'and so very little time to do it, and I know it is more than the result of a refined work ethic. My theory is that we are all doing more than ever *simply because we can*' (her italics). Although the picture above the letter shows Martha in her garden, smiling and holding a basket of delphiniums (an article on them appears in the same issue), the georgic trope here has nothing to do with agriculture, but with technology. Faxing (which Martha insists 'has become nearly passé'), cell phones, and the Internet are the purported objects of concern.

In the course of this tour of her own technological acuity, Martha asks her readers two good questions: 'And what is the result of this new, overcrowded style of living? What problems does this "speeding up" create, and what problems has it solved?' But the last paragraph takes an unexpected turn. 'We know', Martha assures us, 'that these glitches are going to be worked out. Until then we should really all step back and see how far we've come – so fast, so soon'. The last paragraph performs the step back that it directs, but the action creates no distancing. 'These glitches are going to be worked out', which could refer grammatically either to the slowness of Martha's website or to the 'new, overcrowded style of living' in general, delivers precisely the opposite message from the rest of the essay. It refuses to evaluate the consequences of a speed that spawns more work, assuring its readers instead that everything will be OK when the world (or the website) goes even faster. The signature follows abruptly, a vacuous marker of selfhood beneath the command to evacuate the self. Susan Stewart (1993: 14) has pointed out that 'writing by hand assumes the speed of the body . . . handwriting is to space what the voice is to time'.[6] Here the signature – and by extension, the whole concept of 'letter' – registers a nostalgic glance towards embodiment, a simulation of a simulation of self. The rhetoric of self-improvement that structures the letter reaches its culmination in this signature, in which work empties itself into meaningless gesture: the labour of writing one's signature becomes a glitch that has been 'worked out'.

The letter ends: 'P.S. Thank heavens the garden still grows as it did twenty years ago: My favorite tomato ripened in seventy-two days when I first started gardening, and it still does'. Classical georgic returns as the cosy antidote to modern speed. The garden answers to its own rhythm, and our labour must slow itself down to match it. An antidote to Adorno's bourgeois self-evacuation seems to emerge at last, as Martha and her readers 'step back' into the natural world. But the reverse is true: natural beauty achieves existence through human desire. The tomato has to ripen in exactly 72 days in order to give us our wished for perspective. The 'favorite tomato' is thoroughly reproducible: every year it grows and tastes the same. We may see that 'favorite tomato' tomorrow on Martha's television show. We will receive it willingly, like a victor's laws.

Notes

1. For a much debated but important analysis of the relation between Franklin's Protestantism and the American work ethic, see Weber (1985).
2. It hardly seems accurate to refer to Martha Stewart exclusively by her surname, as a large part of the effectiveness of her persona consists in the liberal use of her first name to inculcate a sense of personhood and intimacy. Therefore I will maintain that convention.
3. The URL is no longer active (February 2005).
4. For one exploration of the politics behind Martha's trial, see Shaw (2003).
5. 'In American conventional speech,' observes Adorno (1978: 279) with characteristic bleakness, 'having a good time means being present at the enjoyment of others, which in its turn has as its only content being present'.
6. See also Derrida (1977: 20): 'By definition, a written signature implies the actual or empirical nonpresence of the signer'.

Part II
Home front

5   Home truths?

Ruth Holliday

> The traces of the occupant ... leave their impression on the interior.
>
> (Benjamin 1978: 155)

The explosion in home improvement programmes has been a remarkable phenomenon on British television. Looking through the television guide for the week I am writing, to take a typical example, there are no less than sixteen and a half hours of airtime given over to home improvement on terrestrial television alone, not including the large number of programmes aimed specifically at gardening. The shows range from the 'high class' (such as *Grand Designs*, where we get to watch someone building or renovating their home from scratch, or *Sunday Homes and Gardens*, a restful and upmarket magazine slot) to the 'low budget' – *House Doctor* and *Selling Houses* (which concentrate on how to present your house for maximum sale price), *Changing Rooms* (MDF heaven where two teams of neighbours make over a room in each other's home with the help of a designer); and *Big Strong Boys* and *DIY SOS* (where teams of specialists rescue deserving casualties of DIY). There are programmes aimed at improving one house to buy another more expensive one (such as *Property Ladder*, *Safe as Houses* and *Trading Up*), or giving advice on where to buy your home for maximum resale or rental value (*Location, Location, Location* and *Relocation, Relocation*) in the countryside (*Escape to the Country*) or abroad (*A Place in the Sun*). You can also reorganize your house and get rid of all that clutter ('excess baggage') with *The Life Laundry*. These programmes can effectively be split into two categories – interior decorating and house buying/selling – and both categories claim to add value to your home, either through its immediate sale or purchase, or through its future sales potential.

It would be a mistake, however, to assume that the popularity of DIY programmes in the UK is a uniquely contemporary phenomenon. In fact, the first of their kind appeared in the early 1960s on the BBC (see Brunsdon 2004). *Do it Yourself* (1961) and *Bucknell's House* (1962–3) were both presented by Barry Bucknell, a respectable, skilled and besuited member of a family-owned building and electrical firm. Bucknell's style neatly fitted the BBC's remit to 'educate and inform' (although 'entertainment' was clearly not the highest priority). His particular expertise lay in 'modernizing' Victorian houses by affixing plywood covers to panelled doors and boxing in or removing Victorian fireplaces and baths (procedures which 'yuppies' spent the 1980s trying to reverse). These practices became almost ubiquitous throughout the 1960s and the popularity of the television shows meant that houses modernized in this way were described as having been 'Bucknelled'.

In the 1970s Bucknell was superseded by Yorkshire Television's Mike Smith, presenter of *Old House, New Home* and *Jobs around the House*. Both shows also focused on the modernization of Victorian houses. During each episode various tasks – putting in a central heating system or assembling and fitting kitchen units – were demonstrated in real time, stressing the skill and labour that went into each task. As Brunsdon (2004: 124) explains, time was key in constructing Smith's trustworth-iness as a television presenter/instructor, as 'doing a job properly takes time, and this is exactly what the use of real time [in the show's format] guarantees'. However, by 1975 London Weekend Television had begun to experiment with DIY show formats. In *Furnishing on a Shoestring* the host, Judith Chalmers, was introduced as a busy working mother and owner of large Victorian house in Islington, North London. The show focused on renovating homes and furniture, but whilst Chalmers presented and controlled the pace of the show, renovations were demonstrated by skilled craftsmen – George Dixon and Robert MacDonald – who showed 'ordinary' home and furniture owners how to 'have a go' at restoration. Restored pieces of furniture were then revalued at the end of the show. *Furnishing on a Shoestring*, as Brunsdon points out, introduces a more contemporary format through the display of transformation and resulting increase in cash value; the interplay of ordinary people, experts and presenters; and the narrative of a deadline. However, it also introduces a new narrative – of class distinction. Chalmers dressed in casual and unisex clothing (her gender mobility signifying class mobility), whilst Dixon and MacDonald wore suits. Chalmers controlled the programme, often interrupting the detailed and unhurried instruction of the craftsmen in addressing her audience. The 'ordinary people' on the show were also 'noticeably "posher" than the experts' (Brunsdon 2004: 127). All these factors lead Brunsdon to conclude that *Furnishing on a Shoestring*:

> is a programme of gentrification, not modernization, because, in the teaching of craft skills to these bourgeois entrepreneurs, the programme stages the reclamation of 'junk' – dilapidated furniture, inner-city housing – and its restoration. It is not Mr Dixon and Mr MacDonald who will be living in Islington in the

future ... and this is signified partly through their lack of televisual manner. They are, paradoxically, not modern enough.

(128)

However, despite their roots, newer DIY programmes differ from the earlier models in three important ways: in their emphasis on entertainment and viewing pleasure, in their focus on the 'makeover', and, importantly, in their redefinition of the audience – the British Public.

In *DIY SOS* (a BBC home makeover programme that regularly attracts more than eight million viewers), for example, we witness the banter of the plasterers as they mock the show's host Nick Knowles for his television presenter privileges and lack of participation in the 'dirty jobs'. The team's playful pranks aimed at electrician Billy and the constant verbal sparring between him and Nick add humour and develop the show's characters in an obvious move away from informing to entertaining when compared to earlier DIY programmes. *DIY SOS* gives us a flavour of what it might be like to work in or with a team of housebuilders and the close and interdependent bonds that might be formed as a result. It is a representation of the 'workplace family' (Taylor 1989) that substitutes for the difficulties of our real ones.

The pleasure of these exchanges for viewers is revealed in the show's online message board (despite its remit – 'Planning on a spot of DIY? Whether you're a first time DIYer or an experienced hand, swap your tips and advice in this message board'), which combines requests for DIY advice with viewers confessing their allegiances or attractions to particular members of the DIY team. In fact one of the plasterers, Julian Perryman, was recently awarded a 'pink tiara' (for sex appeal) by gay viewers of the programme, and this was acknowledged graciously on the show.

Another of the most striking aspects of the new genre homes programmes, then, is their inclusiveness. As these programmes represent 'the public', so they simultaneously construct it. Thus, the households presented as 'ordinary British households' include black, Asian, multinational and mixed 'race' families, lesbian and gay families (sometimes, but not always, euphemistically described as 'friends') and single-parent families, and the programmes include a similar mix of both male and female craftspeople among their cast.

The final significant change to the structure of homes programmes is the move from demonstrating skills to the 'makeover'. The dénouement of each programme is the juxtaposition of *before* and *after*, known as 'the reveal'. The pleasure of the new genre is very much the pleasure of consuming a design idea. In earlier programmes the (relatively little) pleasure induced was the pleasure of learning skills – of production.

Given that *DIY SOS* begins by showing the horrible situations that DIY enthusiasts have landed themselves in, and finishes with the transformation effected (against the clock) by a professional team, the message is loud and clear – *Do not try this (yourself) at home!*

Another striking narrative of *DIY SOS* is that of *failed masculinity*. Each episode encourages audience participation through a viewer vote for the candidate most deserving of a makeover. Time and again we witness men (and sometimes women) who have quite literally pulled their houses apart but lack the skills to put them back together. Rooms with no plaster, semi-removed chimney breasts, half-demolished walls, unconnected toilets, showers dripping dangerously onto live electric wires are routinely paraded before us. In many cases the men who began these 'improvements' have now absented themselves from the family home, leaving their children playing amongst damp piles of rubble and their ex-partners preparing meals amongst disconnected taps and cookers. This is the DIY disaster from which the team quite literally rescue women and children. Such a setting gives much weight to Iris Marion Young's (1990) assertion that men act as subjects whilst women are both subject and object. Women, aware of themselves as objects in the world, curtail their orientation to act in a moment of reflection which asks, 'Can I achieve this?' Young argues that this awareness of the culturally constructed limitation of the female body prevents a woman from simply 'acting'. Men, on the other hand, unaware of themselves as objects, are oriented only towards the task, the idea that they may be unable to accomplish it expelled from their subjectivity. In this way men are likely to fail whereas women are unlikely to try. Whilst Young importantly states that these gendered traits are 'tendencies' rather than universal characteristics, *DIY SOS* repeatedly presents us with (absent) men who have 'bitten off more than they can chew'. In order to reconcile this failure with a masculine subjectivity it may simply be easier to remove oneself from the evidence and begin a new unchallenged masculinity somewhere else.

Overall, however, the programme still has wide appeal to both working-class and middle-class viewers. The 'dis-ease' created by the representation of failed masculinity is effectively compensated through the arrival of a 'heroic' team of builders who transform homes and liberate their occupants. The craftspeople are presented as (respectable) working-class heroes and celebrities who 'save' single mothers deserted by their DIY-obsessed husbands, parents halted halfway through a renovation project by serious illness, or those simply too broke to complete the transformations they began. For middle-class viewers the fantasy of inviting tradespeople whom they 'know' (though watching them on television) into their homes, who treat them respectfully regardless of age, gender, 'race' or sexuality, with whom they do not have to negotiate a price, and who transform their homes in 48 hours and clean up afterwards, all under the supervision of middle-class presenters and designers, is a dream come true. The viewing pleasure here is not difficult to decipher.

However, the response that the programmes elicit is not simply viewing pleasure. The popularity of home improvement programmes (together with low interest rates) has also helped to increase spending on DIY, according to the research firm Datamonitor (see BBC News 2002). In 2003, the UK's DIY market was worth more than £23bn, and Britons borrowed £13.6bn to fund home improvements. DIY is now the third most common reason for taking out a loan, and Datamonitor forecasts that lending for this purpose will reach £17.6bn by 2006. Thus, DIY is also serious business, and we might argue that television is a key component of this. Up and down the country people are spending the few hours a week they are not at work doing DIY on their houses. Could this constitute the rational and productive organization of leisure time by bourgeois media professionals acting on behalf of big business?

Home improvement specifically incorporates two aspects: (a) design, which involves imaginary consumption, and knowledge of styles obtained through cultural capital; (b) decoration – practical skills as well as time and labour. Hence this chapter attempts to address two issues: the origins of the contemporary emphasis on *design*, and currently that means modernism as an almost ubiquitous style; and the *practice of DIY* as a regulation of leisure towards productive ends. In order to investigate these two issues it is necessary to look at the origins of interior decorating on a mass scale. Through this I will also demonstrate that interior design and decoration are both *moral* projects that are specifically gendered. I will then show how these moral projects remain part of contemporary DIY television by looking in detail at Channel 5's *House Doctor*, a programme that combines the two genres of home improvement and house buying/selling identified earlier.

Design and the bourgeois home

In the nineteenth century UK and US 'ladies' from the growing middle-class found domestic life to be the limit of their world. Socializing depended on entertaining or being entertained by others of similar status. Thus the home became an essential site of identity – a place where status and 'good character' could be displayed to the (limited) outside world. Interior design and moral worth are not, therefore, incidentally connected, and the arrangement of domestic space was seen as reflecting the character of its occupants. As Penny Sparke (1995: 25–6) explains: 'The "good" was also the "beautiful" and woman, the embodiment of beauty, was also the personification of morality, responsible for the moral dimension of family life ... and beauty found a direct material form in the objects and arrangements which made up the domestic interior'.

Arranging a beautiful home was one of few *activities* a middle-class woman could engage in, alleviating some of her boredom and signifying her virtuosity. Furthermore, the level of devotion a woman gave to her family was assumed to be inscribed in her décor, and providing a harmonious and cultivated environment was central to a woman's ability to 'civilize' her husband and children. Finally, the relative luxury of a woman's parlour might also indicate the relative success of her marriage and the amount of money bestowed on her by her husband, signifying the state of her relationship with (or at least influence over) him. However, feminine décor treads a fine line – it is simultaneously valorized for reproducing an ideal of beauty linked to virtue, and castigated for its falseness. Feminine décor is thus ideally reproduced within an extremely narrow range of femininities – too little attention to decoration and the woman is marked negatively as masculine or eccentric; too much attention to decoration and her home is showy and pretentious (if not chintzy). Against femininity's artifice, however, masculinity is unmarked, unremarkable, and simply natural.

An important characteristic of the Victorian home, derived from the gendered division of labour, was the ideal of the home as sanctuary. Work was absolutely central to middle-class men's identities and was characterized as heroic toil in the provision for a dependent family. To escape the harsh world of work, men needed a refuge from the public sphere, a complement to the masculine space of the office or factory – a place where they could rest and be restored – and thus *comfort* became a central theme in the construction of the home. This ideal was aesthetically expressed through soft and luxurious furnishings, smooth, curved furniture and decorative patterns, epitomized in rouched curtains and an abundance of cushions. Comfort was signified most powerfully in the chesterfield sofa, its buttons quite literally reining in the bulging upholstery, accentuating the depth of its padding.

Even in the two-up, two-down terraced house it was extremely common to create the 'front room' as a parlour containing display cases for the exhibition of trinkets and ornaments. However, in working-class households, 'the social standing of the household appears to be ... strongly reflected in the criteria of respectability, expressed as keeping up standards of cleanliness and tidiness, rather than overt striving for "good taste" or a "sense of distinction"' (Madigan and Munro 1996: 47). The ideological connection between femininity, beauty, comfort and virtue thus held considerable sway in validating and elevating 'feminine' taste within the bourgeois home.

However, the connection with the narrative of progress that men obtained at work was also mirrored by women in the home through fashion. Being up to date with the latest ornaments and gadgets imported through expanding global trade networks took considerable time and expertise. Women were connected to the expanding economy, to colonization, the strange, the rare and the new through fashion as well as being able to signify their distance from necessity through the obsolescence of their things. At the end of the nineteenth century, the decoration of the home, so imbued with the virtues of respectability and gentility, was highly valued in displaying not just the taste of the wife, but the status of the whole family. Central to this 'feminine' style were decoration, ornamentation, craft (accomplishment) and ephemerality (fashion).

The working-class home and the pub

The nineteenth century was the heyday of bourgeois 'feminine taste', but the working-class home had its own different tradition. The migration of labourers taking up new jobs in the factories meant massive overcrowding in working-class homes as workers moved from rural areas to stay with relatives in the city. With two or three families to each small terraced house, and heat and light usually restricted to one room where domestic tasks were also inevitably performed, there was literally no space for 'sitting'. The country pub meanwhile had a long history at the centre of the community, fulfilling a multitude of functions.

As workers arrived in the city in the nineteenth century, the local pub became the sitting room that they lacked at home. Pubs provided food and warmth, space away from cold crowded houses, public meeting spaces and places of popular entertainment. However, the division between the public and private spheres, so central to nineteenth-century bourgeois thought, is disrupted by the *public* house. Commentators of the time turned their attentions to the sheer numbers of people congregating on the street, especially at the newly enforced pub closing times. This was partly fuelled by an anxiety over the gathering strength of the Whigs, and partly by concerns over work-time discipline. However, anxieties were frequently targeted at the large groups of men, perceived as dangerously unmanageable, who met for popular recreations. Popular recreations not only incited outright condemnation, but also a paternalistic desire to reform, aimed at the improvement of the 'deserving' poor through rational recreation. Rational recreation began in the 1860s and can be defined as:

> a set of beliefs and practices which operate in a paternalistic way to offer the kinds of leisure deemed to 'improve' the lives of those individuals who are less fortunate (read also less educated, less moral, less cultured or civilized) than the provider.
>
> (Green et al. 1990: 138)

Middle-class reformers were interested in rooting out 'poisoned' working-class cultures. Despite this, women in general, unlike (working-class) men, were not usually seen as needing control or direction in their leisure. Given that women have rarely been considered in their own right, they have been far less subject to the kind of leisure provided by the proponents of rational recreation (Green et al. 1990).

One way to avoid public assemblies of working-class men for politics or leisure according to the rational recreation ethos was to confine recreation to the home. But this was a good deal easier in the spacious and comfortable bourgeois home than it was in a cramped terraced house. Nevertheless, by the end of the nineteenth century 'good' recreation was undertaken indoors. But just as the connection between femininity, moral behaviour and domestic leisure had been consolidated as a national ideal, then feminine taste came under attack from a new cultural force – modernism.

Modernism began in the last decade of the nineteenth century with a comprehensive attack on Victorian values (Wolff 2000). Located initially in architecture, it castigated 'bourgeois' standards which it saw as decadent, rooted in the emulation of aristocratic taste, and thus fundamentally undemocratic. Adornment, ornamentation and display had no function, and anything within the home excessive to the basic purpose of the room should be hidden away in plain cupboards or behind screens. In attacking bourgeois taste, modernism posed a fundamental threat to feminine tastes which relied on display as a mechanism for producing identity and esteem. Decoration was firmly equated with the uncivilized – the savage, the childish and the feminine: 'modernism [opposes] a set of binary "others" – ornamentation, decoration, craft and ephemerality – which are typically mapped onto the masculine/feminine distinction' (Leslie and Reimer 2003: 295). The pre-eminence of the designer in modernism also produced an opposition between (feminine) consumption and (masculine) design (Attfield 1999). But what can these nineteenth-century preoccupations with homes and leisure tell us about contemporary lifestyle television?

DIY television as rational recreation: *House Doctor*

In the remaining sections of this chapter I will argue that the themes identified earlier – the rational organization of leisure and denigration of feminine taste – still run clearly through contemporary lifestyle television shows. Many DIY and home enhancement programmes still carry a moral message of *improvement* – of homes, but implicitly of lives and, importantly, leisure. This is not surprising in the UK, perhaps, given the long tradition of paternalism enshrined in the BBC's mission, but the paternalist ethic I will argue, is part of *all* home improvement shows. In order to support this argument I now intend to analyse one particular show, *House Doctor*, to demonstrate a recurrent theme of many lifestyle television shows – the way in which gender is played off against class.

The format of Channel 5's *House Doctor* begins with a property that has been on the market for some time and has been identified by estate agents as being difficult to sell. Three potential purchasers are then shown around the house and hidden cameras record their responses to it (in the owner's absence). These responses are then played back to the owner along with a critical commentary from the show's host – 'Californian real estate stylist' Ann Maurice. The comments are usually very negative. Maurice then explains to the owners what they need to do to make the house more saleable (all on a tight budget so as to retain as much profit from the sale as possible). Towards the end we witness the transformation, the 'reveal', and the show ends with the three potential buyers returning to express their now favourable views on the house.

In the particular episode that I want to discuss, Chris and Debbie Jones, a white couple in their early forties, are getting divorced. Before they can separate, however, they need to sell their property in order to buy two new homes. Chris is first mate on a tugboat and Debbie is a psychiatric nurse who has recently been promoted to ward sister. They have three children. The house is a large modern semi on an estate in Kent. The episode begins with Debbie showing Ann Maurice into the living room. It is decorated with a deep red carpet, a cherry red leather chesterfield suite, and an oak-beamed ceiling. But it is also apparent that the living room has been divided into two, not by walls or screens, but by a clash of furnishing styles. At one end (Debbie's) the furnishing is sparse – a lone Kandinsky print hangs on the wall. In the centre of the room is an enormous brick fireplace, built by Chris, and this marks the style transition: the fireplace is adorned with horse brasses and the other end of the room (Chris's) is cluttered with model boats, brass ornaments and antique tools. Overall this area has the look of a country pub. Debbie explains that she and Chris occupy different ends of the room:

We've got Kandinsky at one end, boats down the other and horse brasses in the middle.

To which Ann Maurice responds:

This house is caught between two universes and can't seem to escape ... I'm beginning to understand why you're getting a divorce.

The 'universes' that the house is caught between are stylistic, but seem to stand in for more than this. Style represents the different social and moral positions that Chris and Debbie have come to occupy. The couple's decision to separate is thus posited as self-evidently manifest in their décor. Without any knowledge of their relationship the viewer is led to believe that the couple's separation is being expressed through (if not caused by) their different tastes.

After the living room, viewers are taken through various other rooms accompanied by a critical commentary from Maurice. The kitchen is too dark and gloomy, and is also (to Debbie's detriment) rather dirty. The spare bedroom is too floral, especially since Chris is now sleeping there. However, the greatest criticism is reserved for the living room. In another room Debbie tells us that there used to be a minibar here but she had made Chris take that out. She explains: 'This is more my room', to which Maurice retorts, 'This is more *my* room! ... I'm very happy with this room'.

The couple are then shown a video of the potential buyers' responses to the house as they look around it, including edited clips showing a number of comments: 'It's very dark'; 'The fireplace is enormous'; 'It's very brown and dark, not very inviting'; 'There's lots of different things crammed in there'. The house even reminds one buyer of a 'gothic mansion'. In an earlier period the house might have been described as 'cosy' or decorated with 'warm' colours, but we are quickly told that Debbie's taste is superior to Chris's and that the house must be overhauled to reflect a 'contemporary' look.

Chris is highly resistant to this change. He argues that as a mock tudor house it is reasonable to have a 'traditional' interior. His objections are quickly quashed, and Maurice and a decorating team set about stripping everything from the house that seems to mark Chris's presence there – boxing in the fireplace and painting it white, removing the ornaments and horse brasses. Upstairs the floral wallpaper is painted over and the kitchen units are brightened up with a touch of paint. In the garden there is a pile of old bricks next to some bins which must be hidden behind a screen. Chris is asked to undertake this task, as Maurice comments to him, 'I'm sure you know about bricks'. The camera shows him briefly labouring with his shirt off and then leaves him and follows Debbie, who is taken shopping for cushions.

After the makeover, the potential viewers are brought back. Their (now positive) response is captured on camera:

> It looks much cleaner. You could cook in here now whereas before it really put you off.

Finally, the commentary informs us that the house was sold three weeks later.

Modernism as 'movement'

Throughout the narrative of this episode of *House Doctor*, then, Chris is consistently positioned as 'holding back' the sale of the property by defending his taste, which is clearly 'bad'. In holding back the sale of the house he is also holding back Debbie from 'moving on' in her life. He is defined as fixed in time, unable to see the benefits of a 'contemporary' style and, by implication, contemporary gender relations. He is also fixed to his class through affinity with a décor that signifies the pub, as well as darkness and clutter. Finally, he is fixed in production. His productions – the fireplace and model boats – have to go. They hold no value (and we do not see the results of Chris's labour in the garden). Debbie, on the other hand, is 'on the move'. She is changing her relationship and she is changing her class position by embracing modern design and consumption. These aspects are highly valued by *House Doctor*. Debbie is a modern woman; Chris, quite simply, a dinosaur.

In another time the audience may have had more sympathy with Chris. The sooner the house is sold, the sooner the couple go their separate ways. But maybe it would be better for them to stay together and try to make their relationship work – to compromise on their respective tastes. However, Giddens (1992) has convincingly shown a new moral logic at work in relation to the separation of partners. Rather than staying together through good times and bad, the 'pure relationship' requires that couples stay together only as long as this is equally fulfilling for both partners. *House Doctor*, like many other current lifestyle television shows, harnesses this logic to effectively play off gender against class. Modern gender relations signify class movement. Traditional (sexist and racist) values are repeatedly overdetermined onto working-classness.

At first glance, then, this episode of *House Doctor* seems to contradict my earlier argument about 'masculine' (modernist) and 'feminine' (decorative) tastes. It is Debbie who wants the 'clean lines' and art prints associated with modernism, Chris who wants to hang on to the clutter, the 'excess' of decoration. However, as Lury (1995) points out, analysing the consumption of 'modern' design in a postmodern era that collapses high and low culture is by no means a straightforward endeavour. It is unreasonable to expect that the significations of modernist style have remained unchanged since the turn of the twentieth century. Instead, as Leslie and Reimer (2003) have argued, 'feminine style' has come to be associated (unsurprisingly in many respects) with *traditional* femininity and all of the related impositions on women which that entails. Through the development and success of UK magazines like *Wallpaper, Elle Decoration* and *Living Etc.*, which target a young, professional, child-free, urban loft living clientele of men and women, straight or gay, modernism has come to signify gender neutrality:

> At a time when women increasingly reject traditional notions of femininity, new 'lifestyle' magazines have begun to suggest that it is acceptable for women to have an interest in the more masculine realm of design ... These magazines articulate the notion that it is not oppressive for women to take an interest in their home, nor to view the home as an extension of fashion and their body. There is an implication that a flexible and modern style is liberating for women. At the same time, downplaying the gender specificity of home-making also enables magazines to target male readers.
>
> (Leslie and Reimer 2003: 304–5)

In this case Debbie's job, nursing, especially since her promotion, has given her access to middle-class cultural capital which identifies modernism as the only currently valued decorating style. Chris, as a tugboat worker, embraces the traditional décor of the pub. But this style, as we have seen, holds little value, and even attracts condemnation as morally suspect. However, if we return to the argument that women are *morally* responsible for their families, that they are charged with civilizing their husbands and children, then we can see that Debbie is simply trying to impart moral knowledge to her family, in this case through the valued aesthetic of modernism. This has the double advantage that modernist style has now come to signify modern (ungendered) relationships and connects to a narrative of progress through fashion that is no longer its 'other'.

The narrative structure of *House Doctor*, then, centres on the 'makeover' and the accumulation of capital – both cultural and economic. It also gives us an insight into the lives of 'people like us', and demonstrates the transformative potential of the expert who can improve both our homes and our lives, economically and morally. In this way it draws heavily on the central themes of rational recreation as moral improvement through leisure. However, perhaps the defining moment of *House Doctor* is the level of symbolic violence meted out against those whose tastes are found wanting. As Bourdieu (1984: 435) famously says: 'Taste classifies, and it classifies the classifier' – and *House Doctor* is certainly an exercise in classification. Viewers are encouraged, through a process of identification and dis-identification, to judge the featured participants' taste, to find it lacking, and to learn how to resolve this.

The democracy of style

However, there is also a sense in which homes shows are democratic in a way that first wave modernism never was. Although modernism was designed as anti-bourgeois and utilitarian, it was designed by middle-class men 'on behalf of' and 'for' the working classes, and thus embodied normative middle-class ideals of how the working classes *should* live. Central to modernism was the opposition of designer versus consumer. There are countless documented examples of designer–client struggles from the period of high modernism – frequently centred around the client's desire to personalize her domestic space, the specific national culture's resistance to the universalized International Style, or working-class disenchantment with modernist state housing. However, this opposition is now played out on television for our consumption. Participants in *Changing Rooms* vociferously register their dismay (sometimes crying) when the designer has clearly ignored their stated wishes – the pink room for the woman who hates pink, the painted-over pine cupboard that had been lovingly stripped, the boxed-in treasured Victorian fireplace – and we share their dismay, shouting at the television from our own beloved interiors. Thus the authority of the designer is sometimes undermined by their failure to orient their design to customer specifications.

But how far does this 'discourse of DIY', of home improvement, translate into actual practice? How far can homes programmes impose their logic onto individual consumers? I have already noted that there is a booming economy in DIY and design-related products which might suggest that they are extremely successful. However, there is significant evidence that actual DIYers do not embrace the wholesale makeovers that shows like *Changing Rooms* present. Instead, house styling is likely to be more incremental, marked by compromise or individual interests. In their study of working-class home consumption, for example, Madigan and Munro (1996: 51) show that the majority of people actually acquire household furniture and decoration gradually so that 'there was a tendency to adopt what might be called an evolutionary or incremental style', mixing fashions current upon setting up home with those acquired since. In particular there was an emphasis on the display of 'the memorabilia of family life: trophies, pictures, ornaments'. In fact one respondent to their study was singled out as being highly unusual in her insistence on producing a co-ordinated look:

> The desire to have a co-ordinated style was followed to the extent that she rejected her son's gift of a picture because it did not tie in with her décor and he was told to take it back and get 'something in peach'. For most of our respondents this would be an outrageous thing to do, breaking the canon of family life in which all sorts of gifts and memorabilia, particularly from children, are displayed regardless of 'taste'.
>
> (Madigan and Munro 1996: 53)

Ian Woodward's (2003) study of middle-class consumers in Australia also finds considerable resistance to the prioritization and adoption of homogeneous consumerist styles of décor over personal, intimate, individual and emotional arrangements. For Woodward, home decoration is not about commoditization per se. Dreaming of what a purchase might mean, exploring its possibilities in imagination, consuming its meanings, was seen by his respondents as more pleasurable than the purchase itself. Thus his respondents tended to consume home television shows and magazines rather than actual items of furniture or decoration. Some respondents resisted decorating styles altogether, opposing 'design' with 'comfort' and insisting on the heightened importance of the latter:

> Recent rounds of commodification of design, style and decoration within the domestic sphere have constructed the home as a site that allows for the assertion of conspicuous forms of individual style, luxury, aesthetic expression and the management of identities. Yet on the other hand, the home is also an authentic, even therapeutic ... space of shared experience, relaxation, intimacy and emotion, where style, design and conspicuousness matter little.
>
> (Woodward 2003: 394–395)

Interestingly in Woodward's study, however, there is an unacknow-
ledged split in his middle-class consumers. One group is younger, more
newly middle-class and involved in the gentrification of a particular area
of Sydney. The other group is more 'comfortably' middle-class and
occupies an older, more established upmarket area. It is the new middle-
classes that prioritized style and the more established group that
preferred comfort. This suggests that the already established may have
little need to display status and identity in the way that the 'new'
middle-classes do.

Design dreams

Alison Clarke's (2001) study of home improvements in North London,
moreover, shows not only that many consumers reject a fixed Western
definition of 'good style', but that some reject the practice of home
improvement completely. Two of her respondents, Sharon and Dave,
showed a keen awareness of the *discourse* of home consumption – Sharon
bought homes magazines and watched homes television shows while
Dave, a part-time builder, was trained in all the skills necessary to carry
out home improvements. However, a 'circular logic' prevents the
successful completion of any redecoration plans the couple have:

> Dave will not rearrange the kitchen until he has completed the
> loft [conversion] they have been discussing for years. But he
> refuses to do this as a rogue squirrel has made a nest in the roof
> and 'it gives him the creeps'. While Sharon uses this in defence
> of her husband's inactivity [she explains] 'He's not really scared
> of it. It's just that it might jump out at him and you know [mock
> scream]! I rang the council but they want twenty-five quid to
> come out and I thought "bugger that"'.
>
> (Clarke 2001: 41)

During Clarke's three-year ethnography, this situation did not change,
and repeated references were made to the squirrel. Although 'twenty-five
quid' may not have been easy to come by on one part-time wage, this is a
very small amount compared with the expense of the proceeding
building projects. Thus, it is doubtful the squirrel is really to blame for
Sharon and Dave's inactivity. Although they are clearly *aware* of the
discourse of home improvement, they consistently resist *acting* according to its logic. Importantly, then, it is the *dream* of a better home and
life that is central to the pleasure of home consumption, not its actual
practice. This is where homes television shows are truly democratic, in

that they offer us all the potential to know about, to experience and to consume the *idea* of the ideal home. Many commentators have shown us that it is consumption in fantasy that affords us pleasure, and that the actual acquisition of goods frequently brings only disappointment (Campbell 1987; McCracken 1988; Falk 1994). Despite their sometimes heavy-handed moral judgements on taste, then, as well as their encouragement of the 'socially useful' practice of home improvement, I have cited examples of those that resist these discourses. It is perhaps a relatively small group of precarious young, new middle-class, urban loft dwellers that follow home improvement television recommendations most precisely. It is exactly this group, currently most committed to modernism, that are likely to foster modernism's demise. The first rumblings of anxiety over the lack of distinction that modernism affords can already be heard in that bastion of young middle-class taste, *Elle Decoration*:

> Can you remember the last time you had a truly bad-taste experience? When you walked into someone's home and were overwhelmed by their lack of cohesive interiors ethic; had to bite your lip to stop yourself bitching over a colleague's taste in desk furniture; or winced at a parent-in-law's take on busy, chintzy, overly ornamental crassness. Well, can you? Probably not ... Is mass ownership of good taste merely making it bland?
>
> *(Elle Decoration* 2002: 31)

Design magazines like *Elle Decoration* and *Wallpaper* are exclusive. They are expensive to buy and circulate only amongst those that take good design seriously. Television homes shows, on the other hand, have a mass audience, disseminating 'good taste' to millions of viewers each week. Modernism is a highly recognizable style – 'less is more' – which makes obtaining the cultural capital necessary to appreciate it a relatively straightforward exercise. The pleasure of homes shows is their consumption in the imagination, rather than the consumption of the actual products of modernism (although budget furniture manufacturers are increasingly producing modernist lines). Thus, almost anyone can fantasize the modernist makeover of their home (and their lives/relationships) – were it not for the children, pets, squirrels in the attic, and so on. Furthermore, since the makeover relies heavily on building and decorating *skills*, it may in practice be more difficult to effect those 'clean lines' for middle-class professionals than for their working-class contemporaries. Given the broad appeal of homes shows, they potentially represent a democratization of taste that is a cause for concern for those that most value distinction – the young, urban, new middle-class. Perhaps this time around modernism can offer the democracy it promised but never delivered at the beginning of the twentieth century.

Acknowledgements

I would like to thank Jon Binnie and Mark Jayne as well as the editors for their helpful comments on earlier drafts of this chapter. Special thanks should also go to the MA Gender Studies students at Leeds University, in particular Zowie Davy, Rosa Mas Giralt, Lee Middlehurst and Fiona Philip, who watched lots of DIY television with me and gave me their comments.

6 Monoculture versus multiculinarism
Trouble in the Aussie kitchen

Felicity Newman and Mark Gibson

In a recent essay on transformations in Australian society and culture since the Second World War, writer and social commentator David Malouf settles on food as a particularly potent signifier of change. As a point of reference, he remembers the diet of his childhood growing up in Brisbane in the 1930s and 1940s. Despite his Lebanese background, this was overwhelmingly derived from the British Isles:

> For tea at night, Shepherd's Pie or Irish Stew ... Or pork sausages with mashed potato or mashed pumpkin, and peas of an unnatural greenness from the good pinch of bicarb that has gone into the boiling water. Or corned beef and cauliflower with white sauce. At the weekend, a baked dinner – beef with Yorkshire pudding. And on Saturday mornings the week's leftover bread turned into cold Bread Pudding. And the puddings! Diplomat Pudding, Golden Syrup Pudding, Queen of Pudding.
>
> (Malouf 2003: 9)

Then, after the war, 'things changed':

> There was an intermediary period in the '50s when food was represented on menus all up and down the country by T-bone steak, often in the form of 'Steak and the Works', which in Brisbane at least meant spaghetti, chips and salad (nothing more transitional, surely, than this early version of fusion) or Wiener Schnitzel. The first clear move from an entrenched English style to a rather eclectic 'something different', half Italo-American, half Central European, and the first timid indication that we were ready to break away and experiment.
>
> (p. 11)

The trend reached its full-blown extension in the 1980s and 1990s, with the development in Australia of a certain West Coast American/

Mediterranean culinary style: 'outdoor café-tables, espresso coffee, gelato, octopus, rocket and parmesan salad, pasta' (pp. 11–12). The transformation is captured, for Malouf, in a response from a laid-back waiter in a Perth bistro to an innocent question, 'Do you do an espresso?': ' "Ristretto, sir?" he asks with a slight curl of the lip. "That'd be great," I say. "Coretto?" Put thoroughly in my place, I tell him meekly: "I don't think we need to go that far" ' (p. 12).

In this chapter we want to examine this shift in Australian culinary culture, particularly as it has been mediated through the television cooking show. Food is ubiquitous on the small screen – most obviously, of course, in endless advertisements for burgers, ice-creams and breakfast cereals, but also as a focus for an increasing number of dedicated programmes and segments. The 'cooking programme' proper has been associated in Australia with public service broadcasting, appearing first and most prominently on the government-owned Australian Broadcasting Corporation (ABC, the Australian counterpart of the BBC) and 'multicultural' broadcaster, the Special Broadcasting Service (SBS). The examples we discuss are ABC's *Kylie Kwong – Heart and Soul, Gondola on the Murray* and *Secret Recipes*, the SBS's *Food Lover's Guide to Australia* and one from commercial television, Channel 7's *Surprise Chef*.

Cooking shows belong somewhere on the edge of the category that Frances Bonner (2003) has called 'ordinary television'. The celebrity status of their presenters and aestheticized style sometimes separates them from the familiar image reservoir of homes, gardens, pets and children. They nonetheless deal with a subject – food – which could hardly be more everyday, and share with other 'ordinary' formats in their conversational mode of address and in an erosion of boundaries between programme and audience. But more than that, they *problematize* ordinariness, worrying away at the boundary between the mundane and the distinguished. This makes them an ideal site for considering the scope and definition of 'ordinary lifestyles'. We are particularly interested here in the relation between ordinariness and *class*. This follows recent calls for a return to questions of class in cultural studies (Bennett et al. 1999; Milner 1999). But it also responds to a new sensitivity to questions of class, with the success of conservative populism since the 1990s in representing cosmopolitanism, cultural pluralism and indeed many of the concerns of cultural studies as obsessions of educated 'elites'.

'Contemporary Australian'

Until recently, the transformation of Australian food has generally been represented in the public culture as an unambiguous cause for celebration (Symons 1982; Ripe 1993; Newton 1996). Speaking at the Third Symposium of Australian Gastronomy in 1987, Anthony Corones expressed this general optimism through the term 'multiculinarism':

> In a multiculinary society ... we have the co-existence of many different cuisines, I wish to use the word 'multiculinarism' in a strong sense – to point not just to the presence of many cuisines, but to the awareness of other cuisines, to mutual comparison and influence. And multiculinarism, in this sense, has the consequence of raising our consciousness of food.
>
> (Corones 1987: 2)

Indeed, it has been widely accepted in many circles that these new culinary influences have been the making of Australian food. As noted Sydney food writer John Newton has put this view:

> It took a bunch of immigrants from the Mediterannean, arriving with their rolling pins and mortars and pestles, and with absolutely no intention, like Rosa Matto's mother, of 'falling into whatever the natives of the new land ate', who taught us, finally, how to be comfortable here, and how to eat.
>
> (Newton 1996: 5)

Lamb chops, mashed potato and other Anglo-Australian foods have become a standard marker, in an influential political rhetoric, of all that Australia must leave behind – a bland, homogeneous culture, dominated by stultifying British precedents and lacking in innovation or flair. With the development from the 1970s of formal government policies on multiculturalism, food became an effective way of persuading a some-times sceptical Anglo-Celtic population of the benefits to be found in embracing change. Who, after tasting a satay or a bowl of chilli mussels, could wish a return to the past? As Sneja Gunew (1993: 13) put it, food became 'the acceptable face of multiculturalism'.

With the opening up of the Australian economy in the 1980s, the proliferation of smart restaurants and cafés in the major cities seemed concrete evidence of the benefits of participating in global exchange. As if to crown the new cosmopolitan vitality, Australian cuisine gained an enviable reputation overseas, beginning to match the wine industry with its claims to quality and innovation. Sydney competed with San

Francisco as a leader in 'fusion' cuisine – merging the flavours of various ethnic cuisines with local produce. An eclecticism, inventiveness and imaginative use of local ingredients has been more recently captured, in gastronomic circles, in the idea of 'Mod Oz cuisine', or more widely and generally as 'Contemporary Australian'. Australians reject a conflation with 'Californian', citing the early and independent initiatives of Adelaide's legendary Cheong Liew. The claims for Australian innovation have been accepted by many international food writers. As Veronica Horwell has argued recently in the *Guardian Weekly*:

> The real missionaries for fusion's casual freshness were a new international catering corps of Anzacs ... The antipodean recruits' active approach suited the California styles, which they loosened up, jettisoning the waffly philosophy and the foot-notes; then, as vineyards spread across Australia through the 1980s, Sydney rather than San Francisco became a leading model for good times, while culinary hands with Oz experience could work their way around the world's kitchens.
>
> (Horwell 2004)

As top Australian chefs were feted in London and elsewhere, it appeared for a time that the incubus of the past had been decisively laid to rest.

The fish and chips revolt

From the mid 1990s, however, troubles have emerged in the Aussie kitchen. A shift in political and cultural climate in Australia has been well documented in other spheres, particularly in relation to govern-ment policies on issues with ethnic or racial overtones – multi-culturalism, the handling of refugee claims, relations with Asian neighbours and reconciliation with Aboriginal people (Burke 2001; Hage 2003; Marr and Wilkinson 2003). Among the more potent symbols of this shift was the hardline refusal by the conservative Howard government in 2001 to permit the entry into Australia of the Norwegian container ship *MV Tampa* with a cargo of asylum seekers rescued from a sinking vessel. Such actions, and the widespread support they gained in the electorate, marked a sharp reversal of what many had come to believe was a natural trend towards increasing tolerance of 'foreign' intrusions or influences. The turn has been matched by an increasing reassertion of what Prime Minister John Howard has called 'mainstream' values. As historian Judith Brett (2004) has cautioned, this should not be mistaken for a simple return to the 1950s – Australia has changed too much for that – but it has involved a reconnection with certain totemic sites of Anglo-Australian identity.

One of the more important of these has been food. A good illustration can be found in the case of Pauline Hanson, whose extraordinary impact on national politics in the late 1990s marked the most dramatic turn against the earlier celebration of cultural pluralism. Hanson's brief but sensational political ascent was launched by a maiden speech in parliament in which she argued that the country was being 'swamped by Asians'. It was central to her political persona that she spoke not as a sophisticated cosmopolitan, but as a fish and chip shop owner from Ipswich, an outer satellite of Brisbane. While attention often focused on her simple language and lack of polish in the media spotlight, her identity was also deeply rooted in this culinary reference.

As John Walton has argued, fish and chips have powerful historical associations with Britishness:

> This set of perceptions attaches fish and chips to potent patriotic images of land, countryside, industrial might ... and above all, the notion of Britain as a gallant seafaring notion whose little ships do battle with the elements and the foreign enemy to feed and protect the people.
>
> (Walton 1992: 2)

But the connotations are more specific still. Fish and chips are particularly associated with British *working-classness*: 'there remains something shamefaced about the acceptance of fish and chips as a component of "Englishness" among the "better classes"' (p. 2). There is an interesting way here, as in a number of other domains, that national identity is mapped onto class identity. While Frenchness might be signified by fine wines, Parisian fashions and haute cuisine, Englishness is often signified by the 'ordinary' – football, popular music, tabloid journalism, unsophisticated tastes in food (Gibson 2001).

Some of these oppositions can be clearly traced to longer histories. Since the refinement of cooking techniques and table manners in the courts of early modern Europe, culinary sophistication has been a highly sensitive marker of social distinction (Elias 1994; Mennell 1996). As Bourdieu (1984) argues, class differences in food consumption have never been a simple function of income. There is a relation, of course, but it is at the level where economic determinants have been abstracted into more general values:

> The true basis of the differences ... is the opposition between the tastes of luxury (or freedom) and the tastes of necessity. The

former are the tastes of individuals who are the product of
material conditions of existence defined by distance from
necessity ...; the latter express, precisely in their adjustment,
the necessity of which they are the product.

(Bourdieu 1984: 177)

This explains how a foreman can remain attached to 'popular' tastes,
even though earning more than clerical and commercial employees.

The point has particular significance for the case of England, where
the cultural history of relations with France has meant that refined tastes
have been overlaid with strong connotations of foreignness. Many of
these connotations have survived migration to Australia. In a memorable
1970s episode of the *Paul Hogan Show*, for example, the simplicity of
Hogan – the archetypal working class Anglo-Australian – is set off for
humorous effect against the pretension of a bow-tied, French-speaking
waiter and stuck-up diners in an exclusive restaurant:

> *Hogan*: How ya goin' viewers? I brush up a million dollars don't
> I? A little education piece for you tonight. One of the most
> daunting experiences for a young man is going on that first
> important dinner date to a really posh restaurant – y'know the
> sort of place where they make you dress up in a suit and tie and
> go out of their way to make you feel uncomfortable ... A lot of
> them speak French just to impress ya. The best way to sort 'em
> out is to answer them back in French: *Mon chapeau est sur mon
> pomme de terre*.

The fish and chip connection was confirmed independently of the
Hanson affair in media coverage of the winner of Australia's 2003 *Big
Brother* – 'Tassie Sheila', Regina Bird. Bird's popularity shared something
with the support which flowed to Hanson. Both were accepted as
'ordinary' Australians and, yes, Reggie owned a fish and chip shop too.
Australians have adopted global fast food as readily as any country, but
in the emerging class tensions, fish and chips have had a particular role
to play. There are complications here. While the steaming paper-
wrapped product itself has long signified homeliness and familiarity, the
troughs of boiling oil have been toiled over, in both Britain and
Australia, by Jewish and Greek migrants or more recently, in Australia,
by the Vietnamese. Yet Hanson's occupation of this terrain placed her
perfectly to articulate the backlash against change. No spicy laksa for our
Pauline; she spoke from and for the security of the known.

For all its ugliness, the Hanson incident was important in drawing
attention to one of the central problems of discourses of multi-

culturalism – the widespread neglect of class (Kingston 1999). Food, again, is centrally placed in this connection. What was often missed in the celebration of the new pluralism and sophistication of Australian culinary culture was that the revolution was quite uneven. It would be too strong to claim that there has been any simple correlation between uptake of 'ethnic' (i.e. non-Anglo) foods and class. The majority of post-war migrants to Australia made their way, at first, in working-class occupations and suburbs. From the 'steak and spaghetti' years referred to by Malouf, there has been extensive borrowing and domestication within lower income populations of ingredients and styles of cooking that would once have been regarded as foreign.

The context was altered, however, by the more assertive cosmopolitanism which developed during the 1980s. In retrospect, the conditions for the backlash are clear. Much of regional and outer suburban Australia found that its taste was being disapproved of as 'backward', 'lacking', somehow connected with dubious attachments to older cultural loyalties. At the same time, they were excluded economically from some of the major forms in which the new cosmopolitanism was expressed – the fashionable restaurants and cappuccino strips of the increasingly expensive inner suburbs (Barcan 1998).

Macca's and the latté set

It is possible to distinguish between two sites of tension here. The first has developed around a rural/urban divide and is referenced to a nexus between culinary traditions and actual food production. As Elspeth Probyn has argued, Australia has a 'rather schizophrenic relationship to food and the land upon which it is produced':

> In the cities and in the urban media, eating in Australia is vaunted as the best in the world. For the middle-class and the élite, the fetishisation of 'local produce' is a cliché that is consumed on a daily basis. At the same time, rural white Australia (where the beautiful ingredients are produced) is often blamed for the reactionary politics that seemingly erupt spontaneously from the land. If the divide between urban and rural has long been established ... it is now commonplace for urban dwellers to blame or in some cases praise rural inhabitants for everything from Hansonite racism to the no vote in the referendum for a Republic.
>
> (Probyn 2000: 118)

The promotion of post-war immigration as the saviour of Australian cooking has tended to ignore, and in doing so devalue, traditions of skilled baking, preserving and other domestic arts practised in rural and regional communities. These traditions have often been reduced to a narrow range of stereotypes such as the humble roast dinner. Yet, as Marion Halligan notes, pre-war cuisine in Australia involved considerably more than this:

> They [roast dinners] weren't what made you a good cook. That depended on baking which got done once a week, and kept the cake and biscuit tins full so there was always something to have with cups of tea. It was a kind of shame to serve shop biscuits with cups of tea.
>
> (Halligan 1990: 4)

It is not surprising, as rural and regional Australia has felt itself increasingly left behind by change, that resentments around the new culinary hierarchy should begin to emerge.

The second site of tension has been less traditional, more suburban and articulated around fast food. As the local 'milk bar' has been displaced by trendy cafés and global fast food chains, outings for suburban families on lower incomes have increasingly gravitated towards the latter. There is, of course, an irony here in that Burger King, Kentucky Fried Chicken and McDonald's are no less 'foreign' than a Mediterranean bistro or smart Thai restaurant. The difference, however, is that they have been rapidly indigenized. McDonald's in Australia is no longer perceived as an American import, but can be spoken of affectionately as 'Macca's' – almost as if the golden arches had sprouted spontaneously from the soil of a vacant lot beside the local service station or shopping mall:

> In this narrative of national belonging, unlike most immigrants, McDonald's can exactly date when it truly belonged as Australian: 'About 1985 we ceased being perceived as an American organisation and became an Aussie icon ... when Australians nickname us Macca's we are here to stay.'
>
> (Probyn 1998: 234)

As Probyn has shown, McDonald's has worked assiduously to defuse local/global tensions by adapting its image to suit particular national identities even as they also promote a feeling of global connectedness.

It should be said that class tensions around food in Australia have often been strategically seeded rather than spontaneously expressed.

Incipient resentments against middle-class epicureanism have been exploited by conservative journalists and public commentators – almost exclusively themselves middle-class – in rallying popular support against progressive causes. It has been a commonplace in recent years to dismiss critical positions on a wide range of issues, from the treatment of Aboriginal people and asylum seekers to the war in Iraq, as restricted to the 'latté set' or 'chardonnay socialists', imagined sitting in pretentious downtown brasseries plotting the demise of an older Australia. But the strategy only works – and it has worked quite spectacularly – because the tensions are there to be played upon. There are real questions to be asked about the distribution of benefits of the social revolution in Australia over the last 20 years. For those at the rough end of change, the new culinary hierarchy offers itself all too readily as focus for articulating distress and anxiety.

The food media clearly have a crucial part to play in defining and negotiating ethnic and class identities here. As in other areas, the print media are more concerned with defining than negotiating. Given the extreme segmentation of the magazine market, individual titles can afford to mark out highly differentiated positions appealing to quite specific demographics. At the top end, the sumptuous photography and stylish prose of *Vogue Entertaining*, *Australian Gourmet Traveller* and *Delicious* make no concessions to the 'battlers' searching for weekly bargains in the aisles of local supermarkets. At the other end, the food advice the latter might find in those aisles – in *Super Food Ideas*, in the cooking pages of *Family Circle* or *Australian Women's Weekly* – is quite resistant to strong implications of ethnic difference. While the recipes may now include soy sauce, sometimes even calling for the use of a wok, they do so only as an extension from a solid 'Anglo' base. The supermarket magazines have remained compulsively focused on a familiar *topos* of beaming fair-haired children and wholesome (read predominantly Anglo) fare.

Television, however, is faced with different imperatives. It is, in John Hartley's (1998) terms, a 'population gathering' medium, engaged by necessity in developing modes of address that can operate across demographic boundaries. There are some mild exceptions where food is concerned, indicating perhaps that the subject presents particular challenges. As Frances Bonner (2003: 104) has remarked, 'cooking programmes remain one of the few types of ordinary programming where there is any direct address exclusively to the middle-classes or any fraction of them'. Food, more than other topics, also appears to invoke cosmopolitanism. Cooking programmes are unusual within non-fictional programming in being widely traded internationally: Jamie Oliver and Nigella Lawson are almost as well known in Australia as they are in the United Kingdom; as Bonner notes, 'food seems "naturally" to encompass exoticism' (p. 177). Food on television is often associated with travel, a whole subgenre being dedicated to what Niki Strange (1998) has called the 'tour-educative'. Yet, of any medium, television has the capacity to domesticate and reassure, to erase the more obtrusive markers of difference. In the context we have sketched above, it plays an important role in managing and negotiating tensions and antagonisms.

Murray cod *alla Mildura*

One of the most successful programmes in negotiating tensions around multiculinarism has been Stefano de Pieri's *Gondola on the Murray* (ABC). De Pieri works what might be called the 'peasant' paradigm, drawing on humble Italian origins to establish a comfortable, democratic mode of address:

> Hello, my name is Stefano de Pieri and I prefer to be called a cook rather than a chef. My food is from the school of the untutored and I rely on the memories of my mother's cooking on the Veneto farm in Italy where I grew up. That's what I try to do in my restaurant in Mildura.

But the programme goes well beyond an appeal to familiar Mediterranean stereotypes of earthy conviviality. What makes it work in the Australian context is a highly original fusion of the rustic Italian with the Australian bush. In one episode, for example, de Pieri gives an outdoor demonstration of how to prepare and cook the prize Australian native fish, the Murray cod. Stooped over the campfire in Panama hat and open-necked shirt, under a gum tree on the banks of the Murray River, he appears an eccentric, 'ethnicized' version of the bushman – one of the central figures of Anglo-Australian mythology.

Gondola is particularly significant for bridging the urban–rural divide. Mildura is an unlikely location for gastronomic adventures. Set in the hot, dusty plains of Victoria's Mallee region, it has carried until recently the full weight of urban prejudices against the Australian country town. As journalist Tom Gilling (2003: 14) puts it in one of a number of features marvelling at de Pieri's success, the town 'offered a daunting challenge. To city-dwellers, the bush was a gastronomic wasteland where even a decent loaf of bread could seem like a miracle'. Yet de Pieri himself is more unassuming in his claims. While *Gondola* did seek to promote regional Australia, it claimed not so much to present a miraculous transformation as to reveal a complexity which has always been there. An important aspect of the programme was to draw attention to the freshness and variety of local produce. Many of the producers are Anglo-Australian, like the cod fishermen in their aluminium 'outboard', but de Pieri also drew attention to a rural ethnic diversity which is often overlooked: fresh eggs are purchased from an elderly, black-clad Sicilian woman; Cambodian immigrant workers at an Italian-owned factory are observed cooking on a wok over an open fire.

Gondola owed much of its success to the timeliness of its project. It coincided with the development of boutique food production and increasing culinary tourism. Stefano's role in establishing the Mildura arts festival and his association with the Murray River Tourism Association point to this connection. Trips to the country increasingly offer more than cellar door wine sales or orchard fruits. Olive oil tastings, pasta-making classes, and specialty artisanal produce have provided new economic development in areas like Mildura, Margaret River and the Swan Valley. ABC's hugely popular drama *Seachange* captured the new middle-class yearning for the 'slow living' offered by regional Australia.

Certain aspects of *Gondola* have been followed or borrowed by Kylie Kwong in *Heart and Soul* (also ABC). The bridge between the Anglo-Australian ordinary and ethnic 'other' might even be found in her name. 'Kylie' has a certain suburban, girl-next-door resonance – most famously exploited by Kylie Minogue – and is sometimes contracted in the programme and spin-off book to 'Kyles'. Kwong uses this ordinariness to counter possible suspicions of inaccessibility or elitism. In almost an exact echo of de Pieri, she emphatically instructs the viewer, 'Don't call me chef, my name is Kylie, call me Kylie'. Yet the alliterative linking to 'Kwong' effectively articulates her Chinese heritage. Kwong is, in fact, a fourth generation Australian, personifying in herself a stylish integration of an Australian location and experience – in this case very urban – and an Asian heritage. De Pieri's references to the Veneto farm of his boyhood are paralleled to some extent in descriptions by Kwong of her grandfather's herb collection: 'I never dreamed I'd be using these exotic ingredients in a restaurant of my own'.

But *Heart and Soul* has been less successful in bridging differences than *Gondola* and it is instructive to consider why. First, the programme is set within a very urban milieu. While Kwong addresses the slow food agenda in her choice of ingredients and love of good food, she does not connect with that privileged site of Anglo-Australian identity – the bush. Second, it is important that she is a she. De Pieri's formula is rooted, to a certain extent, in a knockabout masculine identity that eases the way, in a similar way to Jamie Oliver, to a genial familiarity. Third, the 'peasant' reference for Kwong is much more remote. The problem here becomes painfully evident in a segment where she cooks 'humble' fried duck eggs. These are, she tells us, 'rustic peasant stuff', but the effect is altered by the difficulty of believing that she has had close experience of anything approaching a peasant existence. In an urban context, and with several generations remove, the class significance of the rustic is completely transformed. However humble the cooking technique may be, it is tempting to ask where we are to find our duck eggs. 'Peasant' references are particularly open, in Australia, to this kind of resignification. As Michael Symons points out:

> This is the only continent which has not supported an agrarian society ... Our land missed that fertile period when agriculture and cooking were created. ... Almost no food has ever been grown by the person who eats it, almost no food has been preserved in the home and indeed, very little preparation is now done by a family cook. This is the uncultivated continent. Our history is without peasants.
>
> (Symons 1982: 10)

Symons overdraws the point, insisting that 'there has never been the creative interplay between society and the soil'. This denies British and Irish traditions and Aboriginal foodways (an argument more fully developed in Gallegos and Newman 1999). But it is certainly true that Australia lacks any real history of pre-capitalist agriculture. In this context, the 'peasant' is easily appropriated to romanticized fantasies, sanitized of worrying connotations of feudalism and poverty. The new peasant is thus absorbed in a middle-class discourse as 'egalitarian' Australia seems increasingly less so.

In view of these problems, *Heart and Soul* is compelled to narrow its appeal and fall back on style. It should be said that it does this very effectively, with cinematic use of luscious red on black background, flaming wok theatre and beautifully composed arrangements of dishes and objects. The address is limited, however, to an upper segment of the 'tour educative' market, producing uncomfortable tensions aplenty. As we make our way through Kwong's stylish restaurant, with its uniformly attractive and well-dressed clientele, the problematic nexus between food and distinction reasserts itself.

Ethnicizing Englishness

Another response to tensions around class and ethnicity has been to attempt to include the 'Anglo' within the multiculinary fold. This is part of a wider 'ethnicization' of Englishness (Stratton 1998; Brabazon 2000) which can be seen in the arrival in Australian supermarkets of 'good old British bangers', pork pies and other products emblazoned with the Union flag. English might still signify 'ordinary', but in the backlash against multiculturalism of the nineties, ordinary was made special.

In 2001 ABC viewers began a 13-week romp through the culinary diversity of Australia, via the series *Secret Recipes*:

> Immigration has changed the way we live, challenged the way we think – and seasoned what we eat! Australians everywhere are cooking their secret recipes and creating *the new world cuisine*.

Each week host Jacques Reymond takes us on a journey into a different culture to meet the characters who are the keepers of their families' culinary secrets: 'Be it gran's apple pie, or nonna's goat's cheese, you can be certain there's a secret recipe involved and that it's been passed on from one generation to the next' (*Secret Recipes*).

The choice of upmarket French restaurateur Jacques Reymond as presenter indicates the target audience of *Secret Recipes*, invoking the class associations of culinary sophistication and authority claimed by France. France's nuclear testing in the Pacific and the *Rainbow Warrior* incident have ensured an ongoing ambivalence to all things French. Yet Reymond's manner was oddly compelling, with viewers mesmerized by his endless interference. Despite offering viewers recipes 'passed on from one generation to the next', Reymond had no compunction about suggesting adaptations.

Secret Recipes, as with other offerings in ABC's 8 pm cookery spot, found a solid middle-class audience, as did its tie-in publication, *Delicious Magazine*. But our interest in it here is that there amongst all the other 'ethnic' cuisines was episode 12: 'English'. Reymond's French origins were played up, even more than usual, for comic effect:

> It's aprons on and gloves off in this episode of *Secret Recipes* as John 'Hoppy' Hopkins and Jacques engage in some good-natured cross-channel repartee. They also share magnificent tipsy pheasant, delicious kedgeree and traditional homemade English marmalade. (*Secret Recipes*)

The programme begins with Reymond breathlessly informing us that Hopkins 'is going to show us how interesting English food can be if it's done with flair and care' – the patronizing tone is maintained throughout the episode. The programme opens with Jacques and Hoppy riding through a field of farmed deer on the back of a 'ute' – as one does.

They are on their way to buy their live pheasant, of course, and we are treated to a lot of masculine backslapping and repartee:

> *Reymond* (on the subject of kedgeree for breakfast): Typical English guys
> *Hoppy*: At least we don't eat snails

This is followed by more back slapping. *Secret Recipes* is significant for its inclusion of Englishness as an ethnic cuisine, but despite Hoppy's gregarious pub style and the cooking of bread and butter pudding, all those deer and pheasants make clear that it is the England of the stately home, not the fish and chip shop, which is being celebrated. The Britain of *Secret Recipes* remains firmly within the 'tour educative' framework.

Food Lovers Guide to Australia diffuses class tensions and the spectre of gastro-fetishism by a thoughtful and inclusive appeal to audiences. Presenters Maeve O'Maera and Joanna Saville are both experienced and knowledgeable food journalists and yet they project a sensible 'mum next door' persona. Though *Food Lovers* appears on public broadcaster SBS, Maeve's regular cookery slot on commercial Channel 7's *Better Homes and Gardens* enhances its unpretentious image, as does the magazine format in which Maeve or Joanna visit cooks, chefs, and growers around Australia. The programme is an example, as Frances Bonner has put it, of the 'multicultural ordinary':

> The items in each episode are linked geographically by a map indicating to where the next move is, but no attempt is made to present a unified picture of the nation, and the format and its production by the multicultural broadcaster makes doing so impossible and also undesirable ... Ideologically its message is of plenitude and infinite variety.
>
> (Bonner 2003: 175)

While *Food Lovers* does not overtly trumpet a 'unified' identity, the multicultural message of strength via diversity is clearly enunciated. What is most significant about its model of inclusion is that many of the food producers featured speak from the marginalized regional perspective described earlier. One recent episode featured a segment on the Country Women's Association, a group who have suffered the slings and arrows of cosmopolitan scorn. Often relegated to the status of regional relics of the settler past, the CWA actually perform much of the slow food mandate in the regional Australian context. So Joanna visits a smalltown baking champion as she performs her all-night baking marathon for the next day's 'show'. The programme does not employ

Reymond's snide tone; there is no deprecation of the 'British' origins of her wondrous marble cakes. Instead we witness an experienced baker preparing her products and the context of the community in which she competes.

The 'tour educative' format is still in evidence in *Food Lovers*, yet the inclusion of 'Aussie' providores and cooks and the unaffected manner of its presenters work towards the multiculinarism originally called for by Corones. Though the programme is cosmopolitan in its appeal, its use of regional and urban subjects reflects an easy relationship between the two.

The challenge ingredient

A completely different formula is represented by Channel 7's *Surprise Chef*. Australian-Greek-Cypriot Aristos Papandroulakis borrows something of the 'blokiness' of well known Anglo-Australian identity, Iain Hewitson of *Huey's Cooking Adventures* (Channel 10). In the Australian context, the masculine discourse of 'mateship', à la Paul Hogan, is a time-honoured response to suggestions of 'distinction'. But Aristos takes the formula further than Hewitson, constructing an effective bridge between a culinary cosmopolitanism and suburban Australia. *Surprise Chef* breaks not just with the peasant paradigm, but also with the compulsive reference of more middle-class programmes to idealized rural landscapes. Aristos eschews the tour educative model to embrace the everyday suburban realities of the supermarket, industrial food production and, most shockingly, tinned food.

The approach has drawn flaming criticism from a number of food writers. 'Who the hell is Aristos?', asks Sydney columnist Ruth Ritchie, continuing, 'just about the most annoying man on Australian television, that's who ... If Aristos deserves another food show, than [sic] the guy who dreamt up Chicken Tonight should be anchoring the news' (Ritchie 2002a: 27). Aristos's exuberant manner isn't everyone's cup of tea, but the extremity of Ritchie's reaction must raise suspicions. As Sydney broadcaster and columnist Alan Saunders wryly points out, there is a certain kind of food writing that has a lot to answer for:

> I can still hold my head up high because whereas you employ generic own-brand stuff from your local supermarket, what I drizzle on my radicchio is extra virgin oil cold-pressed in Tuscany and available only from a special importer. But, of course, I use it on very simple salads so I can proudly proclaim that I am not a snob. Which is how you know that I am.
>
> (Saunders 2004: 50)

In upmarket food writing, the supermarket is the site of all evil – pre-packaging, industrial production, the subordination of quality to appearance and efficiency. In these terms, Aristos provocatively plays the devil. As the programme website brazenly puts it: 'Aristos is out there, lurking amongst the supermarket shelves and hoping to snare a dinner party somewhere' (*Surprise Chef*).

Surprise Chef borrows from game show formats and shares much in common with reality television. Each week, an unsuspecting supermarket shopper is persuaded to allow Aristos into their homes to cook a meal with whatever ingredients come to hand. Attention is drawn to a 'challenge ingredient' – a particularly ordinary item such as three bean mix or tinned pineapple which appears radically at odds with culinary refinement. This gives the programme a familiar competitive focus and narrative interest – how will the challenge be met? It also functions as an effective mechanism of audience inclusion. The challenge ingredient is almost always a 'despised' item, with strong connotations of older Anglo-Australian identities, but Aristos demonstrates that nothing is beyond redemption. The three bean mix can be included in a tasty minestrone soup. Tinned pineapple works well in fruit muffins. The approach has allowed Aristos to break through resistance to the cosmopolitan implications of cooking 'fancy' or 'ethnic' food. His broad Australian accent and use of British-derived Aussie rhyming slang (referring for example, to salt as 'me old mate Harold Holt') all aid the process.[1]

Of all the programmes we have reviewed here, Aristos most clearly refuses the opposition between cosmopolitan good taste and the ordinary Anglo-Australian. The bridge between the two is nicely reflected in his own career. After starting business in fish and chip shops with his father, he now runs an upmarket seafood restaurant in Perth. His recipes continue to invoke both ends of this continuum, ranging from lobster mornay and wok fried beef fillet to 'bronzed Aussie chicken' and horseradish hotdogs (preparation time ten minutes). While he extends popular knowledge of unusual ingredients and cooking techniques, he also shows that good food can be prepared without the aid of pheasant or duck eggs and in a time frame that is realistic given the mounting pressures of contemporary life. Most significantly, he shows that social differences can be negotiated without retreating from the primary sites – the supermarket, the suburb – in which they are inscribed. The culinary ordinary is not to be disavowed, but a challenge ingredient to be embraced.

Conclusion

We have not wanted, in this chapter, to pit middle-class epicureanism against the culinary 'mainstream'. Rather it has been our intention to map the ways in which opposition between cosmopolitan notions of good taste and the image of the ordinary Anglo-Australian plays out in food programming. We have argued that Australia's food media have, by and large, adopted an attitude which privileges 'ethnic' and chic urban foodways whilst denigrating the culinary traditions of Australia's settler heritage. In doing so media have overlooked the powerful semiotic value of foods such as fish and chips, which now play a role in signifying opposition to the imposition of European notions of 'distinction'. In such a climate, British culture, and particularly food, has been 'ethnicized'. We have argued that programmes such as *Food Lover's Guide, Gondola on the Murray* and *Surprise Chef* owe their success to an understanding of the importance of the place of the 'ordinary' in the way in which working-class and rural Australians see themselves. If the ordinary is the challenge ingredient, performing mediation between middle-class sensibilities and the everyday comfort of the ordinary is the challenge.

Notes

1.   Australia's twenty-second prime minister, Harold Holt, disappeared off Portsmouth Beach on 19 December 1967. Despite the tragic nature of his demise, its mystery has assured Holt a lasting place in Australian popular humour.

7   Cookbooks as manuals of taste

Danielle Gallegos

They peddle vicarious 'gastro-porn', provide travelogues for exotic locations, and are utilitarian manuals, and as such cookbooks have finally emerged as objects enmeshed in the cultural and social fabric of life. As examples of lifestyle media, cookbooks fulfil mundane needs by assisting in the preparation of food; at the same time they give material form to a particular narrative of self-identity (Giddens 1991). Their significance lies not in the reproducibility of their recipes; rather, their significance is their emergence as the vehicles and tools used to maintain the communication between the web of flows that is 'culture'. An examination of cookbooks, therefore, serves to tell us more about 'a people's collective imaginations, symbolic values, dreams and expectations' (Fragner 2000: 71).

Along with magazines and television cooking programmes, cookbooks are proponents of taste and fashion and have a role in inscribing the self with a sense of place, belonging and achievement (Appadurai 1988; Mennell 1996; Heine 2000). They 'set standards and attempt to influence consumption' (Ireland 1981: 108), and in so doing provide a means through which changes in taste can be discerned (Santich 1996). Yet to describe cookbooks as simply discerning taste perhaps constructs them as cultural objects of little significance, as simply reflecting changes in taste rather than actively shaping it. Cookbooks facilitate the production of a moral self as 'good' cook, 'good' parent and 'good' spouse. They also facilitate the production of 'good' citizen by providing standards through which pluralism can be explored.

This chapter maps the evolution of Australian cookery writers as intermediaries for developing and communicating taste of the 'other'. As cultural intermediaries they bring knowledge of taste to ordinary people who can use them to master a lifestyle that embraces the notion of what it is to be 'multicultural' and, in this case, 'Australian'. Cookbooks enable a collective national identity to be forged that is always debated and contested. They elevate, in late modernity, hybridity and inclusivity as the contemporary lifestyle offering distinction.

Taste has emerged as one technology that the self can use in order to undertake the ongoing project of identity building. However, any discussion of food and its consumption highlights the dual meanings of 'taste'. First, taste refers to the biological manifestations utilizing the sense of tongue-taste and smell to discern sweet, sour, bitter and salt nuances. Second, taste denotes a socio-culturally linked concept, where to have 'good taste' is a sign of distinction. In other words, the ambiguity of taste-for-food captures the dilemma that involves reconciling the body, or the corporeal, with the transcendental. This duality of taste, first highlighted by Kant (1790/1952), can result in confusion as to whether taste 'always refers to the preferences and choices of the individual and is totally private by its very nature', or if it 'offers a universal standard, potentially applicable to all members of a society' (Gronow 1997: 91).[1] In other words, taste provides a bridge between the public and private and, as we shall see, between global and local.

As a result of the ambiguous nature of taste, there has been intense speculation over the mechanics of food choice and the taste acceptability of food. The answer to the food choice question, however, remains a riddle – and while complex, continues to be routinely simplified. This simplification is exemplified by Santich (1996: 18) who concludes when posing the question 'So why do we eat what we eat?' with 'Because that's the way we were born, the way we are – and because we like those flavours'. The question then remains largely unresolved: what is it that determines our 'taste' for some foods over others? Taking another angle, and going a little further than Santich, Falk (1994: 79) poses the question 'How can the others' food become our food?'; how do we learn to adopt food that we have not been exposed to historically or culturally? In this vein, considering distinctions between 'our' food and 'their' food, Bourdieu (1984) and Campbell (1987) have both problematized the taste, fashion and pleasure nexus with more subtle responses. Both have embedded the question of taste in a group of related and more fundamental concepts. For Bourdieu, these concepts are socially driven; for Campbell they are psychological. The two (while appearing to be the opposite poles of the taste debate) preserve the Kantian public–private duality.

For Bourdieu, taste is primarily about class and the affirmation of class boundaries. Food choice is about 'positioning people in accordance with their class expectations and their collective consciousness, it is therefore what distinguishes one group from another' (Coveney 1996: 50). For Campbell, modern consumption is reduced to modern hedonism, and is characterized by a longing for pleasures generated through the action of daydreaming. In this sense, as technologies of practical subject formation, these very theories can be ranked with other technologies of taste such as cookbooks, magazines, television cooking programmes and cultural tourism. They become tools in the attempt to harmonize the binaries that constitute the self: public–private, global–local, universal–particular, risk–pleasure. Taste emerges, then, as an ensemble of techniques for reaffirming a very particular and limited story about ourselves in both public and private spheres. Cookbooks provide the requisites for the implementation of both socio-political and psycho-emotional taste. They provide the social stratification, knowledges and experiences for a contextual framework in which taste can perform. This framework does not just appear but rather evolves over time. In order to develop an appreciation of the importance of cookbooks within an Australian context it is relevant to provide some historical context.

Australian cookbooks

The first 'home-grown' Australian cookbook is thought to be *The English and Australian Cookery Book: Cookery for the Many, as Well as for the Upper Ten Thousand* by an Australian aristologist, also known as Edward Abbott (Pont et al. 1988: 5). The book was published in 1864 in England, 76 years after Australia was founded as a British penal colony. During this time, and for many years after, Australia was an outpost of Britain. All inhabitants were British subjects, British law was enforced and migration was restricted to British subjects (Jupp 1991). The majority of non-convict migration for the next 150 years, due in part to the operation of the White Australia Policy, remained largely British in origin.[2]

The British legacy of overcooked, bland food is the starting point for Australian culinary heritage, one that is often overlooked 'in the rush to proclaim the new food' (Raymond 1999: 30). The charting of the development of ethnic cookbooks for the Angloceltic community (as opposed to ethnic cookbooks produced by and for specific ethnic communities) is an attempt to tell one story with due consideration given to the evolutionary process.[3] Newman and Gibson (this volume), tell another version of the story by problematizing Australian mono-culture and multiculinarism via television cooking programmes. The emergence of ethnic cookbooks in Australia can be roughly divided into four phases: the 'foreign' (1890s–1920s); the 'continental/oriental' (1930s–1950s); the 'international/multicultural' (1960s–1980s); and finally the 'Australian' (1990s–2000s). Each of these is dealt with in turn.

The foreign phase (1890s–1920s)

During this phase, the White Australia Policy was in full operation and, as a result, the Australian population was almost entirely white and Angloceltic. Therefore, cookbooks during this time were not about introducing readers to foods that they may, through the course of the everyday, come into contact with. Instead, Australia's isolation created an interest in the foreign, and recipes acted as curios, complete with foreign names and ingredients that helped to satisfy that curiosity. The recipe names were simple descriptors; they were not an attempt to accurately represent 'foreign' food (Pillsbury 1998: 127). Collecting these recipes provided an opportunity to feel part of a larger global community; they were, therefore, a technique of inclusivity, not for the 'other' in Australia but for Australia as part of the world. Consequently, from these recipes, Australia was viewed as a part of Europe. Asia made a tokenistic appearance represented by Japanese sukiyaki and Chinese chop suey. Regardless of the motive, there was an understanding of Australia as part of a larger global community.

The continental/oriental phase (1930s–1950s)

In order to ensure its long-term viability as a 'nation', Australia had to embark on a systematic process of immigration that has been and remains politically and socially divisive. This process began in earnest immediately after the Second World War and continues today. The social management of this large influx of migrants has progressed through a number of stages. During the 1930s to 1950s, the exclusionary practices of the White Australia Policy were marginally relaxed and gave way to a policy of assimilation. Here the emphasis was on immigrants becoming archetypal Australians with no visible signs of difference. Assimilation failed and moved on to become integration, where 'the best characteristics of each [culture] would be used to form the basis of a single Australian identity' (Theophanous 1995: 5).

The interest in 'foreign' food re-emerged in the late 1930s as 'continental cookery' with the publication of *The First Australian Continental Cookery Book*, 'printed in Australia for Australians'. This book aimed to 'flash a ray or two of light into the occasionally somewhat obscure recesses of traditional British cookery' (quoted in Bannerman 1998: 57). This aim is not unlike Elizabeth David's (1951) *A Book of Mediterranean Food* (published some 20 years later), which was described as her attempt to 'escape from the spartan conditions of post-war Britain' (Hardyment 1995: 91). In 1952, *Oh for A French Wife!* (Moloney and Coleman) aimed, in a fun way, to blow away 'any mystique surrounding Continental Cookery'. A few years later Maria Donovan's (1955) *Continental Cookery in Australia* 'brought together French, Italian, Viennese, Hungarian and other continental recipes which had appeared in the Melbourne *Age* and *Sun*' (Bannerman 1998: 57). This book endeavoured to improve accessibility to continental food:

Continental cooking, often regarded as extravagant and laborious, has now come within the reach of the Australian housewife. In a simple, everyday style, which makes immediate appeal, the author of this book initiates the reader into the mysteries of continental cooking – till now closely guarded by blue-ribbon chefs and made difficult by the lack of foreign ingredients.

(Donovan 1961: back cover)

Moloney, Coleman and Donovan mimicked, to some degree, Elizabeth David in that recipes were delivered in a chatty style and given some contextual framework. This framework did one of two things: it either placed the recipe in its country of origin, turning the books into travelogues, or, alternatively, it placed the recipe in the reader's home, making, at least in the imagination, all things possible. However, unlike David, who made very few concessions to ingredient availability, Moloney, Coleman and Donovan and their predecessors were all about accessibility rather than 'authenticity':

There is not one [recipe] here that I have not tried myself, and each is adapted to conditions prevailing in Australia, such as the shortage of domestic help and the supplies available of foreign ingredients. No ingredient is mentioned that cannot be easily obtained in the larger cities of Australia.

(Donovan 1955: xiii)

In fact, David and her Australian counterparts were striving for the same outcomes. All these cookbooks were improving access to what was 'foreign' and largely inaccessible – providing the novelty required by both Campbell (1987) and Bourdieu (1984) for the projection of idealized pleasure and the shoring up of class distinctions respectively. At the same time, they were reaffirming 'authenticity' and 'tradition' as antidotes to the increased fluidity and permeability of modernity.

The primary locus of this phase is again Eurocentric, which is not surprising given that the White Australia Policy was still fully operational. However, it is in this phase that we begin to see the significant introduction of Asian food and cooking. Despite the long history of the Chinese in Australia (from the 1840s), the first Australian book devoted to Chinese cookery did not appear until 1948 (Geechoun's *Cooking the Chinese Way*).

The 'foreign' phase was about creating 'good' global citizens; cookbooks during this time were an attempt to insinuate Australia into the global. This continues in the 'continental/oriental' phase, and is joined by the emergence of the individual as a cosmopolitan. Engaging in cosmopolitanism requires curiosity and is an intellectual and aesthetic openness toward the 'Other', 'a search for contrasts rather than uniformity' (Hannerz 1990: 239; see also Lash and Urry 1994). Cosmopolitanism also relates to a consideration of the self. By increasing one's understanding of the other 'a little more of the world is somehow under control', resulting in 'a curious, apparently paradoxical interplay between mastery and surrender' (Hannerz 1990: 240). While this phase sees the initial emergence of the cosmopolitan, it is not until the next phase that cosmopolitanism as a balance between 'mastery and surrender' and 'anxiety and pleasure', fully emerges.

The multicultural/international Phase (1960s–1980s)

In the 1970s the social policy for 'handling' migrant populations moved from integration to the more ambiguous policy of multiculturalism as active encouragement of cultural diversity. It was not, however, until the mid-1980s that multiculturalism become accepted as an integral, inescapable part of the Australian political and social landscape.

Initially the 'foreign' and the 'continental' were viewed as curiosities, worthy of separating out and encapsulating in an entire book. This being the case, these were probably purchased by those already interested, who had travelled, or who were looking at ways of maintaining cultural capital and improving social status. Readers, were they to cook anything from these cookbooks, had to possess a degree of culinary skill and a willingness to move outside their culinary comfort zones into largely unfamiliar territory; they had to become cosmopolitan. In other words, the taste for the ethnic or the 'other' was confined to those with the required social and cultural capital. This changes during the international/multicultural phase. Here the taste for the ethnic is incorporated as an 'international' section or as recipes designated as 'other' in more generic cookbooks. That is, such recipes were included in cookbooks that were popular, espoused by the 'experts' and being purchased by a wider variety of people. The large influx of migrants into Australia was unsettling for both the migrant and the predominantly Angloceltic resident population and generated anxiety for both parties. Given the failure of assimilation, a public policy designed to reduce anxiety for Angloceltic Australians, food and cooking was one area where the ethnic could be 'mastered'. In this process, anxiety was reconciled with pleasure. At the same time, Angloceltic Australians willingly surrendered and the cosmopolitan became another facet of the self.

This move to a more eclectic approach is exemplified by the Western Australian *CWA Cookery Book and Household Hints* (Barnes 1936). Since 1936, this book has been revised and reprinted through 42 editions.[4] One measure of the success, or otherwise, of multiculturalism could be the degree to which non-Angloceltic recipes are represented in this bastion of Angloceltic Australia. The 1963 edition of this book incorporated a new section called 'Here and There'. At about the same time as this section was introduced, the aims of the Country Women's Association were altered to include, 'to be a loyal citizen of Australia and the British Commonwealth of Nations and promote international understanding' (Townsend 1988). This quest for international understanding is revealed in the 'Here and There' section as a cautious, qualified embracing of the ethnic. Pillsbury (1998: 129) found a similar phenomenon when looking at the international theme in the *Better Homes and Gardens New Cook Book* in the United States. He found 'a not-so-gentle Americanization of these "foreign" recipes – they are foreign, but not too foreign'. So it is for the *CWA Cookbook*. Yet, unlike Pillsbury, who made a careful comparison between these recipes and those of specialty cookbooks, the content of the recipe is not so important. What is important is the intent – the inclusion of an international theme encouraged readers of the *CWA Cookbook* to think outside their own knowledge base. It was a step in the process of understanding, a way of bringing the ethnic into their homes and of promoting cosmopolitanism as a common ideal of Australian society.

The two most popular cookbooks of the time – *The Margaret Fulton Cookbook* (Fulton 1968) and *The Australian Women's Weekly Cookbook* (Sinclair 1970) – took on an overt pedagogic role, teaching their readers with thoroughness. Margaret Fulton and Ellen Sinclair were the food editors for *Woman's Day* and *The Australian Women's Weekly* respectively. The popularity of their cookbooks was due in part to the following these women developed in magazines. The *Margaret Fulton Cookbook*, for example, has been continuously in print since 1968 and has sold over one and a half million copies (Pont et al. 1988).

As a pedagogic text, *The Australian Women's Weekly Cookbook* sets out to teach readers about a diverse range of foods. The section on pasta exhorts readers to make the effort to discover the 'different macaroni foods – or pastas, as they are called', for it is 'a treasure hunt that will reward you with good food for all the family' (Sinclair 1970: 94). In introducing the section on 'International Cookery' what is emphasized is the contribution made by migrants:

Each year, as a nation, our food tastes are changing, becoming enriched by the national cuisine of migrants from other countries who have now settled in Australia. Restaurants of many nationalities flourish; we've found that Chinese, Italian, Indian dishes – as well as the food of many other countries – each have their own subtle blending of flavours. Because Australian housewives are always interested in new ways with foods, new, delicious tastes, dinner parties with an international flavour have become popular.

(Sinclair 1970: 120)

The Complete Margaret Fulton Cookbook does not have a separate 'international' section, but consciously decides to place them throughout the book, with the rationale being:

Today's trend of cooking seems to be international. British households no longer confine their cooking to English foods nor do Italians eat only Italian style. Take one street in any one city of the world and you find different cuisine being prepared in every second kitchen. With this in mind, it seemed logical that each section would have to include recipes from all over the world. Soups, for example, include Minestrone from Italy, Short Soup from China, the French soup so often served at weddings, Madreline, and Mulligatawny from India.

(Fulton 1968: 7)

The cookbook dedicated to one particular type of cuisine was not a new one and during this period it belonged to the explosion of cookbooks in general. Rather than emphasizing authenticity, these cookbooks appeared to emphasize novelty, simplicity and fun. Margaret Fulton in her *Italian Cookbook* (1973: 6) describes Italian cooking as 'good cooking and best of all it is fun cooking'. Charmaine Solomon (1973: 8) in her *Chinese Cookbook* describes Chinese food as 'extremely simple to cook', 'there are no complex sauces, no tricky techniques, no mysterious procedures that need a master chef to explain'. Solomon's book was, however, more than just an exploration in the kitchen. With a glossary of Chinese ingredients and a list of places selling them, Solomon was attempting to get Australians to explore their environment and expand their knowledge: 'visit your city's Chinatown and find them [vegetables] in cans, dried, or freshly grown by Chinese market gardeners' (Solomon 1973: 84). In this respect she continues a task commenced by the earlier writers of Chinese cookbooks.

The last books to be examined in this phase are Alexander's *Stephanie's Menus for Food Lovers*, published in 1985, and *Stephanie's Feasts and Stories*, published in 1988. The recipes in these books, like Elizabeth David's, are accompanied by stories – the recipes are named after people and are given context – making them close and personal: 'ordinary' recipes from 'ordinary' people. Alexander has deliberately not separated out recipes with an international flavour, arguing instead, 'I have learnt never to say "this is the only way" or, "this is the best way". The more one travels to eat, the more one reads, the more one listens, the less definite the ethnic boundaries become' (1988: vii). Alexander acts as a local interpreter, in the same way that Bonner (this volume) describes television cooking presenters as interpreters, in that she continues the process of moving the 'ethnic' away from being a mere curiosity – a peripheral oddity – towards becoming an integral and central component of Australian culinary heritage.

The Australian phase (1990s–2000s)[5]

In the 1990s multiculturalism was reworked to apply not only to non-English speaking Australians but 'equally to all Australians, whether of Aboriginal, Angloceltic or non-English speaking background, and whether they were born in Australia or overseas' (National Multicultural Advisory Council 1997: 5). These efforts were an attempt at inclusivity, an attempt to define what being 'Australian' meant.

The Australian phase is characterized by an abundance of eclectic cookbooks affiliated with celebrity chefs, well-known restaurants, magazines and television programmes. Cookbooks became the ultimate marketing device not only for personalities and products but also for concepts and policies, including multiculturalism. All cookbooks in this phase 'celebrate' diversity. Some do it under the banner of 'Australian', others are 'Asian' or 'Mediterranean', or more generic. All of them have become a modality through which multiculturalism is celebrated as a success.

As we look at the evolution of cookbooks in Australia, what becomes evident is that they are vehicles for defining the boundaries of community. The incorporation of 'bush tucker', as the indigenous food component, into the genesis of Australian cookbooks appears, at least on the surface, to be a leaning towards a new democratic inclusivity for the Australian community. Consequently, cookbooks that circulate what is described as 'Australian cuisine' operate as technologies of citizenship (Miller 1993). In other words, these cookbooks are tools that are being used to construct a sense of community both within the text, amongst those who read the text, and where the text circulates. This is a public affirmation of community, defined by Arendt as 'a shared world', 'a common space of appearance' and 'a fundamental condition of selfhood' (Villa 1996: 7).

As a technology of citizenship, Australian cuisine, as exemplified in cookbooks, has become a means through which a collective identity can be affirmed. Via other means, this affirmation can prove to be a problem for settler and/or postcolonial societies. Turner (1994: 123) argues that the formation of collective identities is complex in that 'among other things, they must be plural: identities rather than identity. They must be built on the recognition rather than the overriding of cultural difference, and they must accept and negotiate Australia's dual history as colonised and coloniser'. Australian cuisine, as has been shown, has always been hybrid, a collection of identities rather than a single 'pure' identity. Over time, these identities have been continually contested and (re)negotiated, emerging in late modernity with increased intensity and explicitness.

Bush foods provide a link between these identities. They have been described as the 'indigenous ingredients of our cuisine' (Bruneteau 1996: 8) and as the 'wild flavours' that 'might be a unifying influence in our contemporary multicultural cuisine' (Beckett 1999: 15). They are used 'because they taste wonderful', 'excite our palates' (Robins and Robins 1994: vii) and 'expand the frontiers of taste' (Bruneteau 1996: 8). The big picture of Australian cuisine – the hybrid, multicultural, indigenous combination of foods acting as a citizenship device – is functional as a public affirmation and modality through which Australia can be seen to extricate itself from 'global food', 'Pacific Rim cuisine' and 'New British food'.

To eat Australian food is to be Australian, to be non-traditional, to be innovative, open minded and sophisticated. However, unlike some hybrid forms such as Australian music that have erupted 'naturally', Australian food is orchestrated. The conductors have been the chefs of fine-dining restaurants in tandem with food producers. The Australian chef has become, rather than the creator of something new, a bricoleur in the same vein as Coco Chanel. Floch (2000: 108) describes Chanel as being 'concerned with a need to find means to ensure that the baroque counterpart remains essential to the affirmation of her vision'. He also suggests, however, that bricolage is 'not a mere transportation of a unit from one semiotic system into another', but rather involves some form of calculated transformation. Therefore, to suggest that Australian cuisine acts as a technology of citizenship, through which individuals and groups can stake a claim in a collective plural identity, is tenuous. Australian cuisine has arrived from the top down, not from the bottom up. For it to become *the* food chosen by the people for self-identification, all groups within Australia would need to become equal stakeholders.

The food presented in these Australian cookbooks, despite their claim to provide recipes that are 'easy-to-prepare', and for 'the home kitchen' (Ross 1995: 6; see also Beckett 1999) are not recipes for the entire population. Instead, they are directed towards those who have access to ingredients, those with culinary skill, time to both cook and reconnoitre for ingredients, and those with the economic and cultural capital to want to indulge in such tasks. Australian food is, therefore, still very much the domain of the upper middle-classes, but there is some evidence of a trickle-down effect. Popular cookbook producers associated with women's magazines, such as *The Australian Women's Weekly* and *Australian Family Circle*, have both published their own versions of Australian food cookbooks, interestingly, minus the indigenous component. In a recent article, Pamela Clarke, who runs the test kitchen for *The Australian Women's Weekly*, is quoted as saying that the cookbooks produced by *The Weekly* provide recipes for 'Mrs Average; not the elite bracket, nor right down the bottom' (O'Neill 2001: 54).

By following the evolution of cookbooks, we find that they are technologies that shape how we see ourselves and where we place ourselves in the world both individually and collectively. Cookbooks provide recipes for life but, as with all recipes, perfection remains elusive. Cookbooks do not resolve the tension between public and private, local and global, risk and pleasure, universal and particular. They do, however, provide a space where these tensions can be tested; a space where the Kantian harmony of imagination and understanding can be played out. As techniques of taste, cookbooks demonstrate how the individual is trained to implement both socio-political and psycho-emotional taste almost at the same time. Cookbooks instil us with a sense of place, belonging and achievement; a means by which we can employ taste and create and recreate being 'Australian'.

Notes

1. Kant (1790/1952) makes the distinction between taste that is 'simultaneously subjective', in that it relates to individual perceptions, and 'universally subjective', in that to rise to the status of the 'beautiful' it needs to be communicated and validated with others.
2. Jupp (1991: 53) asserts that the White Australia Policy was exactly what it appeared to be: 'an assertion that the white race was superior to all others and must preserve that superiority by excluding others from the continent'. As a form of immigrant exclusion, it was almost completely effective between the 1890s and the 1960s (p. 51). Those that were permitted entry under the White Australia Policy included British, Irish, Scottish and Welsh. Scandinavians were also permitted entry and because the British royal family

was known to have direct German links, Germans. Based on prevailing race theory in Britain and elsewhere the ideal Australian was English in culture and German or Nordic in appearance (p. 69).

3. The term 'Angloceltic' is used to describe those Australians with ancestry dating back to colonization. It is acknowledged that this term conflates a range of ethnicities that may or may not be mobilized.

4. The Country Women's Association (CWA) is found in all states and territories of Australia. First formed in 1922 in New South Wales, it is an organization whose primary aim was and remains to improve the life of women and children living in the remote and rural areas of Australia. The inclusion of the CWA cookbook here provides the background noise against which comparisons can be made. The organization was fundamentally Angloceltic and while overtly apolitical and non-sectarian, its motto 'Honour to God, Loyalty to the throne, Service to the Country, through Country women, for Country women, by Country women' provides a political contextualization. The organization exemplifies the female version of Australian 'mateship'. Today it remains an icon of the Australian landscape and continues to champion the rights of, and opportunities for, women and children living in areas outside major cities.

5. I have given this phase the title 'Australian' as it is during this era that the nominator comes to collect notions of cultural difference and diversity. It is also the phase where 'Australian' cuisine emerges as a distinct entity (see, for example, Dunstan 1976).

Part III
The great outdoors

8 It was beautiful before you changed it all

Class, taste and the transformative aesthetics of the garden lifestyle media

Lisa Taylor

The 'ordinary' domestic garden has become the site where most garden lifestyling in the British media is staged. Arguing that the 'ordinary' people and places of lifestyle are always classed, this chapter interrogates the transformative aesthetics of the lifestyled garden. With reference to British weekend lifestyle journalism, such as *Observer Life,* and lifestyle programmes like *Home Front in the Garden* (BBC2, 1997–), it asks: if the lifestyled garden is more 'ordinary' who, in class terms, is the implied 'ordinary' viewer? Is there a dominant set of garden aesthetics or are there competing versions vying for authentication? And whose aesthetics are given national legitimation and whose are relegated to the local margins?

The sustained popularity and expansion of the lifestyle media needs to be set against the backcloth of a wider cultural shift: the ascent of 'lifestyle' must be seen as part of the transition from civic to consumer culture (Bauman 1987). Locally, social agents have experienced this shift through the decline of traditional, communal 'ways of life' which have been replaced by consumer lifestyles (Chaney 1996, 2001). For subjects no longer reliant on the stability offered by the traditional way of life, lifestyle projects are utilized as coping mechanisms in face of the changes delivered by modernity (Chaney 2001). Seen in this way, the lifestyle media offer viewers the stabilizing potential to help them cope; the formal construction of lifestyle hooks into the ordinary rhythms, practices and sites of everyday life. In the context of late capitalism, the media and culture industries have a vested interest in providing a central arena for the organization of the transition Chaney describes. Hence, there is an interlocking, mutually lucrative relationship between the lifestyle media, the display of lifestyle ideas and consumer culture.

In his most recent work on lifestyle, Chaney (2001) argues that traditional ideas about culture are no longer tenable in social theory. Whereas culture was once conceived as a firm set of beliefs and normative expectations, shared within a relatively stable community, in mass societies there are a 'multiplicity of overlapping cultures with differing relationships with social actors' (Chaney 2001: 78). In a time of mass communication and entertainment, culture is in part about the relationship between the identities represented in media discourse and how people identify both themselves and members of other social groups. For Chaney, culture has become a 'symbolic repertoire', adapted from images and symbols available in a mass-mediated environment which are then assembled into performances associated with particular social groups. A repertoire is a set of practices through which people symbolically represent identity and difference.

Chaney argues that traditional conceptions of culture have virtually given way to new social forms. One of the most significant examples of a new social form that typifies social change is the growth of lifestyles. Lifestyles draw on the resources provided by consumer choices out of the symbolic repertoires on offer in contemporary culture. In contrast to the traditional 'way of life', the lifestyle is utterly dependent on the leisure and culture industries and consumer patterns. Playfully and reflexively constructed by those who invest in them, lifestyles are performed improvisations; unstable and open to reimprovisation, they converge in 'loose agglomerations' (Chaney 2001: 86).

One of the key strategies that the British media have employed as a means of urging people to incorporate lifestyle practices into their everyday lives is that of 'ordinaryization' (Brunsdon et al. 2001: 53). The presentation of lifestyle knowledges, for example, has altered since the early 1970s: the authoritative tone of public service has been replaced with what Ellis has called 'popular public service' (Ellis 2000: 32). One of the ways this more popular address is achieved is through the inclusion of more 'ordinary' people in garden lifestyle television: ordinary gardeners are embraced in lifestyle programming and garden experts act as 'personality-interpreters' (Taylor 2002), packaging lifestyle ideas from the symbolic repertoires on offer in consumer culture (Chaney 2001). The inclusion of ordinary subjects is an 'ordinari-ization' strategy that constructs a discourse of achievability and accessibility (Moseley 2000) for viewers which pervades programmes such as *Ground Force* (Bazal for the BBC, 1997–).[1] In this way, ordinariness has been awarded a crucial place in garden lifestyle culture in ways that potentially offer a positive location to the ordinary gardener. Ordinary people are included, addressed as equals and given a positive site of identification in the lifestyle media. Indeed it might even be argued that ordinary people have a real stake in the ongoing construction of mediated garden history. Yet these assertions beg a central question: who are the 'ordinary' people of lifestyle?

Ordinariness has taken on increased significance in both the contemporary media and in lifestyle culture (Moseley 2000; Chaney

2002; Bonner 2003). Here ordinariness is defined as a mode of experience that belongs to everyone's everyday life; it is not just the authentic preserve of particular social groups such as women or the working class.[2] Rather, ordinariness is always subjectively *positioned* by the social variables of class, gender, 'race' and sexuality. Lifestyles never float free of class. The 'ordinary' people of terrestrial lifestyle television, for example, are usually at least lower middle-class; the embrace of working-class people is extremely rare in lifestyle programming (Taylor 2002). Diversity might exist amongst the ordinary people of lifestyle in terms of age, gender and sexuality, but it is a lower middle-class type of diversity.

Acknowledging that the people of lifestyle have been 'ordinari-ized', this chapter turns to the question of how gardens are represented in the lifestyle media. The first section investigates garden aesthetics. Drawing on Bourdieu's approach to taste and aesthetics (1984, 1990a) and his theory of symbolic violence (Bourdieu and Passeron 1990), I argue that the 'ordinary' garden in national lifestyle texts offers a middle-class version of the contemporary garden. Indeed, the national media act as a forum for competing middle-class tastes about how the garden should look – from the traditional, patrician middle-class to the playful, eclectic codes which would appeal to the postmodern stand-alone subjects described by Chaney (2001). Arguing that the national lifestyle media imposes barriers against working-class garden aesthetics, the chapter then turns to elements of the local lifestyle press as a means to investigate the visual language of ordinary working-class garden aesthetics.

Drawing on Bourdieu's (1984) concept of 'new cultural intermediaries' and using Marxist perspectives on history and postmodernism (Jameson 1991; McGuigan 1999), the second section investigates how historical conceptions of the garden, given through the interpretative advice of personality-interpreters, act as a capital resource for the group identified as the 'postmodern' fraction of the British middle-class (Savage et al. 1992). Postmodern aesthetic design codes, available only to those with the capital to access them, proffer the means to showcase the most consecrated moments from garden history 'at the least cost' (Bourdieu 1984: 370). As a result, it is – once again – middle-class audiences who are the main beneficiaries of the national lifestyle media. 'Lifestyling', as Chaney argues, is mainly the preserve of middle-class destabilized subjects with sufficient cultural capital to realize garden lifestyle projects.

Aesthetics of the contemporary garden

From the lifestyle press to the makeover: national garden lifestyle aesthetics

Solid, traditional middle-class commentary on garden aesthetics is subtly explicated in Monty Don's Sunday gardening column in the *Life* supplement of UK broadsheet the *Observer*.[3] Like most contemporary lifestyle personality-interpreters, Don avoids a directly instructional approach to gardening. Rather, he implies that the practice of effective gardening can only be understood by adopting a liberal humanist approach to the arts, from the highbrow (literature, painting and music) to the middlebrow (photography). As a result, Don's column is frequently strewn with cultural references and allusions. For example, an October 1997 piece about apples, entitled 'Cider with the Roses', alludes to the writer Laurie Lee. More specifically, Don loosely adopts a quasi-Keatsian perspective both in relation to his own journalistic style and as a guide to gardening appreciation. Implied in this approach is the idea that aesthetic understanding can be acquired through the development of a sensuous appreciation of beauty. For Don, the creation of a garden is about being quintessentially alert to one's own senses. 'Last night', begins his apples column, 'I jogged around the Herefordshire lanes and came home almost drunk with the scent of apples. Every breath was a slug of strong cider ... not enough is made of how smell is such a feature of the countryside, from the fetid sweetness of the May blossom and the chaffy greenness of haymaking' (Don 1997: 56). Elsewhere, sight becomes the privileged sense, as Don describes 'a wigwam of purple sweet peas, the occasional iridescent petal back lit against the sky like a butterfly wing'. Similarly, the tactile quality of plants is likened to 'a kind of delicate floral Braille' (Don 1998: 38). Thus, according to Don, the ability to distinguish beauty leads to an understanding of the visual language of gardening.

The extreme close-up photographs which accompany Don's copy, most often supplied by acclaimed photographer Fleur Oldby, work in tandem with Don's sensuous recommendations. Instructional, literal images of plants in situ are avoided in favour of the more subtle visual strategy of allowing the reader to survey the finite, detailed minutiae of the colour, form and texture of plants. In this way, Oldby's photographs are aimed at those in possession of elite taste, who are able to cultivate an aesthetic of disinterested contemplation and who have the capacity to appreciate the representational form over the function of a photograph (Bourdieu 1990a). Just as Don's column has more to do with the act of writing as opposed to practical gardening, Oldby's illustrations are about enjoying the visual play that plant close-ups allow the photographer to access. Gardening aesthetics, within the pages of Don's middle-class weekend supplement, begin with a cultivated state of mind that is attuned to arts appreciation. The visual organization of the garden, it is implied, is the natural addendum to a cultured approach to lifestyle. In these ways, *Observer Life* offers a traditionally educated, patrician middle-class, yet specifically English approach to the garden as a lifestyle space.

Other compartments of the national media are equally unapologetically middle-class in their demand for knowledge of the type of contemporary visual codes that reference high artistic enclaves. It is virtually impossible to discuss the visual aesthetics of the garden makeover without setting the idea of contemporary gardens against the backcloth of postmodernism. A number of central features characterize accounts of postmodernism in the arts: the obliteration of meaning as a result of the prominence of design and aesthetics; the stylistic tendency towards eclecticism and the juxtaposition of visual codes; the decomposition of the staunch distinction between high and popular culture; and parody, irony, playfulness, intertextuality and a celebration of the depthlessness of cultural forms (Featherstone 1991a; Rojek 1995). A glance at the typical garden makeover reveals an explicit correlation between the visual composition of these gardens and the stylistic features of postmodernism. These kinds of playful, reflexive codes appeal to the destabilized middle-class social subjects discussed by Chaney (2001). Stand-alone postmodern people, as Chaney describes, are more open to the new symbolic repertoires required by lifestyle projects.

The post-makeover contemporary garden is a space that above all has been subjected to the principles of design aesthetics. The decomposition of meaning through the prominence of design is a key strand of thought among postmodern writers. Jameson argues that postmodern culture is characterized by superficiality: 'Depth,' he argues, 'is replaced by surface' (Jameson 1991: 12). In *The Condition of Postmodernity* (1989) Harvey discusses the shift in the conception of space from urban modern planning to postmodern design:

> Whereas the modernists see space as something to be shaped for social purposes and therefore always subservient to the construction of a social project, the postmodernists see space as something independent and autonomous, to be shaped according to aesthetic aims and principles which have nothing necessarily to do with any overarching social objective, save, perhaps, the achievement of timeless and 'disinterested' beauty as an objective in itself.
>
> (Harvey 1989: 66)

While Harvey's claim is made in relation to urban design, his comment holds credence for the consideration of the typical garden makeover: they too are most often conceived as gardens within wider urban spaces. The pursuit of a rigorous and consistent garden design concept without any recourse to a wider communal or social goal is therefore a characteristic of the makeover. In these ways, one can see how the traditional 'way of life' with its recourse to shared communal codes is discarded in favour of the design remit of the 'lifestyle' that Chaney (2001) describes. Design is often presented as a desirable end in itself, and the possibility of underlying meanings is disregarded in favour of immediate surface impressions. Yet the idea of placing design above all else incurs costs, with real effects, for working-class subjects.

As part of the back garden makeovers in *Gardening Neighbours* (BBC2, 1998–), for example, presenter Ali Ward persuades older members of the terrace, Terry and Joan, to wipe every trace of their old garden away in favour of allowing the makeover team to produce a classical formal garden.[4] By way of introduction to the feature-segment, Ali Ward's voiceover sets the scene: 'The central feature of Terry and Joan's original garden at No. 4 was a raised bed full of Bizzie Lizzies'. This is clearly a loaded introduction for the viewer of taste; if these are the plants and structures these gardeners choose, they need the tasteful features that a design concept provides. The saddening aspect of this act of gardening 'benevolence' is that these gardeners clearly wanted to keep their homemade concrete raised bed of impatiens, because it contained valued personal aesthetic meanings for them. 'It was beautiful before you changed it all', remarks Terry as the camera pans the crisp formality of the newly installed box hedges and standard bay trees. The raised bed provided colour and centrality that the new design, which Terry and Joan call 'interesting', fails to provide. This instance is typical of the values of makeover aesthetics. There is an almost clinical obsession with maintaining a coherent design (even if that theme is one of postmodern eclecticism), at the expense of plants or objects invested with value, memory or meaning. It is also an example of symbolic violence par excellence (Bourdieu and Passeron 1990). The programme encourages the removal of local working-class aesthetics to make way for the imposition of a middle-class coherent design concept. The message is clear: get rid of vulgar working-class aesthetic attachments which lack reconvertible capital and surrender them to the cosmopolitan eclecticism of desirable middle-class design principles (see Holliday, this volume). This typical instance is one of the conventions of the genre where the makeover expert and the makeover subject battle over the sentimental attachment people are accused of harbouring to garden plants or objects. Most often the casualties are working-class objects or aesthetic features. In the world of the makeover, the depth of personal (working-class) meaning must be sacrificed to the cleansing agency of design aesthetics.

In order to deliver audience entertainment, each new makeover is constructed on the principle of difference; its central dynamic therefore becomes the endless pursuit of novelty. This is also manifest in the eclecticism of visual codes which typically characterize the makeover. In an episode of *Home Front in the Garden*[5] for example, presenter Anne McKevitt's[6] makeover is based on providing a series of 'rooms' for the garden which include modern features – a heated swimming pool, a grass and bamboo garden and a lit patio area – as well as such 'updated' historical features as a perspex version of the eighteenth-century ha-ha and a brightly painted khaki, aubergine and maroon representation of a walled garden. The result is a mélange of stylistic trends, or what some might even regard as a miscegenation of cultural and historical codes. This kind of playful eclecticism is also at work in the community makeover of back gardens in *Gardening Neighbours* (BBC2, 1998–). Here, eight back gardens of a terraced row in Sheffield are made over around themes of choice – African, white city roof top, cricket, child safe, classical formal, herb and seaside – so that the experience of strolling past is almost akin to choosing lunch in a shopping mall restaurant from an array of world cuisines.

In this way, one can see how postmodern aesthetics carry little value for working-class audiences, who lack the requisite capitals to enable them to 'play' reflexively with high cultural artistic knowledges. Rather, such codes appeal to those interested in the lifestyle practices Chaney (2001) describes. For stand-alone, educated, middle-class subjects in post-industrial societies, who have left behind the communal 'way of life', the interpretation of postmodern aesthetics enables the refashioning of new forms of identity. Yet postmodern middle-class codes reside uneasily next to the established, traditional forms of middle-class aesthetic advocated by writers such as Christopher Lloyd and Monty Don.[7] Postmodern aesthetics, which rely either on elite artistic knowledge of both modernism and postmodernism or a familiarity with the sanction given to aestheticized objects by commodity culture, strike a jibe at the patrician 'establishment' aesthetics promulgated by Don in his *Observer Life* column. After all, the makeover provides spectacular visual spaces which seem exciting, youthful and hedonistic in comparison with the rather pedestrian emphasis on the colour, texture and relationships of form provided by companion planting. Garden lifestyle texts not only showcase different kinds of (middle-)class aesthetics which demonstrate the internal divisions within class groups, but also testify to the contiguous friction between different fractions of a social class.

The Sunday lifestyle press: local garden aesthetics

The contemporary garden looks entirely different in local aspects of the media. For instance, Howard Drury offers weekly gardening advice in the 'preview' supplement in the *Sunday Mercury*, a Birmingham and West Midlands local Sunday newspaper. This example is typical of the kind of publication to be found across local, regional newsagents in the UK. *Howard Drury's Gardening Diary*, which is specific to the locale of Birmingham, is a cheaply-produced, largely black and white annual 'special publication'. It offers the reader a month-by-month breakdown of the gardening year, highlighting the seasonal requirements of the garden. Hard-sell advertising for products such as orthopaedic chairs, ceramic tiles, Capo Di Monte figurines and credit agencies reveal a working-class, white, 'grey' readership.

The pamphlet offers the reader ways of constructing a practical, sensible garden space; an aesthetic is provided, but it denies anything that might be regarded as ostentatious. In this way, the supplement alludes to the kinds of lower middle-class values that appealed to the British working class of the 1980s: economic thrift, hard work and an ascetic approach to leisure. These key components of the cultural aspect of Thatcher's brand of Conservatism inform the few photographs provided. The magazine promotes an aesthetic ethos of plain orderliness based on conserving the respectability of traditional garden elements. Elsewhere the magazine uses close-up photographs to illustrate the copy in a utilitarian way. Where images of a garden are provided, the colour scheme is traditionally wrought: outdoor landscaping materials, such as stone paving flags, creosoted wooden fences and trellises, gravel pathways, aluminium and glass greenhouses all utilize neutral, outdoor colours such as brown, beige, grey and green. The images draw upon conventional, stock garden elements such as the lawn, the flower bed containing common shrubs and space for annual bedding, trees, the shed, the greenhouse, the rockery, and pots and hanging baskets.

The only full colour photograph which focuses on a plant display shows a summer flower bed arranged in blocks of white and pink bedding plants consisting of begonias, pelargoniums (geraniums) and impatiens. There are no spectacular constructions, no novelty themes, no bright colours and no structural references to transnationality. Within the pages of this advice supplement, the reader is encouraged by the personal address of Howard Drury the author to focus down on the essential information: the plants themselves. Thus, the simply conceived advice sections – 'The Lawn' and 'The Vegetable Garden', for example – steer the reader away from what might be seen as the ostentatious excesses of consumption towards a moderate conception of how a garden should be practically constructed. In these ways, Drury's recommendations have nothing in common with the national 'art' codes of *Observer Life* or *Homefront in the Garden*. Based on plain orderliness, sincere tidiness and respectable traditional garden elements, Drury's garden is generated locally using local aesthetic visual codes.

These examples show that while 'ordinary' people are given an identification point by aspects of the media which use the private domestic garden as a setting for interpreting lifestyle ideas, the garden remains a classed space at the level of representation. Internal antagonisms within the middle-class are illustrated by the differences between the traditional, educated and somewhat staid middle-class aesthetics embodied by garden writers such as Monty Don, and the new middle-class who are receptive to the postmodern cultural goods and experiences offered by the makeover. The middle-class consists of dominant and subordinate fractions who 'are engaging in endless though reasonably genteel battles to assert their own identities, social positions and worth' (Savage et al. 1992: 100). Bourdieu (1986) reminds us that the upwardly aspirant 'new petite bourgeoisie' keeps discovering that the social field it wishes to have more purchase upon is already dominated by a more patrician, longstanding middle-class generation, and in a bid to mark new territory, 'previously well-established cultural traditions are thus increasingly treated in a "pastiche" way' (Savage et al. 1992: 128). Concomitantly, in counter-response, those higher in cultural capital struggle to ensure that 'culture' remains autonomously scarce and exclusive, and intellectuals attempt to find ways to maintain the value of their specialized knowledge. In this way, Bourdieu's work enables one to understand the specific class context from which different aesthetic modes of lifestyle emanate. It also shows the ongoing struggle between the culturally more outgoing and the more respectable and conformist fractions of the contemporary British middle-class.

Moreover, Bourdieu's (1984) economistic metaphors show that the national media deploy techniques as a means to institutionalize particular forms of capital. As the examples from *Observer Life*, *Gardening Neighbours* and *Homefront in the Garden* show, it is middle-class gardening tastes, competencies and aesthetics which are ordained as legitimate by the national media. Not everyone has the resources to enable them to access the display of middle-class taste in the media, yet the garden lifestyle media sanctions the symbolic power of the middle-class as the primary arbiter of symbolic capital. Monty Don, for example, constructs a resoundingly middle-class presence in his *Observer Life* column; his reference to literary allusions and antiquated knowledge offers a means to display a high volume of capital. Moreover, through the use of middle-class tastes, as the example of the imposition of a postmodern design remit on working-class couple Terry and Joan in *Gardening Neighbours* illustrates, the media enacts symbolic violence (Bourdieu and Passeron 1990) against working-class viewers. Yet legitimate knowledges and aesthetic codes require recognition based on the 'transferable dispositions' of one's habitus and on access to forms of capital (Bourdieu 1984). In this way, Bourdieu's model enables an understanding of how class inequalities are perpetuated, since those with meagre capitals simply cannot exploit the pedagogic action of the garden lifestyle media, hence they experience problems in their attempt to accrue, exchange and capitalize on them. No wonder working-class audiences turn to aspects of the local press for affirmation of their own local garden aesthetics.

Indeed, some forms of cultural and symbolic capital, in a bid to retreat from legitimate taste, are generated locally. *Howard Drury's Garden Diary* uses different garden codes and conventions, which arguably function to contest legitimate capital. Yet these local conventions only hold value within local settings; at national level, media institutions have a vested interest in conferring the symbolic power of middle-class aesthetics. In these contexts, local aesthetic codes are devalued and their tradeability is therefore limited: they simply lack the institutional channels through which to disburse their calls for legitimacy. In these ways, the 'ordinary garden' of the lifestyle media is shot through with classed aesthetics.

Evocation of history and the contemporary garden

Identified as a more culturally extrovert fraction of the middle-class, the new middle-class are argued to have emerged in Britain in the early 1980s (Savage et al. 1992). Critics have argued that this group is marked by its receptivity to postmodern cultural goods (Featherstone 1991a). Indeed Savage et al. identify a 'postmodern' fraction of the British middle-class, which they argue is characterized by its indulgence in a 'wide range of disparate consumption practices' (1992: 130). Even more pertinently, Savage et al. argue that this group is also marked by its tendency to treat previously 'auratic' forms of culture in non-auratic ways. Hence, they give weight to the argument I mounted in the previous section: postmodern lifestyle garden aesthetics offer this new class fraction a means to challenge auratic or at least highly legitimate middle-class garden aesthetics, while allowing them to indulge in the depthless, self-parodying commercialized art found in lifestyle compartments of consumer culture. In this section, I argue that the lifestyle media is sentient of the new middle-class and its needs and, acting as guides for living, lifestyle texts promulgate the idea that the aestheticiza-tion of components of everyday life – such as the garden – will lead to a more gratifying lifestyle.

Bourdieu (1984) identifies a whole swathe of cultural workers devoted to the production and dissemination of symbolic goods for the expanding new middle-class. Obsessed with the promotion of appearance, identity and presentation techniques in occupations such as the media, advertising and public relations, these workers act as 'new cultural intermediaries', ferreting out new artistic and intellectual trends, producing and crystallizing particular symbolic ideas, in a bid to educate publics. A key part of their project has been to break down previous barriers to elite forms of knowledge. As cultural interfaces, the new intellectuals have striven to formulate 'an art of living which provides them with the gratifications and prestige of the intellectual at the least cost ... they adopt the most external and most easily borrowed aspects of the intellectual lifestyle ... and apply it to not-yet-legitimate culture' (Bourdieu 1984: 370). As Bourdieu argues, the new good which ciphers aspects of the intellectual lifestyle 'is still able to fulfil functions of distinction by making available to *almost* everyone the distinctive poses, the distinctive games and other external signs of inner riches previously reserved for intellectuals' (Bourdieu 1984: 371).

Mindful of the new middle-class who Bauman (1987: 135) describes as 'neither coarse nor fully refined, neither ignorant nor educated to the standards boasted by the elite', the new cultural intermediaries are concerned with the project of tutoring the new petite bourgeoisie in how to make discriminatory judgements about the positional value of symbolic goods. Taste configurations and lifestyle preferences are associated with social class and occupational status, making it possible to plot out the world of taste and its minutely graded distinctions. Within late capitalism, however, where the ever-increasing proliferation of symbolic goods can shift the value of 'marker goods', there is a potentially endless supply of work for new intellectuals (Featherstone 1991a). In a context where the positional value of symbolic goods is relative, the anxiety of members of the new petite bourgeoisie to consume legitimate aspects of culture is potentially assuaged by the work of the new cultural intermediaries. Their task is to supply the self-conscious consumer with the knowledge required to both judge the cultural value of the latest goods and be attuned to the culturally befitting ways of how they should be consumed. I argue that the role of the personality-interpreter is to display and proffer the social and cultural value of postmodern modes of history to the self-conscious middle-class consumer so that they might be consumed judiciously and in the 'right' ways.

For postmodern writers, the experience of the present no longer entails the possession of a coherent sense of the linear progression of history. 'Eschewing the idea of progress', asserts Harvey, 'postmodernism abandons all sense of historical continuity and memory, while simultaneously developing an incredible ability to plunder history and absorb whatever it finds there as some aspect of the present' (1989: 54). Similarly, for Jameson, postmodern culture is characterized by a 'weakening of historicity' (1991: 6). As a result, the past becomes a series of malleable signs without any concrete sense of the forces or narrative trajectory of material history. Other writers have identified a crisis in the representation of history. Taylor, for example, argues that the television viewer's experience of history is presented as 'an endless reserve of equal events' (Taylor 1987: 104). Television is, he argues, 'the first medium in the whole of history to present the artistic achievements of the past as a stitched together collage of equi-important and simultaneously existing phenomena largely divorced from geography and material history'. This kind of approach produces what has been called a 'flattening out of history' (McGuigan 1999: 72). In this way, the relative importance of certain events is lost, since history becomes merely a surface area without volume. Instead, intertextuality dominates postmodernism to produce an endless free play of signs detached from their referents. The result is a 'new depthlessness' since the logic of intertextuality is that everything, including history, is reduced to textuality. Past historical moments are deliberately raided, using allusion, imitation and pastiche, to produce a simulacrum of historical reality. 'The history of aesthetic styles', Jameson argues, 'displaces "real" history' (1991: 20).

Indeed, a consideration of the way in which the garden makeover provides reference to the historical antecedents of gardening reveals a will to ransack the surface image of historical styles in a manner which floats free of the depth of their historical significance. For example, in *Homefront in the Garden*, Matthew Vincent explains Anne McKevitt's intention to put a 'contemporary spin on a very old idea' – they decide to construct a perspex ha-ha. The ha-ha was essentially a large ditch placed at the end of a garden boundary. When the eighteenth-century landowner looked to the garden edge, the ha-ha generated a visual illusion: the garden merged with the landscape beyond to create a vista, while simultaneously deterring both animal and human 'undesirables' in surrounding fields from entering the garden. 'Capability Brown copied it from the French', remarks Vincent, as he proceeds to illustrate their intention to produce a similar visual effect using perspex as opposed to a cordon sanitaire. Yet while Vincent's explanation provides a sense of spurious historicity to the makeover programme, an actual encounter with this ha-ha would almost certainly amount to a profoundly ahistorical experience. For these makeover experts the ha-ha is useful as a design concept, interesting because of its surface appearance. The wider context of its meaning as a signifier of the great age of gardening is neutralized. In the context of this garden it is no more than an allusion or an empty textual signifier, as Jameson argues, 'a "connotator" of the past' (1991: 20). Yet while what lies beyond the historical allusion is of little consequence, the ability to be able to offer a cursory nod at historical knowledge is: the ability to drop a flattened historical vignette into the commentary on the design remit is an important signifier of cultural capital. Historical allusion is used as a means of conferring legitimation and power on those who can couch their choices in a trajectory of garden history. It is these distinctive poses that the lifestyle media are concerned to transmit to the new self-conscious middle-class consumer.

Yet as the camera moves away from Matthew Vincent's commentary on the ha-ha, Tessa Shaw's voice-over introduces the viewer to another refashioned signifier of the past. We are told that 'Anne had created her version of another classical design – the walled garden'. Anne's version, however, has very little in common with the walled kitchen garden William Cobbett described in *The English Gardener* (1996) in 1829. The ideal design he recommends is for a south facing, brick walled, rectangular enclosure which is divided within and provides space for fruit and vegetable plots, a hotbed and a toolhouse. The walled garden that Cobbett advocates is a working garden, often owned by country families, which had been tended in the English countryside for 500 years. McKevitt's version is more akin to an outdoor living room: its walls are angular, textured and painted in a variety of fashionable colours, and it provides seating and a coffee table as opposed to offering a space to grow food. The experience of history in these gardens is based on the juxtaposition of different ephemeral, fleeting moments: from the ha-ha to the modern patio to the walled garden. Historical chronology or development is a moribund concept in the typical garden makeover: in these postmodern spaces designers feel free to quote images of history in any order they choose. Yet the ability to choose from a body of historical knowledge, no matter how superficially it is retrieved, confers power on the beholder. Such references may lack depth, but they stamp the authority of history onto the garden. As such these programmes work to show the potential consumer how to use a sense of history as a means to legitimate taste.

One can see the same kind of strategy in the glossy monthly magazine *Gardens Illustrated*.[8] Here a sense of garden history is pivotal to the entire magazine, from the features about historic gardens to the commodities that imitate objects from the past. A feature entitled 'Playing Tag', for example, offers the reader a series of photographs of potted bulbs and herbs in order to showcase a variety of plant labels currently on the market. These labels are evocative of various moments in garden history: Victorian hanging alitag, antique small and large glass and aluminium alitags, steel 'tournefort' label. Most of them, as in the case of a verdigris copper tag which can be purchased from the Conran Shop, offer a pre-designed patina. They offer the consumer the opportunity to venerate the garden with a sense of antiquity. Such features tutor the reader about the newest symbolic goods and offer interpretations of how history can generate cultural capital in the garden.

In these ways, one can see that the lifestyle media acts as a commercial site where personality-interpreters use the garden as a space for interpreting new, yet classed, symbolic lifestyle ideas. For the new middle-class, however, 'cultural assets need not depend on the legitimacy offered by the state. Cultural assets can be deployed and valorised in the market' (Savage et al. 1992: 129–30). In this way, the media act as a commercial guarantor for the value of new positional goods. Lash (1990) argues that the middle-class use symbols as a substitute for things, enabling them to 'produce symbols which help realise the value of other symbols' (Lash 1990: 251). In this way, the lifestyle media show consumers how to use distinctive historical symbols as forms of power and as a means to make the garden a legitimate middle-class space.

Conclusion

While the 'ordinari-ization' of garden lifestyle television can be read as part of the wider cultural move to help people to make the social and cultural transition from ways of life to consumer lifestyles (Chaney 2001), this chapter argues that the 'ordinary' lifestyled garden is a middle-class space. Despite the egalitarian embrace of more 'ordinary' people and the concomitant strategy of staging lifestyle ideas in the private domestic garden, lifestyle garden projects are comprised of middle-class aesthetic codes. It is the gardening tastes of those who are – or who aim to become – culturally enriched that are lauded and consecrated. Indeed, the garden lifestyle media acts as a forum for the competing interpretative ideas that emanate from different, and at times contiguous, fractions of the contemporary British middle-class. Working-class garden aesthetics have no positive location, except perhaps as a negative foil for the 'desirable' visual aesthetics of the national lifestyle media. It should come as no surprise, therefore, that working-class audiences turn to the local press for endorsement of their own locally created garden aesthetics in a bid to preserve gardening – not as lifestyle – but as a 'way of life'.

Notes

1. *Ground Force* was the BBC's flagship garden makeover programme. A family member secretly colludes with the makeover team, comprising celebrities Alan Titchmarsh and Charlie Dimmock, to produce a surprise gift of a transformed garden for a nearest and dearest.
2. For a discussion on the relationship between ordinariness, everyday life and issues of class and gender, see Felski (2000).
3. As the main presenter of Britain's most long-standing popular gardening programme *Gardener's World* (BBC, 1956–), Monty Don is marked as the most prominent British media garden expert. In this way, he comes closest to a public service gardener. He has worked as gardening correspondent for the weekend *Life* supplement of the middle-class Sunday broadsheet *The Observer* since 1994.
4. Presented by lesser known experts Ali Ward and Andy Sturgeon, *Gardening Neighbours* was a community makeover programme. Typically, the makeover team would work to transform the gardens of a shared residential area.
5. *Homefront in the Garden* is a typical example of a popular, terrestrial British lifestyle makeover programme. Originally screened on BBC2, the series has since been repeated on prime time television.
6. Anne McKevitt is a Scottish celebrity interior designer. However, as lifestyle programmes often seek to emphasize, a lack of knowledge about gardening is often embraced within lifestyle programming. For a discussion of the role of the shift from authoritative to interpretative modes of address in garden lifestyle programming see Taylor (2002).
7. Christopher Lloyd has written a number of influential books about how to select tasteful plants for the garden; see for example, *The Well Chosen Garden* (1984). He has a long-standing career as a gardening journalist in middle-class quarters of the British press such as *The Guardian.*
8. *Gardens Illustrated* is a BBC publication. It is aimed at a firmly middle-class readership.

9 Playing the tourist
Ideology and aspiration in British television holiday programmes

David Dunn

> Television is an invention that permits you to be entertained in your living room by people you wouldn't have in your home.
>
> (Sir David Frost)

This chapter is about British television holiday programmes, a genre which pre-dates and in some ways stands at a slight angle to more recent developments in lifestyle. Holiday programmes are as much about the getting of taste as are other lifestyle strands; but whereas programmes about home improvement, gardens, fashion and the like have favoured the makeover of ordinary people with the climactic moment of revelation at the heart of a linear narrative structure, programmes such as BBC1's *Holiday* and ITV's *Wish You Were Here?* have conventionally offered surrogate sightseeing and advice through the mediation of presenters. These presenters have stood for the ordinary viewer-as-holidaymaker without necessarily engaging with the diversity of popular democratized tourism. There are logistical reasons for this. Holidays do not necessarily occupy the conveniently compact unities of place and time which are afforded by the televisual makeover. They involve often unfamiliar space, not the ordinary of home and garden. Their narrative is not a linear one with the resolution of transformation, but is cyclical, offering fragmented experiences which are given order in the memory and in the retelling back home. However transforming holidays are, beyond a few photographs, a few displayed souvenirs, they do not leave much mark as physical signifiers of taste and achievement in ordinary people's homes.

In other words, holidays have to be interpreted. Elsewhere in this volume, Frances Bonner draws attention to the centrality of the presenter in lifestyle subgenres which do not feature linear narratives of personal transformation; and much the same has applied in holiday programmes, where the need to condense holiday experiences into five minutes has privileged the professional presenter. Palmer (2004: 178) suggests that at the heart of lifestyle is the acquisition of 'good taste' and consequent class status, and that viewers 'who lack self-assurance may put themselves in the hands of lifestyle experts (whose success is measured and reaffirmed daily) and the old established bourgeois middle-class'.

Although they have the ex officio authority of celebrity with its connotations of high socio-economic status and lifestyle, holiday programme presenters are not necessarily experts in travel. To that extent they differ from Bonner's celebrity chefs. The kitchen demands practical skills; the tourist destination suggests the need for cultural and material capital. Conventionally, holiday reports have been informed by the scopic; a discursively limiting discourse which has paralleled the influential critical thinking within the academy of MacCannell (1976) on the sacralization of the tourist sight, and of Urry (1990) on the institutionalizing of the tourist gaze. The privileging of the scopic suits the television camera's gaze, even if it does not replicate the practice of many holidaymakers whose photographs construct memories of family or friends in which sights are relegated to soft-focus backgrounds (Haldrup and Larsen 2003). This regular televisual recycling of the familiar has led to stagnation, yet for three decades the format of holiday programme reports has remained clearly defined: presenters mediate destinations and facilities by performing the role both of tourist guide and tourist, buttressing the essential round of sightseeing with consumer-oriented shots of accommodation, poolside and shopping. Underpinning this has been an ideological ambivalence towards demotic holidaymaking. The stuff of tourism, the sun and the sand, it is implied, is remission or reward for previous good conduct as a dutiful sightseer.

In the 1980s and early 1990s, BBC1's *Holiday* and ITV's *Wish You Were Here?* had UK audiences of over ten million, while BBC2's *The Holiday Show's* alternative destinations and C4's *Travelog's* televisual equivalent of the travel essay were strong players in networks which positioned themselves as being, albeit marginally, more aspirational. By 2004, however, *Holiday* had dropped to an average of 6.5 million while *Wish You Were Here?* no longer featured in the top one hundred television shows. *The Holiday Show* and *Travelog* had disappeared from screens before the millennium, the latter, in 1997, a victim of increasing budget cuts.[1] Now mainstream terrestrial television holiday programmes are having to diversify to maintain an audience. BBC1's *Holiday* has spawned a 'brand' which includes *Holiday Memories, Holiday Celebrity Memories, Holiday Swaps* and *Holiday – You Call The Shots*, while *Wish You Were Here?* has experimented with consumer-led strands and constructed glimpses of the exclusivity of celebrity holidays.

This chapter begins with how holiday programmes have represented popular touristic practice in the main through the mediation of presenters, with how their presence on screen has privileged a discourse of mild enlightenment and improvement over consumption and pleasure seeking, desire and transgression. After a brief account of the genre's growth and the constraints of its public service ideologies vis-à-vis popular culture, it will consider the impact of increasing media personalization of lifestyle (Dovey 2000; Macdonald 2003) on its representations and on the roles which its presenters are required to perform. It will address the ways in which holiday programmes have reflected the increasing nexus between consumption and celebrity in constructions of lifestyle, making particular reference to a *Wish You Were Here?* report from Turin by former *Big Brother* contestant Alex Sibley. Finally, it will discuss how the genre has responded to the makeovers of lifestyle and the confessionals of daytime and 'trauma' television, using BBC1's *Perfect Holiday*, and will suggest that for ordinary holidaymakers to appear on screen they must in some way be extraordinary.

Conventions and constraints of UK holiday programmes

British television's first holiday series, *Passport*, appeared on the BBC in the late 1950s. Presented by the patrician Richard Dimbleby, it was informed by a Reithian ideology which privileged information and education over entertainment. Clips from the series have subsequently been transmitted on BBC2 in the first of a historical survey of the genre, *The Way We Travelled* (17.7.03), where they were amplified by comments from Dimbleby's son Jonathan. According to the latter, Dimbleby had been the first person to spot the need for a holiday series, and had made it with his own production company (the first independent commission for BBC television). A decade after *Passport*, the production of *Holiday* was, according to travel journalist John Carter, delayed for two years before its first transmission in 1969 because of concerns expressed by the BBC governors about its need to feature products and prices.[2] It is fair, therefore, to assume that it was Dimbleby's gravitas, achieved by his years of war reporting as 'the voice' of the BBC, as much as his programming acumen and his consumer interest in foreign holidays, which got *Passport* on air.

The first programme opened with Dimbleby père and his wife Dilys being handed down from a railway carriage at an unnamed station. She is in fur coat, he in tweed jacket, waistcoat and tie, coat over arm. She, speaking impeccable received pronunciation, says, 'Look, the cabs are on skis. Let's take one of these'. He, with an approving 'Fine', and a boomed 'Taxi', raises an imperious hand to summon a horse-drawn carriage. Settled in it he addresses the camera directly, 'Well this is *one* way of starting *one* sort of holiday in *one* part of Switzerland, the Jungfrau region of the Bernese Oberland. Now my wife and I chose this area because in many ways ... oh!' The horse whinnies and the carriage is jolted out of shot before he has finished. Dimbleby the informing and educating presenter, carefully contextualizing and clarifying his choice, is in that dangerous abroad where for two centuries or more an English milord has been subject to the whims of the *vetturino* and his horse.[3]

The series was claimed to choose locations that were within the reach of most viewers. This may say more about the BBC's construction of television viewers as members of an exclusive club whose ideology differed little from that of its pre-war radio audience (Frith 1983) than it does about the popular practices of holidaymaking of the time. The series also chose locations for their visual potential, yet after two shots of skiers it is Dimbleby and his wife who feature, framed in a shop window. With a firm, 'Now darling, you're the expert on all forms of shopping so will you go in and find out what the prices are and we'll meet later', he departs. The camera pans into what is revealed as a ski hire shop and into a wifely, and stilted, conversation about costs conducted in English. What will be the enduring importance of consumer information to the genre is thus established, and a caption shows minimum and maximum prices. Transmitted at a time when package tours were in their infancy, Dimbleby's series suggests an ideology both of middle-class aspiration matched by fiscal caution, and of holidaymaking as an activity for the normative family. Indeed a subsequent programme about Brittany featured the whole family, filmed in wide shot sitting formally at a restaurant table. Dimbleby the paterfamilias is at the centre, and on the periphery waiters in long aprons bear salvers. A platter of shellfish is brought to the table and son Jonathan, 14 and clad in sports jacket and tie, is shown in close up smiling approvingly and appreciatively, and then, in a two shot, shares that gastronomic moment with his blazer-clad father. Such sequences support Hall's (1986) claim that, historically at least, the BBC as the embodiment of public service broadcasting may have reflected popular culture but made no commitment to it. Indeed what *Passport* had in common with BBC1's subsequent long-running and more relaxed but similarly purposeful *Holiday* was an anti-touristic discourse manifested more in concerns about avoiding the vulgarity of the tourist than about travelling 'off the beaten track'.[4]

Holiday began in 1969 as a studio-based consumer programme, but with the advent of colour in the following year it moved to the format of three or four location reports fronted by a loose team of reporters and linked by a regular presenter, a format on which it has relied ever since. *Holiday*'s first presenter was Cliff Michelmore, previously the anchorman of BBC's flagship early evening news and current affairs programme *Tonight* – as authoritative, if less patrician, a broadcaster as Dimbleby.

Holiday established itself in what was a televisual era of scarcity, marked by limited choice, clearly defined public service values and a concomitant singleness of ideology rather than a celebration of difference, an era which Ellis[5] suggests left its mark on the subsequent decade:

> Public service broadcasters throughout the 1980s were dominated by their inheritance from the era of scarcity. The provision of definitive programmes went hand in hand with a notion of providing a service that lived up to the ideals of a social improver's agenda rather than those of a simple servant of market forces.
>
> (Ellis 2000b: 86)

The evidence of *Holiday* and other mainstream programmes indicates that the failure of their reports to reflect an increasingly democratized tourism created narrative and ideological tensions. These were often reflected in sequences where presenters sat beside swimming pools determinedly doing nothing while postponing the hard work of sightseeing: former model Linda Lusardi in bathing costume reclined on a sun lounger in Rhodes while contemplating the sights which the island would offer some other day (*Wish You Were Here?*, 6.2.95). Eamonn Holmes lay in a hammock slung between palm trees with a Barbadian sea in the background saying, 'And here there's the freedom to laze the days away doing absolutely nothing at all', before setting off on the obligatory round of sightseeing (*Holiday*, 17.3.92). John Carter, also in a hammock, but this time in the Florida Keys, apologized for his laziness, blaming it on the long journey and saying that it would be wrong to have travelled so great a distance just to lie around doing nothing (*Wish You Were Here?*, 16.3.92). Such images offer a very controlled version of the carnivalesque in which the priorities of work and leisure are not completely inverted. The foregrounding of tourist guilt at doing nothing played its part in the discourse of holiday programmes.

Procrastinating by the pool was about as transgressive as the genre got. While docusoaps like ITV's *Ibiza Uncovered* and *Holiday Reps* represented the tourist destination as a place of licence and inversion, mainstream holiday programmes scarcely hinted at the liminal. Broadcasters, doubtless aware of a need for pre-watershed self-regulation, reflected Shields's (1991: 98) contention that even in marginal places social regulation 'tends to moderate the inversions and suspensions of the social order'. Yet the tourist destination has spaces which are free from the usual constraints of hotel or home, heterogeneous spaces 'with blurred boundaries' (Edensor 2001: 64) where tourists and locals mix but which seldom open themselves up to the paraphernalia of the television crew. Although sanitized disco sequences have featured in resort reports, such meeting places offer predictably limited opportunities for transgressive travel in the sense of a stepping across social and psychological borders (Porter 1991). In a rare dip into something more radical, Judith Chalmers (*Wish You Were Here?*, 6.2.95) was shown in a public square in St Lucia which acted as a night-time meeting place. A sequence of candid shots of groups of St Lucians gathered in the darkness in knots, drinking and chatting as well as dancing with white-skinned visitors while a local band played in the background, showed an event apparently unstaged for the camera, and the intensity of the experience suggested little external control. Judith Chalmers observed that it was far too tiring for her and that she was about to return to her hotel for a good night's sleep. A potentially subversive event – subversive because of its anomalousness – was thus brought prematurely to an end, at least for the viewers.

By the mid-1980s women had replaced men as series presenters. Figures like *Wish You Were Here?*'s Judith Chalmers and *Holiday*'s Anne Gregg were established broadcasters whose authority sprang from their association with other factual genres, albeit in the 'softer' reaches of public service broadcasting, women's or regional programmes. There were, however, new tensions. There are parallels between holiday programmes and advertising features (Morgan and Pritchard 1998), and while the former draw also on traditions of reportage and of documentary 'objectivity' they are, at the same time, dependent on good relations with the travel industry. The destination products featured are those offered by specific tour operators, and the practice is for each report to finish with a caption which names the operator and indicates the cost. It is fair to assume that such operators are likely to facilitate travel and offer other help to the production team, and that there is at least some sharing of interests. While the perceived integrity of the presenters, coupled with a gender-associated consumer knowledge, lent credence to the holiday products on show, it was not necessarily balanced by any critical comment in their reports. In addition, the new emphasis on women presenters made assumptions about the masculine gaze of the audience and about production values which increasingly placed entertainment, exemplified by the gratification of that gaze, over authoritative comment about the destinations featured.

In the absence of more conventionally academic comment, it is perhaps apposite to quote from the television page of the satirical magazine *Private Eye* (1997), which highlighted that double tension of commercialism and sexism, suggesting that the camera's leering at scantily clad suntanned women had been sublimated by focusing on an attractive, and increasingly revealingly dressed, female presenter:

Hypocritical on the female flesh issue, *Holiday* remains vulnerable on the charge of free advertising. Apart from a small murmur about the price of one of the packages, every package on offer in the first show of the new series was paradise, the directors of the little illustrative filmlets obligingly providing stunning sunsets wherever possible to close out the reports. To be true to its subject, the appeal of its presenter to male viewers and the journalistic approach of its reporters, the series really ought to be renamed *Getting Off*.

(p. 10)

This is a perceptive analysis, touching on the broadcasters' ambiguous role vis-à-vis popular culture and the bodily excesses of carnival, on the masculine nature of the television camera's gaze and on the complicity between camera and viewer, and raising questions about television's claim to objective representation, not least in the light of its increasing espousal of celebrities as the presenters who mediate tourist destinations. The invoking of journalistic authority, regard for the obligations of sightseeing, very limited collusion with transgression and rather more with the holiday industry: such are the ways in which the relationship between ideological and mercantile establishments and audience existed in an uneasy balance over three decades.

Reflecting diversity: public and private performance

If broadcasters have been constrained by their conventional role as providers of purposeful (if surrogate) sightseeing, they cannot perhaps match the shift which the academy, recognizing the limitations of a scopic reading of tourist behaviour, has made towards consideration of other senses. Television's limited 'sense-scapes' cope more readily with *plaisir* than with *jouissance*, even when Crouch (2002: 217), positing tourism as an encounter with space, offers a reminder that 'the world is grasped through the body and the world is mediated through the body'.[6] Yet a concurrent critical shift towards considerations of performance, not only in the sense that the tourist destination is staged by those who service it but also in that it allows tourists to take on new roles (Edensor 2001), has inevitably found greater resonances in a medium where the destination has always been staged for the camera, and in which presenters have assumed touristic roles which inform their reports and their performances.[7]

Berghoff (2002) argues that tourism is not rooted in basic needs, since it requires an excess of purchasing power. Material consumption is more than matched by dreams and desires and it is, he argues, 'the ultimate consumer commodity because it is almost infinitely expandable as a product' (p. 169). Nor does it offer one mass experience, since different tourists consume different products in an era of market segmentation 'defined by lifestyles as well as by demographic and social factors' (p. 175). Holiday programmes, in common with other leisure and lifestyle strands, are about the tensions identified by Bourdieu (1984) between possession of material and cultural goods. Ellis (2000b) contends:

> The market-place accentuates social differences with the in-evitable consequence of the intensification of social antagon-isms. The role of a public service broadcaster in this new environment is to provide the space in which these antagonisms can be explored, but without appearing to explore them in any explicit way.
>
> (Ellis 2000b: 86–7)

This has, in part, found its expression in television's era of availability, which no longer offers a single authoritative voice but allows viewers to work through a variety of more casual and varied messages. Ellis's 'social differences' are in fact worked through with varying degrees of antagonism, from the class and taste tensions of BBC1 *Holiday Swaps* in which ordinary families are required to exchange holidays, to the increasing foregrounding of celebrities.[8] Television celebrity is grounded in familiarity and the ordinary (Langer 1981), yet at the same time a celebrity lifestyle signifies distinction, public status and wealth, offering viewers an encounter, as Rojek (2001: 18) suggests, with desire and with consumption: 'Celebrity culture is therefore partly the expression of a cultural axis organised around abstract desire. It is an essential tool of commodification since it embodies desire. In particular, it provides consumers with compelling standards of emulation'. It is, of course, also an encounter with performance.

Given the solipsism of television celebrity it is not surprising that *Holiday*'s guest presenters are performers identified with the BBC, most notably stars of *EastEnders*, while ITV's *Wish You Were Here?* has its own loyalty to those who appear on ITV, C4 and C5. A report from Turin by former *Big Brother* competitor Alex Sibley for *Wish You Were Here?* (4.5.03) offers evidence of how the self-referential celebrity of television, performance and conspicuous consumption are increasingly blurring the distinctions between fact and fiction, public and private, in constructing aspirational discourses of holidaymaking.[9] Series presenter

Ruth England's introduction constructed Sibley's credentials as a reporter: 'But first a Mini, a man and a plan. With the *Big Brother* house just a distant memory, Alex Sibley has been making the most of his freedom. He's a big fan of *The Italian Job*, so when he heard they were doing a remake of the classic film he had to find out more. We join him on location in Turin'. There is a cut to Sibley in close profile, impersonating Michael Caine in a scene from the original film, '5, 4, 3, 2, 1 ... you're only supposed to blow the [expletive muted] doors off'. From a wide shot of the city the camera tracks in for his piece to camera: 'This is the city of Turin, the industrial capital of Italy, the most modern in Europe, famed for its architecture, the Holy Shroud, and of course the greatest robbery in the twentieth century, *The Italian Job*'. In the celebrity destination, equal billing is given to unnamed buildings, shroud and movie – a movie whose own star line-up included the Mini cars involved in the bank robbery. Over a sequence of the recently relaunched Mini being driven through arcaded streets Sibley asks, 'So what else would I be driving on my mini-break? You've got it; a new version of an old big screen favourite, and believe me this car was great fun to drive. There are echoes of the film all over the place, so if you're a movie buff you'll feel right at home'.

Intertextuality combined with product placement is underpinned by close-ups of the Mini logo and steering wheel, and product placement continues with Sibley outside a café, holding up a packet of coffee. 'Michael Caine's line is the most quoted line of all time, but it's not the only thing to come out of Turin. There's this. Yea, Lavazza coffee is made in Turin'. There is a cut to a close-up of the pack then to a close-up of a Martini logo as he continues, 'Martini was invented here'. In an ornately decorated bar he downs in one the special Martini cocktail which he confides to camera with a swagger 'was very strong'. He immediately orders another to the feigned surprise, shot in close-up, of the barman, and then 'falls' off his stool. There is another cut to the barman, who, half to camera, smiles on cue. Sibley's laddish performance plays to audience expectations of a *Big Brother* contestant, and his subsequent advice, with its connotations of the licence of all-male weekends abroad, about how to cruise the bars in search of free food during the *aperitivo* hour, is a long way from Judith Chalmers' discreet departure from a St Lucian square as the drink began to flow. Dovey (2000: 7) argues that television is increasingly about pleasure and desire rather than a 'regime of truth', and that illusion and entertainment have flooded 'discursive zones previously reserved for education, information and enlighten-ment'. Sibley's report is, indeed, a performance staged for a series of camera angles, as evidenced by the number of cuts. Like other celebrity reports it is one in which the destination – its ostensible subject – becomes a background for the celebration of celebrity.

Television has to reconcile the individuality required by a personalized story with the generality of consumerism. As Bonner (2003: 106) suggests, 'actual audience members are addressed only in as much as they recognize themselves and their desires within what the programme is offering, but the fantasies on offer are structured to be inclusive wherever possible'. Holiday programmes have made little use of the personalizing makeover, not least because any holiday is in itself a makeover, taking the holidaymaker to a liminal and recreative state before the return to daily life.[10] Holidays also fail to provide the single moment of revelation which Moseley (2000) identifies as the genre's televisual climax, when what has been changed is suddenly revealed to the participant and the camera moves in on the response. Holidays are temporary possessions which rely for their meaning and social value on recorded evidence, often photographs or videos, which however artfully edited and displayed lack the constant impact of, say, new wall coverings or a redesigned garden (Crang 1999). BBC1's most recent spin-off of the *Holiday* 'brand', *Perfect Holiday* (2004), however, is an attempt to combine elements of personalization and makeover with destination reporting.

Perfect Holiday is constructed as a fairy godmother, bestowing on a select few the holiday of a lifetime and displaying what Bonner (2003: 127) defines as television's power 'to dispel dragons and grant wishes' in return for grateful and willing participation in the production processes. *Perfect Holiday*'s beneficiaries are nominated by friends or relatives because of the inspirational way in which they have faced personal tragedy. They are ordinary people chosen precisely because their stories are extraordinary, and in return for their holiday they are required to revisit and make public those stories: the loss of a teenage daughter, lengthy treatment for a life-threatening illness. This element of confessional or 'trauma' television (Dovey 2000: 21), using interviews and personal mementos such as videos and photographs as illustration, is woven into the narrative, first to establish the subject's claim to a perfect holiday and then as counterpoint to the happy experiences of that holiday. There is further intrusion. The first third of each programme is given over to clandestine filming of its subject's house, where three 'experts' construct a profile by examining his or her possessions in order to decide on an appropriate destination. All this is staged as a race against time before the subject is 'surprised' in a public space amidst friends and relatives. Such secret filming is a feature of makeovers, and its claims to profiling disguise an appeal to voyeurism. Given the arbitrariness of the destination suggestions by the 'experts' and the speed with which their decision is turned into a detailed itinerary complete with a caption crediting the tour operator, it would not be difficult to argue both that the 'expert' decision is a fait accompli and that there has been considerable manipulation of the timescale of filming and edited narrative.

For reasons of space, one programme must stand here for the series. *Perfect Holiday* (28.1.04) featured Vicky Doyle, who had been nominated by her partner Craig Catlow. Commentary explained that series presenter Russell Amerasekera and his team had been 'called in' while Vicky was at Guy's Hospital for a regular check-up. Although now clear, she had been diagnosed two years previously with leukaemia, and had needed a stem cell transplant, isolation for six weeks and chemotherapy. Her consequent hair loss is illustrated with photographs. As the team go through her belongings they linger on her collection of stockings, with a comment from Jamie Bowden that 'she's doing her best to keep this company afloat', before Jennifer Cox holds up a showerhead suggestively to camera while speculating on whether it might contain a battery. Cox then rifles through Vicky's bedside cabinet, and while the contents are not shown in close-up she provides a running commentary, 'Something for colds, something for veruccas and', with an embarrassed laugh, 'something for ... later', before quickly shutting the drawer.

Despite the popular connotations of holidaymaking, early evening scheduling means that holiday programmes make little reference to sex. In the case of *Perfect Holiday* the focus is, however, on private individuals rather than on the mediation of a solitary public figure presenter. In this programme Vicky's partner has already confided to camera that after nine years of living together and all the sufferings of the last two years he intends to propose to her during their holiday. Thus an underpinning of prurience might be argued to contribute to this narrative. On the strength of what they have learnt, Amerasekera suggests a 'trophy destination', and they agree on a trip to Venice on the Orient Express to be rounded off with a few days in Florence, in order, as he says to Vicky during the obligatory 'surprising' on camera before running out of words, 'that you can look at the art ... and the food'. The caption which accompanies Amerasekera's description of the holiday lists a price of £2710 per person, which suggests that this holiday of a lifetime is likely to be beyond the reach of many viewers for whom the subsequent narrative will combine the fantasy of armchair travelling with the final resolution of a private story about a proposal of marriage.

Throughout the holiday Vicky and Craig are accompanied by Amerasekera who adopts the role, appropriately enough for the destinations chosen, of a latter day *vetturino*, part guide, part fixer, and even part matchmaker.[11] Such a role would be inappropriate in conventional reports, but here he is delivering a service both to a specific couple and to the generality of viewers. His presence both enables and mediates their holiday. Amerasekera, previously a travel expert on *Wish You Were Here?*, is a flamboyant character with a fondness for deep coloured ruffled shirts with frilled cuffs and long knotted silk scarves. His exaggerated and knowing performance and his ambivalent appearance dominate the screen and construct a presenter-guide whose otherness reflects the liminality of holidaymaking. He controls events, offering advice about the relative costs of a gondola and a water taxi and 'pulling strings' to arrange an upgrade to the Palladio suite at the Hotel Cipriani in Venice. After showing Vicky and Craig its luxuries, he points out the handmade Venetian writing paper unique to the suite saying, 'You'll be able to send notes to all your friends. That'll really cheese them off'. He then offers the coup de grâce, 'I'll leave you with a thought. To stay here for one night is £4300'. Craig responds with the televisually obligatory, 'This is out of this world ... I've never seen any thing like this in my life'. Amerasekera leaves them, the screen discreetly fading to black after a sequence shot in home video style (to connote a more intimate and more spontaneous relationship between subject and viewer) which shows Vicky dancing and flirting with the camera, stretching out in dressing gown seductively on the bed, then Vicky and Craig in the jacuzzi drinking champagne, and finally in dressing gowns jumping up and down on the bed. Even for ordinary people it is no longer enough to say that you are happy and in love; it is necessary to perform that happiness, to act the lover.

It will be clear that *Perfect Holiday* is about aspiration and material consumption, and about its transforming power. As they had cruised under the Rialto Bridge on their way to the hotel, Amerasekera offered, 'Yeah, that's the one you hear about; quite spectacular, isn't it?' before devoting more time to a *palazzo* reputedly recently bought by Woody Allen and to introducing their accommodation with the words, 'Across the lagoon and next to Elton John's *palazzo* is the hippest hotel in Venice'. The association with the lifestyles of the rich and famous, and the shot in which Amerasekera upstages his two charges in the stern of the water taxi, his silk scarf streaming in the evening breeze, the pink of the setting sun a colourful contrast with his blue ruffled shirt, both exist uneasily with the interview which preceded their grand arrival, when Craig was asked 'Do you think that she was scared that she wasn't going to make it?' and replied, 'It was the most scary thing that's ever happened in my life, and it was the most scary thing that's ever happened in Vicky's life as well'. The Reithian discourse of the BBC has not quite been abandoned. For ordinary people at least, such luxury has to be earned.

Craig and Vicky continue to earn their holiday by playing the roles demanded of the narrative. Florence is distilled into a visit to a sixteenth-century *farmacia* to buy perfume and a shot of the cathedral with Amerasekera's injunction to climb its campanile early to avoid both crowds and heat. They stay in the upmarket Villa San Michele overlooking the city where they have been upgraded, Amerasekera informs viewers, to 'the discreet Chapel Room, to help Craig get Vicky in a prenuptial mood', and where they are filmed kissing before closing the door on the camera. At a solitary table set for the camera in the hotel's garden, Craig dutifully proposes and is accepted. The scene is played out as spontaneously as such things can be, the number of angles suggesting something less than spontaneously filmed. The film ends with a balloon flight described as 'the ultimate way to see Tuscany', and while a few superlatives still remain at the programme's disposal Vicky sums up, 'We've had a racy, extravagant, decadent, opulent week together'. Craig adds, 'And lots more words ending with "ent"'. Television's power to change and enrich lives has been duly acknowledged.

Conclusion

Amongst its other credits *Perfect Holiday* includes a talent producer. Whether her care is the presenter or the recipients of the holiday is in a sense immaterial. Macdonald (2003) argues that broadcasters no longer have a choice between entertaining or informing viewers; they must simply interest them. What the existence of this credit signifies is a television discourse in which the rise of celebrity coupled with a need for human interest stories, personified by ordinary people and performed by them on screen, has indeed blurred that distinction between information and entertainment. Holiday programmes have of course in one sense always been about performance and role playing. The presenter, in standing for the ordinary tourist, has performed a public role informed by ideology and discourse as much as by the need to articulate with ordinary lifestyles, and the result on screen has been an increasing tension between the purpose of the anti-tourist and the consumption of the tourist. *Holiday* and *Wish You Were Here?* have thus displayed a shift in emphasis from the sights of the tourist destination to shopping opportunities and the facilities on offer in a chosen hotel or villa, a shift from the public of sightseeing to the private and self-defining of consumption and luxury.

Holiday programmes have always had a subject. Conventionally that was the destination itself. Increasingly they are also required to tell a story, in which the destination becomes the setting for the expression of a range of lifestyle choices, not least the aspirational of celebrity. The performance of Alex Sibley in Turin, while more blatantly commercial and more staged than some, is increasingly typical of holiday programmes' need for new and entertaining narratives and for new presenters who do not privilege purposeful sightseeing. *Perfect Holiday*'s mix of performance, travelogue, fantasy and voyeurism indicates that the monothematic is no longer sufficient to maintain the viewer's interest. The pursuit of art and architecture, the high culture of the traveller, is dismissed in favour of upmarket shopping and gazing on the houses of the rich and famous and emulating, however briefly, their lifestyle. Lifestyle's focus on personal improvement that is as much material as cultural suggests holiday programmes' need to reflect real experiences. Yet *Perfect Holiday*'s celebrity mediated narrative of transformation suggests an unequal balance between producers and participants. Those few ordinary people who are chosen to spend their holiday on camera have been chosen precisely because their stories are not ordinary.

Notes

1. Correspondence between the writer and *Travelog*'s editor Jenny Mallinson Duff in April 1992 indicates that even then the series' budget was being reduced by Channel 4.
2. Carter was featured later in the same *The Way We Travelled* programme.
3. Ever since the Grand Tour, the British abroad have been ambivalent towards the services of the *vetturini* or tour providers who could be 'perfect pests' or protectors from the annoyances and dangers of travel (Hibbert 1987: 108).
4. Buzard (1993) argues that in the discursive struggle between the tourist and the traveller it is the unknown 'off the beaten track' which is constructed as 'authentic'.
5. See also Crissell (2002) on the impact of the Annan Committee in the 1970s on dismantling the Reithian ideology of broadcasting as 'social cement'.
6. See also Franklin and Crang (2001) and Chaney (2002a).
7. See also Crang (1999), Rojek (2000) and Coleman and Crang (2002).
8. This format has been developed by ITV's more confrontational peak time *Holiday Showdown* (2003) which, while not a conventional lifestyle series, does place its emphasis on the material and (often more honoured in the breach than the observance) cultural consumption of the tourist product. This can produce pairings as ill-matched as that of the Littlechilds from Essex 'who like the odd cocktail or two' on their beach holiday in Cancun with the teetotal Curtis family who spend their holidays in Ghana doing missionary work (*Holiday Showdown*, 20.11.03).
9. Sibley came third in C4's *Big Brother* (2002). His celebrity rests on a far from successful modelling career and his conflicts with his fellow contestants on issues of personal hygiene.
10. Turner (1973) posits pilgrimage, sacred or secular, as a journey to 'the center

[sic] out there', a centre with its own rules, a centre of anomalous behaviour and social inversion where people separate themselves from the daily profane life and find themselves in a liminal state. See also Nash (1996) on tourism as personal transition.

11. Despite the credited tour operator, Amerasekera makes regular claims that he is fine tuning the experience for his charges.

10 Holidays of a lifestyle
Representations of pleasure in gay and lesbian holiday promotions

Gregory Woods

The mobile homosexual

In their gay and lesbian travel guide to Europe, Lindsy Van Gelder and Pamela Robin Brandt send their American readers forth into Europe under a proud banner of gay transcultural identification. Their introduction closes with a rhapsodic passage:

> Long before 1992 [the date of the British reissue of this guide], gay Europeans were sharing a culture, which is your culture, too. Walk into a gay bar or center in any country [in Europe], and you stand a good chance of walking out with new friends who've been moved by Walt Whitman, Natalie Barney, Harvey Fierstein, David Leavitt, Edmund White, Alison Bechdel, Armistead Maupin, Keith Haring, and Rita Mae Brown, as well as Cocteau, Gide, Wilde, Woolf, Isherwood, García Lorca, Sappho, Rosa Bonheur, Marguerite Yourcenar, Gerard Reve, Anna Blaman, Magnus Hirschfeld, Jimmie Sommerville, and Tom of Finland; who march in Gay Pride parades at the end of June (but who are inspired as well by Paris in the teens, Berlin in the twenties, and Greece in the fifth century).
>
> (Van Gelder and Brandt 1992: xv–xvi)

Notwithstanding the American predominance in this supposedly cosmopolitan list, it is hard to imagine a clearer statement of the myth of gay and lesbian *universalism*. The idea that not only do homosexually inclined people recognize each other wherever they go, but that they even, also, consume the same cultural products and adopt the same political strategies, may be preposterous, but it is a surprisingly widely and firmly held belief. It raises the possibility, or the dream, of international fellowship on common ground.

Not only that, but in recent years gayness itself has been mythologized – and not only by gays – as being intrinsically *cosmopolitan*.[1] As Dereka Rushbrook puts it, in a discussion of many western cities' use of their gay populations as a tool for urban regeneration: 'gays are more than merely one component of diversity and more than a commodity for direct consumption; they serve as markers of the cosmopolitan nature of the metropolis' (Rushbrook 2002: 190). Gay 'lifestyles' of a narrowly circumscribed type are welcomed because they can accelerate the gentrification of run-down areas of cities; and then they may also become tourist attractions in themselves.

The history of 'gay travel' – to use a contestable shorthand – is long and well documented. Wherever one lived in Europe, sodomy was always said to be spreading from elsewhere – and was therefore always to be sought there (Robb 2003). For those who could afford to do so, travel was one of the ways of finding it without risking one's reputation back home. Indeed, in the 'Terminal Essay' to the 1885 edition of his translation of the *Arabian Nights*, the great Victorian adventurer and scholar Richard Burton identified a 'Sotadic Zone' belting the Earth, in which pederasty was so widely practised and accepted as to have become, to a greater or lesser extent in various cultures, institutionalized (Burton 1970).[2] The zone included the north and south shores of the Mediterranean, Asia Minor, Mesopotamia and Chaldaea, Afghanistan, Sind, Punjab and Kashmir, Indochina, the South Seas and – at least until its conquest and colonization by Christian fanatics from Europe – the New World. Burton was widely travelled in the zone and, as well as having read an enormous amount of textual evidence of the Sotadic customs he wrote about, had gained copious first-hand experience of those same customs. Judging by promotions of gay holidays today, the Sotadic zone is still popular but somewhat shrunken, partly by increased hostility in the Islamic world, partly by new sensitivities to the iniquities of sex tourism. But northerners still travel south for sun, sea and sex, even if their sexual partners now tend to be fellow tourists. Northern European gay men have had an especially rich and complex cultural relationship with the Mediterranean rim and its inhabitants (Aldrich 1993).

One of the characteristics of gay 'lifestyles' that have developed in the West in the past two decades has been a willingness to travel for pleasure – 89 per cent of adult gay Americans hold a valid passport, as against a national average of 18 per cent (www.homearoundtheworld.-com/stats.htm) – and a growing, if smaller, willingness to do so with specifically gay companies.[3] In the present chapter I am interested in the evidence that the publicity materials for these companies offer for the distinctiveness of their product and what that tells us about their perception of the needs of their gay and lesbian customers.

Brochure representations

All package holiday brochures, whatever the target market, offer a promise of physical pleasures (sun, sea, food, wine, perhaps sex). Often, although with less emphasis, they offer a spiritual pleasure derived from stress relief. In the visual imagery of most such brochures these pleasures are on offer to heterosexual couples and nuclear families. If individual bodies are shown in mainstream brochures, as on television holiday programmes, they are likely to be those of the advertiser's familiar come-on, the young woman in a bikini (usually sporting herself in the shallows or tanning on the beach/poolside – a representation echoed on television; see Dunn, this volume). Only since the late 1990s, and only in brochures for young people's sun-and-sex holidays, have young men's bodies started to be used in this way, to attract the relatively new market of independent single women, or groups of such women. Likewise only recently, and in the same kind of brochure, have single-sex pairs or groups been shown with any significant degree of regularity. These pairs/groups of girls/boys are, presumably, meant to represent unattached heterosexuals, hunting in packs. They are *not* meant to be taken as the queers they sometimes appear to be.

Gay and lesbian brochures – and the majority of them are gay – imitate the visual and verbal conventions of the mainstream company brochures in order to lay claim to the professionalism of the mainstream, and in order not to put off those gay consumers (perhaps a majority) who believe that gayness is *the same as* straightness except insofar as it sometimes attracts homophobic responses. The fact is that most gay people buy their holidays from straight package companies. Gay companies have to offer a similar product which, even if it ends up being slightly more expensive, must provide something that is specifically gay without putting off customers who are, in their working lives, to a greater or lesser extent closeted. Although unusual in the amount of male flesh in their illustrations, very few of the gay brochures are what you might call 'flamboyant'. Virtually none are overtly 'political'. That is not their job. The men portrayed are uniformly young and masculine; almost invariably (tanned) white. The holidays on offer are in no respect extraordinary, once one has factored in that they are being sold to gay men.

What does it mean to have a gay or lesbian holiday? What is on offer when a company promises not the holiday of a lifetime but – in the words of a Man Around leaflet – the holiday of a lifestyle? One New Zealand company puts it as follows: 'Your holiday overseas does not have to be a gay holiday to a gay destination. We send gay people away to all corners of the globe. There are many holiday options that are not gay, but are very gay friendly' (www.gayholidays.co.nz). This raises a number of obvious questions: What is a 'gay holiday'? What is a 'gay destination'? What is a 'holiday option' that is 'not gay', and exactly what would distinguish as option that was 'very gay friendly' from another that was not? Regardless of the distinctions suggested by these remarks, the company in question is happy to be known by the apparently straightforward name Gay Holidays.

Many of the male gay brochures attempt a sex-positive informality that often produces embarrassingly poor puns and innuendos about the activities that the advertised holidays facilitate and provide. For instance, the website for Throb Holidays (www.throb.com) includes the following sentence: 'Our travel team have scoured the hotspots and examined many bottoms (oops! we mean underneath beds, of course!) to bring you the best in gay holidays to Spain'. The very name of the company eschews any claim to finesse, but raises the all-important possibility of sexual excitement.

Sex apart, the brochures offer two implicit promises, both of which relate to temporary deliverance from stress. First, like the mainstream companies, the gay ones promise relief from the everyday stresses of urban and suburban living, to be delivered by way of landscapes and seascapes which afford the prospect of relaxation, whether active or inert. Second, the gay companies specifically promise some kind of deliverance from homophobia, or at least from the need to hide one's homosexuality in order to avoid homophobic incident. Clearly, this latter promise can only be speculative and provisional, and on most holidays can only be delivered in part. (A few companies also consider people with HIV's vulnerability to both infection and prejudice.)

So if any holiday is conventionally represented as being a liberation from everyday life, a gay holiday must provide a utopian or pastoral foretaste of Gay Liberation as we do not yet know it. Many brochures address this issue, implicitly acknowledging the limited outness of their potential customers, by speaking of places in which it is possible – unlike 'at home', wherever that may be – for single-sex couples openly to hold hands. This appears to be the main measure of a gay friendly environment. Gayness must be ignored in the street or on the promenade. For the holidaymakers' extraordinary luxury of walking hand-in-hand without being mocked or otherwise attacked, the sight of a gay couple must be treated as ordinary rather than as a tourist spectacle in itself. The promotional website for gay visitors to Key West in Florida offers as its main claim to suitability the idea that 'For gay and lesbian visitors, Key West is a place to be open and relaxed' (www.gaykey-westfl.com). Another such location is Sitges, near Barcelona: Respect Holidays call Sitges 'a heaving hotbed of homosexuality' (www.respect-holidays.co.uk). According to the Sensations '97 brochure: 'Sitges is quite simply the most Gay-friendly place on this planet. A place where you can stroll hand-in-hand with your partner, embrace as the golden sun shimmers on the crystal blue Mediterranean and swear love everlasting as life goes on around you in its own cool, laid-back way' (p. 4). But we are not just talking about pre-existing couples, here, even if the restraint of the brochures often gives that impression. The freedom at issue is the visibility not just of love, but of open gay cruising. Occasionally, a note of warning raises the question of cultural difference in such matters. Speaking of resorts in Turkey, the In Touch brochure (1997) says: 'Turkish men show a great deal of affection for each other, are often to be seen walking hand in hand, and to greet your friend with a kiss on each cheek is a matter of course. These tactile customs should not be misinterpreted unless accompanied by other signals of which only you can be the judge' (p. 20). This latter point is a matter of common sense, in any case, to men who are used to cruising strangers in public spaces back home. The potential problem arises when such men assume that the precautions they take in their home country are no longer necessary in the holiday location.

To be truly gay friendly, a resort must provide not only the facilities of a good beach holiday, but also the gay 'scene' of a town of reasonable size: that is, gay bars and nightclubs. A recommendable scene makes all the difference to a company's ability to promote a resort as being gay. Of one such town, the Sensations '97 brochure states: 'Standing proud like a Gay oasis in the straight desert that is the Costa del Sol, you'll find the long established, popular scene of Torremolinos' (p. 18). In Touch Holidays (1997) claim: 'In Europe we are lucky that a number of the most prestigious resorts have become world famous as welcoming the gay visitor and catering for our lifestyle's every need. From non-stop nightlife to romantic piano bars, from poolside barbecues to just cruising around the beach; it's all here just a few hours flying time away [from Britain]' (p. 2). These requirements of 'our lifestyle' are noticeably identical to the requirements of generic young people's package holidays. If different at all, they will be different in the detail.

A Man Around brochure (1992–3) says of one popular destination: 'Ibiza is an island where the sun always seems to shine, where the air seems electric with the tantalizing combination of raunch and romance, whatever the time of day or night. Ibiza is unique – and is whatever you want it to be' (p. 13). In that round-the-clock promise of sex and love, with daylong sunshine apparently undimmed by a rainy season, Ibiza sounds as unique as all the other resorts that share these same characteristics. It can surely only be 'whatever you want it to be' if you want the expected characteristics of a major gay and straight holiday destination. On the other hand, some resorts simply cannot be offered as providing whatever the gay tourist might conceivably want. As the In Touch brochure (1997) puts it in one case: 'Kalkan [in Turkey] is a non scene resort and not gay in any way beyond the normal law of averages' (p. 20). This, then, sets a test or challenge for the gay tourist: how ordinary are you capable of seeming, even when enjoying yourself and at your most relaxed? Do you really *need* a place where you can hold hands? Do you ever *expect* a place where a straight man will not take offence when persistently cruised? If one is paying extra for a gay holiday provided by a gay company in a supposedly 'gay friendly' location, the answer may well be an emphatic *yes*.

As far as possible, in order to provide a safe haven from homophobia, the accommodation provided in such resorts should not cram the gay holidaymaker in with incompatible lifestyles. The Sensations '97 brochure includes the following note in its small print: 'It is almost completely unheard of for Sensations guests to experience homophobia while staying in Sensations accommodation, but if you are made to feel uncomfortable in any way please contact us or our local office and we'll do our best to remedy the situation' (p. 23). The In Touch (1997) brochure says: 'The [Oasis] hotel [in Kalkan] is run by a lovely family keen to promote a civilised atmosphere, and who operate a no children policy' (p. 21). On the other hand, the possibility of having to mix with non-gay groups is often admitted, as when the same brochure states: 'We have to stress that all [three apartment complexes in Playa del Ingles] have a completely mixed clientele base and particularly at peak season dates, you should expect a fair number of families' (p. 7). This has implications in terms of both the possibility of homophobic responses, whether from parents or their children, and the necessary reining in of overtly sexual behaviour, whether in front of the children or their parents. Some companies even evince, and perhaps invite, a phobic response to families, as when the Respect website says that 'hobnobbing with straights in Mykonos ain't like spending your holidays with Mr & Mrs Ghastly and their snotty kids. Mykonos is far too stylish for that'. But at least this weeds out those of us who would rather holiday alongside the Ghastlys than with Mr and Mr Stylish.

The controlled environment

A gay holiday company can only make cast-iron guarantees about an environment over which it has complete control, which, in the present context, means a heterosexual-free zone. (There is also a gender issue here: gay men may look for a men-only holiday, lesbians for a women-only holiday.) Such conditions are most explicitly foregrounded, as both aim and achievement, in brochure accounts of holidays on chartered cruise ships. At least while the ship is at sea, and assuming its crew have been properly briefed, there should be no occasion for any anti-gay incident to disturb the carefully constructed, gay-affirmative together-ness of a controlled cruise environment. Assuming the gayness of all passengers – or the willingness, at least, of all passengers to have bought tickets for a 'gay cruise' – the enclosed world of the ship will be, for the duration of the cruise (but barring forays ashore), both safe and encouraging for those who wish to relax into open expressions of their sexuality, or of the 'lifestyle' it entails, in the company of others whose intention is to do pretty much the same. Otherwise, if a ship sails with mixed groups of passengers, there is always the danger that groups who are identified as 'minorities' will be resented by those who seek the privilege of 'majority' status. On the maiden voyage of Cunard's *Queen Mary II* in January 2004, some passengers complained that the ship's Commodore Club had been taken over by gays. One wit started calling it the Commo*dorothy* Club.

A leaflet about RSVP Gay & Lesbian European Cruises (1997) includes the claim: 'RSVP always charters the entire ship so that we can create a cruise vacation tailor made for gays and lesbians' (p. 3). Holiday cruises are not for everyone. Indeed, a common theme from people who swear they will never go on one is the fear of confinement in the company of particular kinds of people. Travel companies have to make a virtue of the very same thing, of course. So the Man Around brochure (1992–3) includes this passage, in which one man's confine-ment becomes another's liberation:

> Free to be who you are.
> Freedom takes on a special meaning on an RSVP Cruise. RSVP Freedom. It means having the rare opportunity to relax and be who you are, twenty-four hours a day, seven days a week. In a comfortable, supportive Gay environment. Saying what you want. Acting as you like. Letting the real you come through. RSVP Freedom. ... RSVP Freedom. It means being who you are. Or who you've always wanted to be.

The implicit assumption here, that the target group consists of individuals who do not normally even get the chance to be themselves, let alone to be who they want to become, gives an impression less of a confidently well-adjusted and openly gay client base than of a constrained constituency yearning for release.

An Olivia brochure (1996–7) claims: 'Other travel companies take you to a destination, but Olivia takes you to a whole new world . . . a world where women loving women is the norm'. Asking themselves how this is possible, Olivia respond: 'We charter entire cruise ships and resorts to make sure that everyone is an Olivia guest'. This is a more convincing claim than RSVP's, since for obvious reasons it is easier to be selective in terms of gender than of sexuality. The back cover of this brochure carries the following legend on a familiar theme:

> IMAGINE
> Holding hands . . . without a second thought.

While this would not be much of a promise to straight couples in most Western countries, it clearly holds significant weight when addressed to a lesbian audience. Yet cruise ships do not sail non-stop. A major part of the pleasure they provide is in short visits to interesting or beautiful locations; and it is at this point that the concept of the gay-only or lesbian-only cruise can come unstuck. In December 1997, the government of the Cayman Islands refused docking rights to a ship with the Norwegian Cruise Lines, MS *Leeward*, which had been chartered by the American gay tour operator Atlantis Events. The following April, a 300-strong hostile crowd greeted the arrival of the SS *Seabreeze I* at Nassau in the Bahamas. Most of the 800 American lesbian passengers stayed on board, for understandable reasons. In October 1998, another Atlantis Events tour group of 300 lesbians and gay men was prevented from leaving a resort in Costa Rica when an angry crowd gathered to protest their presence. The country's president had to intervene to calm the situation. Jasbir Kaur Puar makes the crucial point here: were they not on the itineraries of the cruises in question, 'many of these island locations would not be destinations for queer tourists from North America and Europe' (Puar 2002: 137). There is no earthly reason why being visited by a shipload of such tourists should suddenly have turned them into such resorts.

On a land-based holiday a company can create the same conditions as those on a closed cruise more cheaply, and yet can combine them with some of the more valuable features of a gay resort – such as gay restaurants and clubs within walking distance – in the secure environment of a villa complex or chalet-based hotel. Here, a successfully created atmosphere of gayness will depend on the strict exclusion of any hint of non-gayness. We are now thinking in terms of walled compounds, the majority of them being for American nationals within their own nation. The Island House complex in Key West – nominated by one magazine as 'The best gay men's resort in the world' – states the matter clearly on its website: 'Imagine . . . A place where everyone is gay . . . Where it's easy to make friends ... Where you can really be yourself ... Where you can enjoy yourself 24 hours a day ... In a secure locked compound, safe from the outside world' (www.islandhousekeywest.com). The covering letter to the leaflet for El Mirasol Villas in Palm Springs states: 'Our established multi-national clientele returns again and again because they find more reserve and class behind the walls and gates of El Mirasol'. By contrast, in a covering letter to its general leaflet, the Alexander Resort in Palm Springs puts a more positive, less defensive gloss on privacy: 'Our grounds are private ... walled and gated, so nude sunbathing and swimming are permitted'.[4]

Such resorts tend to present themselves in terms akin to the isolationist romantic fantasy of the 'desert' island, but without the connotations of being stranded there indefinitely.[5] As Jasbir Kaur Puar has observed, once the desert island fantasy has been made real beyond the timid confines of the developed West, 'colonial constructions of tourism as a travel adventure into uncharted territory laden with the possibility of taboo sexual encounters, illicit seductions, and dangerous liaisons' are encouraged by the fantasy's implicit or explicit invocation of the idea of a meeting with Man Friday' (Puar 2002: 113). However, since most of these closed resorts are located within the USA, their publicity materials tend not to tap into that promise. In these resorts' fantasies of insular security, Robinson Crusoe is only likely to meet other Robinson Crusoes.

The other resonant image that the brochures rely on is the Garden of Eden, perhaps always with the knowledge of eventual expulsion. A leaflet for Big Ruby's guesthouse in Fort Lauderdale, Florida, says: 'Upon entering through a locked gate (for security and privacy), you find yourself in an exotic secluded garden with cascading waterfall. There is a beautiful large swimming pool surrounded by a tropical sundeck where nude sunbathing is possible'. A similar leaflet for the Triangle Inn in Palm Springs encourages the reader to 'Escape... To a romantic paradise within the privacy of our beautifully landscaped tropical gardens' (p. 4). It continues: 'Finally ... a secluded resort geared to the gay male traveller that will exceed your expectations. As you pass through the gate to our sun-drenched tropical gardens, you will be allured to the refreshing, sparkling pool and soothing Jacuzzi' (p. 5). The inn 'is a delightful feast for the eyes and a soothing embrace for the troubled spirit, a place where one can make new friends or surrender to peace and solitude. Either way there is always something here to remind us that life is worth living' (p. 5). Sad to say, the latter point states a crucial need for many holiday-makers whose careers get them down. But in a brochure where 'us' means gay men, these remarks may carry more sinister connotations regarding the plausibility of gay happiness in straight America.

An insert in the leaflet for the Columns Resort, Palm Springs, speaks of the place as 'A MAN'S PRIVATE PARADISE!' combining the virtues of

The BEAUTY of a lush tropical paradise
The COMFORT of a private retreat
The QUIET of a desert island

A leaflet for The Rainbow House, Key West, says 'Key West's Legendary Women's Guest House Welcomes You to Paradise!' Not quite a desert island – 'The ocean is just two blocks away' (p. 3) – the guest house does, at least, promise an escape from the need to travel outside its walls: 'Most of our guests park their car when they arrive and don't use it again until they leave' (p. 6). The women's resort Pearl's Rainbow in Key West similarly speaks in terms of escape from the outside world, advertising itself as a 'tropical escape in a testosterone-free atmosphere' (www.pearls-rainbow.com). The brochure for a Palm Springs establishment called Inn Exile enjoins the reader to 'close your eyes and fantasize about a place where being gay is a way of life', as if this were not the case wherever the gay individual is living the rest of his or her life. In a felicitous phrase, Man Around advertises 'Holidays of a Lifestyle'. Of its Fiji resort, Man Friday, the same leaflet says: 'Fiji has been welcoming visitors for years and now has its very own exclusively gay and lesbian "Garden of Eden" ' (p. 4). Quite how many lesbians will be attracted by the resort's name is not clear. For gay men, however, the promise of native company and help – a 'Man Friday' instead of Eve in this 'Garden of Eden' – may suggest more holiday perks than are actually on offer.

Queer activities

In holiday terms, desert island and Garden of Eden imagery tends to carry connotations of stasis within pleasurable confinement. But there are other, broader landscapes that demand not merely to be rested in, but to be roamed across. The more active tourist may seek a vacation involving more strenuous physical pursuits than alternate sunbathing and splashing about in the pool. The seventeenth edition of the Ferrari Guides' *Gay Travel A to Z* directory (1996) lists four companies providing 'outdoor adventure' holidays for gay men (three based in the United States, one in Australia), and no fewer than 29 such organizations for women (21 in the United States, two in Australia, one in New Zealand, two in the Netherlands, one in Germany and two in Canada). One such company, Women in the Wilderness, makes this promise: 'On all trips, you can be sure we won't be seeking out hardships to prove our womanhood or build character. You probably like your character fine, and can find all the stress you want in the city. When we do strenuous things, it's for the joy of it'. Much the same spirit is evinced by publicity material for Prairie Women Adventures and Retreat, which promises 'Adventures in being a cowhand on a working cattle ranch. Participants perform actual chores, such as branding, vaccinating and castrating cattle'.

A company with a similar name, Wilderness of Women, takes a more explicitly engaged line: 'We seek to do the work of the women's movement, including our political work, Earth work, healing, and spiritual work. Our goal is to make the experience of the wilderness accessible to as many women as possible. All of our guides are committed to the process of unlearning oppressions and addressing power dynamics. Enjoy delicious vegan-friendly food that is allergy sensitive. Our trips are drug and alcohol free'. One of the major concerns of such companies is the sensitive treatment of the holiday environment, an active friendliness to the natural world, rather than the sun-seeker's need for a backdrop to a spell of rest. The 1997 Wild Women Expeditions brochure begins with a general statement of ideals: 'We believe there are mutual benefits for women and the natural world to experience each other' – and goes on: 'Our relaxed atmosphere is a reflection of our trust in both the women in our groups and in our relationship to the natural environment' (p. 1). A canoe trip up Lake Huron's North Channel promises a symbiotic relationship in which the 'power and majesty of the wind and the water call to the fiery nature of the adventurous woman' (p. 2). And when the day's adventure ends, everyone returns to camp to experience a range of activities designed to fit in with the holiday's broader aims: 'It is the power of nature, the simplicity, the quiet, and largeness of the starry sky that fills us. Our programmes aim to nourish our artistic sensibilities, our need for activity, and restoration' (p. 3). Oddly, perhaps, these activities include boxing. As with Wilderness of Women, the idea of being in nature implies being in a natural condition, free of artificial stimulants. In the small print on the application form, there is a declaration to be signed by the applicant: 'I further understand and agree to refrain from the use of any intoxicants while on a Wild Women Expeditions trip' (p. 5).

As often as not, women-only travel companies do not advertise themselves as being exclusively lesbian. The absence of men may itself be taken as sufficiently lesbian friendly. Although the Wild Women Expeditions (2003) brochure contains no explicit reference to lesbian women, a rainbow flag is displayed immediately below the company director's opening statement on the brochure's first inside page. Prospective customers may or may not recognize its significance. The company certainly thinks it ought to be there. The written copy emphasizes a generic femaleness: 'Wild Women Expeditions attracts a diverse range of women from Canada and abroad who share a love of adventure, a reverence for the natural world and a genuine enjoyment of other women's company. Most women come on their own and make friends here'. If there is a slight hint, in this last remark, of discouragement to lesbian couples, it seems likely to be unintended.

It is clear that the concepts of 'holiday action' and 'holiday adventure' have a very different meaning for gay men. The *Spartacus International Gay Guide* (1997–8) gives an idea of these activities in its notes on gay beaches and cruising areas like Chowpathy beach, Bombay, India ('at the end of Marine Drive and just below Malabar Hill; all the beaches stretching 200 yards and the sands in front; many of the people are gay, some R[ent] and some not, and one has to use one's own judgement and discretion; very active after 18 h[ours] on Sundays; the men carrying large white sheets are masseurs and many of these will play for 30 rupees at your place' [p. 531]); Platya Es Cavallet, Ibiza ('from Ibiza-town follow the signs to the airport, then to Platya Es Cavallet. P[arking] possible at the beach. Walk along the beach or the dunes to the far end with the bar Chiringay. Action is going on in the bushes behind the bar towards the other side of the peninsula' [p. 776]); or Tisvilde Strand, Copenhagen, Denmark ('Public beach in North Sjaelland (Sea-land). Go by train E[ast] to Hillerod, then change to private railroad for Tisvildeleje. The beach is about 2 km from the station; pass the P[arking] lot] and go 1–2 km further west. The beach will gradually get more and more nude and gay. Some action in the dunes and in the wood behind the beach' [p. 186]). Here, the enjoyment of the natural landscape is secondary to the fundamental natural pleasures of sex.

Becoming the same

Most of the holidays advertised in the gay men's brochures I have been looking at – from companies in Europe, North America and Australia – are either city breaks or 'sunshine' holidays, where the adjective 'hot' is used to characterize not so much the climate as the men who inhabit it. These companies' brochures, therefore, promote not the culture and landscape of the hot spot in question, but the accommodation you can stay in there and the men you might meet (and mate with). It is hardly surprising that even a *Gay Phrase Book*, clearly aimed at the holiday market, while anticipating contacts with foreign nationals who do not speak English, will have a heavy emphasis on sexual negotiations. Endorsed by Gay Men Fighting AIDS and the AIDS Council of New South Wales, and published in association with Prowler Press (purveyors of gay erotic magazines, the phrase book includes safer sex dialogues in its seven languages (French, German, Spanish, Italian, Dutch, Portuguese, Japanese). The book also covers what are considered the main subdivisions of the gay travel experience, including the bar/club scene, cruising, personal contact ads, health emergencies and, of course, sex itself (McKay 1997). If you want to say 'Come all over me!' in the language of your sexual partner, this is the phrase book for you. But if you think you are likely to want to hire a car or buy a newspaper or have a wound dressed, look elsewhere. Of course, if you want to talk to strangers in a bar about Walt Whitman and Rita Mae Brown, you may have to transfer to a country whose language you know, or chance your arm with your fellow tourists.

Speaking in the first person plural at the conclusion to an essay on 'extraordinary homosexuals' at the start of the twentieth century, Biddy Martin raises the question of the limited queerness of people who, almost a century later, had taken to calling themselves 'queers':

> An enormous fear of ordinariness or normalcy results in superficial accounts of the complex imbrication of sexuality with other aspects of social and psychic life, and in far too little attention to the dilemmas of the average people that we also are.
>
> (Martin 1994: 123)

This may be true, but we have also to consider that the bulk of people who identify as lesbian or gay, rather than as queer, while possibly being pleased to think of their sexuality as conferring something special on them by way of compensation for the pains they may have suffered as a consequence of being in a social minority much discriminated against, are happy to think themselves ordinary and are determined to make heterosexuals think of them as such. (Self-styled queers are apt to sneer at this as an assimilationist posture, which is precisely what it is.) To such people their gayness is neither strange nor extraordinary, and if, on holiday, there is a risk of heterosexuals treating them as strange, the better option may be to holiday only with other people who think gayness itself ordinary. They may therefore seek a holiday on which, to minimize the risk of stress, embarrassment or even violence, they fit in with rather than stand out from the crowd. Paradoxically, this may entail taking an 'extraordinary' holiday with a gay company rather than a mainstream package.

The predominant impression one gets from the promotional materials I have been examining has been less of a universalizing unity than of a commercially led homogenization. I do not believe this means we are all having the same three or four basic holidays. It is more likely that those who write the narratives of pleasure that make up the brochures and, to a lesser extent, the shapes of the holidays they offer, exhibit a failure of imagination, if, perhaps, one partly forced on them by the economics of mass tourism. There are, however, signs that this narrowness reflects an increasing narrowness in commercial and political representations of lesbian and gay 'lifestyles' worldwide, but especially in the industrialized nations of the West, as a limited range of acceptable modes of liberation are palmed off as some kind of victory in the struggle for gay rights. Especially given the fact of American cultural power, and the virtual supremacy of the English language in the electronic media, it is hardly conceivable that the range of possible gay and lesbian identities will not continue to contract down to a handful of US-led models in a capitalist-commercial mode. Identities that encourage the sale of goods and services will prevail; and the available goods and services will themselves in turn encourage the development of those identities at the cost of other alternatives. Since the commercialization of leisure is central to this process, the development of gay and lesbian holidays over a broader geographical range but still within circumscribed limits of imaginable pleasures will continue to play its role in the consolidation of a gayness that can easily be assimilated into the status quo of 'freedoms' under the yoke of capitalism.

Notes

1. If 'to be cosmopolitan is to display an openness and curiosity about other cultures, to seek out the different' (Rushbrook 2002: 188), one might doubt the cosmopolitan credentials of American tourists who go to Europe hoping to strike up conversations, presumably in English, about Walt Whitman and David Leavitt.
2. Burton named the zone after Sotades of Maroneia, the Greek satirist of the third century BCE, whose scurrilous poetry was renowned for its coarseness. Ptolemy II is said to have had him executed by drowning.
3. There are so many versions of these statistics that they seem unreliable. But the stories that the different versions tell seem similar. Here is another: 'Community Marketing states not only that 88 percent of the gay tourism market [in the USA] is college graduates (compared to the national average of 29 percent) but that 54 percent had taken an international vacation in 2000 (45 percent in 1999), six times the national average of 9 percent, and that 89 percent hold valid passports, more than three times the national average of 29 percent' (Puar 2002: 110).
4. Apparently oblivious to gay men's, and to a lesser extent lesbians', long history of involuntary imprisonments (and even to sadomasochistic fantasy), a brochure for Above and Beyond Tours (1996-7) offers the following

promotion of holiday accommodation in Australia: 'Incarceration is the ultimate gay and lesbian fantasy! There is only one place in the world that visitors can overnight in comfortable surroundings in a once-functional jail ... The Old Castlemaine Jail was once the finest structure among the Goldfields. While the cells have been converted to comfortable sleeping rooms with shared facilities, the dungeon retains its original mystery'.

5. I have written elsewhere about the masculinist and homo-erotic resonances of the desert island narrative (Woods 1995).

11 Countryside formats and ordinary lifestyles

Robert Fish

Rural lifestyles: the ordinary in flight from/to itself

If we wanted to pick on a site of popular cultural imaginings that seemed to function as the antithesis of ordinary experience, we could do worse than settle on the idea of countryside. Widely shared understandings of country life, it is consistently claimed, are fashioned around the idea of a rural idyll, the working label for highly affirmative enactments of community, nature and landscape (Mingay 1989; Bunce 1994). With its heightened and perfected states of meaning and being, this sedentary way of thinking about countryside appears, at first glance, more concerned with exceeding the limits of the ordinary than about grasping or shaping it. Certainly this seems true if we were to reflect on how this sign has been conventionally employed. To speak, for instance, of 'being ordinary' or of 'leading an ordinary life' is often to cast experience in highly unfavourable terms (Williams 1983). It is to emphasize the rather mundane, often unremarkable and typically imperfect events around which everyday life becomes familiar to itself, and through which it is contained and enclosed. In formative histories of critical thought, this reading has also often prevailed. Ideas of ordinary culture have frequently been treated as an issue of 'disenchantment', 'alienation' and 'lack', and it is telling that in accounting for this 'condition' of ordinary life, the imaginary of the city, and the social relations of the disempowered and duped inhabiting it, has tended to predominate. At the same time, affirmative ideas of countryside have often occupied a reflexive place within this critical frame. The radical potential of the everyday has, on various occasions, rested on marshalling the power of 'authentic' ways of living – *a flight from the ordinary* – in which appeals to the rural, apparently far from controlled systems of industrialized and mass media consumption, are by no means absent. In recent years, critical theory has departed significantly from these kinds of (reactionary) distinctions, in part by asserting a version of the ordinary that is overtly more creative, tactical, playful, in a word *optimistic,* in form, and one in which affirmative ideas of countryside might stage a different kind of entrance. The matter under consideration in this book, that of lifestyles, is instructive here, for even the most cursory of engagements with the cultural history of this sign would show up its aspirational tone – its self-conscious desire to elevate, rework and transform experience – and even the most cursory of engagements with the highly mediated objects and practices allowing lifestyles to be enacted would show up an investment in ideas of countryside and country living. As a question of lifestyle, then, pejorative senses of the ordinary are tacitly displaced, and the idea of an idyllic countryside begins to enter, act on and express it. Or, to put this another way, it functions as a *flight to the ordinary;* a category of thought and experience within which the tactics of everyday life can take shape and assert influence, as opposed to being something simply over and above it.

It is this second, less pessimistic reading of ordinary that guides this chapter's reading of the rural, and one that I ultimately come to problematize. I wish to do this by pursuing an account of popular media formats; in this case, widely duplicated ways of putting the idea of rural lifestyle together in the United Kingdom. Ideas of countryside have a long-standing contract with mass media processes in the UK (Phillips et al. 2001), and often express themselves in highly affirmative terms. In this discussion I wish to draw upon two such countryside formats – the lifestyle magazine and the television drama series – to think about the form these aspirational versions of rural life take, and to examine the editorial practices that help to shape them. I do this first through an account of the self-identifying lifestyle magazine *Country Living* (National Magazine Company, 1985–present); a widely circulating media format branding itself as 'a uniquely evocative celebration of country style and all that is positive about the country way of life' (www.countryliving.co.uk).[1] I then consider the long-running television drama series *Peak Practice* (Carlton Television 1994–2002), again, a widely circulating format with the countryside as a central part of its narrative repertoire.[2] The insights that I present are based on almost nine years of extended research with media practitioners creating countryside formats in the British television and magazine industry. They develop from discussions and observation with over 100 key informants, both common to different genres and mediums (such as writers and editors) as well as specific to them (such as directors in television, or photographers working for magazines). These structures of media production are by no means reducible to a British context, and the analysis I develop in relation to my particular category of concern – that of English rurality – should be read as a way into thinking about the relationship between mass media and aspirational ideas of rurality more generally. My initial concern in addressing the two particular texts in question here is to explain the thematic and narrative terms that govern their ideas of rural lifestyle, drawing particular attention to notions of reader self-identification among media practitioners. In both cases, I go on to ask how these affirmative visions are maintained in the light of contravening ideas. That is to say, I consider the tactics that media producers employ to banish signs that threaten to assault those visions, or better still, signs that threaten to make them unexceptional, or *ordinary*.[3] By way of conclusion I consider what these strategies imply for a cultural politics of rurality in the lifestyle sphere. Indeed, while we might say that these texts function as sites of creative and playful acts in identity formation, they rest on a problematic social-spatial imaginary; one that ultimately manufactures the tactics of ordinary lifestyles through a deeply conservative reading of English countryside.

The magazine format: *Country Living* and rural lifestyles

In a recent collection of papers exploring the way ideas of country life are widely envisioned, Cloke (2003) has spoken of the importance of mass media forms in continually reasserting the 'long fingers' of an idyllic rurality, and if we wanted empirical evidence to back up this claim then we might look no further than the magazine *Country Living*, an unashamedly celebratory and didactic meditation on the idea of rural lifestyle and one designed to 'reflect the interests of people living in the country whilst inspiring all those who dream of this ideal lifestyle' (www.countryliving.co.uk). Published in the UK since 1985 by the National Magazine Company, and replicating a format developed successfully in the North American marketplace, *Country Living* is a strong performer in a crowded market for monthly lifestyle titles, one that regularly translates a circulation of 170,000 into a readership of 800,000 (NRS 2003). In the formal and informal imaginings of its practitioners the social identity of this reader is well delineated. *Country Living*'s readers, it is variously claimed, are: 'affluent, educated and caring'; 'value quality and demand the best'; have 'the right attitude and spending power'; are 'three quarters ABC1s, with 89% owning their own homes'; have 'an average age of 48'; 'live in Islington or perhaps Fulham'; are individuals 'who have left the rat race'; and are people 'just like my mum'. The confluence of these different identities is pretty clear in terms of a reader archetype: the *Country Living* reader is an aspirational middle-aged, middle-class woman, with her 'heart in the country'.[4]

Precisely how the magazine constructs its vision for this imagined audience is a matter of theme and form and, as I will go on to explain, is underscored by a specific set of strategies designed to deny, play down or invert contravening ideas. As a theme, country living is evoked around a litany of affirmative ideas: celebrations of landscape type and feature; engagements with nature's rhythms and limits; curiosities of local ritual and heritage; allusions to sites of artistic and literary worth; accounts of craft and workplace; sensual pleasures of the body; dreams and promises of romance; healthy and purified commodities; recipes and cookbooks; soft ornaments and furnishings; living rooms with open fires and sleeping dogs; kitchens with Agas and stone floors; post offices with hanging baskets; village greens with fêtes; flowers and gardening seasons; manicured lawns and conservatories; walks in orchards and along shores – around, in short, every thematic version of what it might mean to envision a rural idyll.

Such themes are governed by high production values and consistently engage in an active process of reader self-identification, both tacit and explicit. Articles become, for instance, the provenance of more general sets of rural taste and competency – 'from front doors and hallways to gates, fences and pathways, our practical, stylish ideas will ensure *your home* always gives the *right* impression' (October 2003, my emphasis) – and often frame their concerns around people, predominantly women, who move into the countryside, gentrify properties and start up a small enterprise. As one media practitioner put it: 'The whole ethos is to persuade people that they would have a better quality of life away from the stress and strain of urban living'. Or more specifically:

> One of the big jobs we have to do is inspire people, particular things by women. ... It's all about what they would like to do with their lives and stuff, so we have this section called 'Change your Life' and it's all about people who move out the city to the country, dropped, you know, stopped being a recruitment consultant and set up a bakery, and that sort of thing. So we always do something on rural businesses. ... And we do quite a lot of campaigns on that as well, like our 'Enterprising Rural Women' awards. We've just done this 'Start your own Rural Business Booklet'.

Country Living fosters these visions in a rhythmic fashion. Themes pertaining to 'House and Gardens', Food and Drink', 'Fashion and Health' may well be compartmentalized 'sections' on the contents page, but they work recursively across the publication: images of the perfect garden give way to images of the fashioned body, which give way to images of the perfect kitchen, which give way to images of the healthy body, which give way to images of the perfect living room, and so forth. In other words, the narrative logic of *Country Living* is designed to add up to an aspirational lifestyle rather than disaggregate it. As one practitioner explained: 'We don't have all the homes, then all the gardens, then all the features: it drifts from one to another, so you end up feeling like you've got this complete package'.

Such a package rests, of course, on fostering neat transactions between affirmative vision and market-based solution: between constructing a lifestyle and then selling it. At the most ostensible and straightforward level *Country Living* integrates commodities by inserting double- and single-page advertisements alongside its different sections. Such acts of positioning often reflect the concerns of the theme in question. A regular feature known as 'Emporium' provides 'inspiration for your house and garden' and is played out alongside adverts of high quality fabrics, wallpapers and soft furnishings to the effect that editorial feature and commodity are not easily disentangled. But then, the Emporium feature itself is merely a series of displayed objects anchored with commentaries on their commodity value – gingham edged tablecloths brought to you by X, bespoke scented candles brought to you by Y, rustic iron egg baskets brought to you by Z. And again, such commentaries are often designed to speak to its imagined readership: 'Inspired by rural success stories in *Country Living* Melissa Fisher decided to leave city life and start her own cottage industry ... this potting shed peg bag costs £15' (October 2003). In other cases, the commodity value of a featured image functions in a more implied fashion. Take for instance a House and Garden section featuring 'practical and stylish ideas' for gate fences, pathways and hallways and carrying with it an image of an entrance hall, complete with reclaimed chapel pew, stone flagged floor and docile dog. We learn in the peripheral footnotes that the reclaimed chapel pew is 'a practical seat for putting on outdoor footwear' at £1200 and the stone flagged floor is 'ideal for a busy entrance hall' at £45 a square metre. But it is the dog which is the key part of signification here, since the image directly faces another marketplace solution, a perfect country kitchen from Aga-Rayburn where, we are told, 'life couldn't be more idyllic', and in it rests a dog, in an identical resting position, laying on a stone floor. In other words, the apparently naturalized vision of country living spills over into the commodified vision.

This scrambled relationship between *Country Living* features and commodity value finds its most advanced expression as an 'advertorial', the process of taking a commodity and elevating it to the status of a *Country Living* feature. According to *Country Living*, through the advertorial 'clients benefit from the perceived endorsement of the magazine' (National Magazine Company 2003). In these terms too objects and services that do not have a literal sense of rural signification – opticians, cleaning products, car rentals – often become extensions of the affirmative vision. In other cases, commodity values are sectioned off and confined to particular areas as if they might otherwise pollute, rather than construct, the vision. As one practitioner put it: 'We wouldn't want any old advert next to our features'. Indeed, policing this distinction between editorial vision and the assaulting signs of advertising is seen as crucial in many instances, a matter that expresses itself more generally through the construction of 'The Well', a series of pages at the heart of the magazine that deliberately avoids overt commodification: 'So for example a really beautiful piece that would be total trash with an advert would go in that section, so it can all just run on seamlessly', explained the same practitioner. This process of containing and banishing adverts is at least one of the functions of its other principal site of commodification, the classified section, or County Directory, a panoply of conservatories, fish sculptures, tree houses and fireplaces that sits quietly at the back of the publication, functioning like the dénouement of a long sales pitch.

Country Living and the negation of conflict

We don't do doom and gloom.

Country Living may well be an evocative celebration of everything positive about 'Country Life', and may well be deeply implicated in the commodification of affirmative rural lifestyles, but how does it create this vision from material social realities? After all, *Country Living* produces meaning not as a self-constructed fiction. Its narrative mode – in editorials, features and design sections – constantly implies that what it is talking about, drawing upon and designating is 'a real'. How, then, does *Country Living* deal with realities that contravene its own versions of rural life? What should a lifestyle format do when confronted with a dilemma such as the foot and mouth epidemic, or social deprivation in the countryside, or the discontents of rural in-migration, or the building of wind farms, or GM crop trials? What should it do, in short, about processes that depart from the text of its aspirational rurality and threaten to make such rural lifestyle shot through with conflict, or even *ordinary*?

The simple answer to this question is, in one sense, 'ignore them': ignore the ordinariness of country life with all its habitual and evolving dilemmas. Such is the way articles on, say, growing food organically, or leaving life in the fast lane, or refurbishing and restoring an outhouse, must be understood. They function as strategies without problems, ideas without conflicts, practices without contradictions. And yet, rather than simply sidestepping premises that might contravene its brand values, *Country Living* also continually engages and translates dilemmas to positive effect. In one sense, it does so by drawing on examples where conflicts over rural space are already resolved, or in the process of being resolved. Recent articles on 'All you need to know about affordable social housing' (February 2004) or 'Melton's Mowbray's fight to safeguard the heritage of the original pork pie' (October 2003) are indicative of this mode of address. Functioning as 'answers' to social deprivation in the countryside and the erosion of local ritual and custom respectively, they only acknowledge counter-visions insofar as affirmative programmes of action are already in place. Or consider the recent feature entitled 'A new school of thought' (September 2003) which narrates the experiences of a village in Devon, responding to the threat of school closure. This is how one practitioner explained it:

> Basically it's about making people ... inspiring them ... giving them positive stories, I mean not in an Esther Rantzen, *Hearts of Gold* type way. For example, we have just done a feature in our September issue for the start of the school year about [a] village school closing down and what a tragedy that is. But we didn't say that, we said we found some parents who have taken [over] their village schools and [are] running them, and saving them, so you cover the issue.

In other instances, the magazine actively creates solutions to self-identified 'rural issues', a process enacted through a series of congratu-latory *Country Living* 'campaigns' designed to gradually invert the problem at stake. So, for instance, declining service provision in rural areas becomes a campaign to find 'Britain's best newsagent', a process culminating in a series of features that celebrate in visual and narrative terms these 'hubs of the community'. Interestingly, one of its 'highly commended' winners was Sue and Peter Knight from Somerset, who, we learn, 'bought their store after deciding to leave London for a new life in the country' (October 2003). In short, social relations that might otherwise function as conflicts to the vision are actually devices for particular aspirations about rural life to be asserted and maintained. And such processes of inverting conflict find expression even in highly contradictory events and occurrences. When, for instance, it emerged in early 2001 that the British countryside was effectively in crisis as a result of the foot and mouth epidemic, *Country Living* engaged in a gradual process of reconstituting this 'crisis' as a narrative of hope, a narrative of communities pulling together, of individuals confronting and over-coming this assault on rural life. As one practitioner explains:

We took an example of an organic farmer down in Devon, Paula Walton, who literally, like a siege mentality, just shut herself off from the outside world to protect her and her livestock, and although three farms around her were taken out and she said she could see the funeral pyres of the livestock she survived it, so we thought that was a great example. A lot of it of course would be luck I suppose, but she managed to get through it. So it's a positive example, in that this female organic farmer, who survived it, was an example to others.

That the protagonist in this narrative was a woman who had moved to the countryside is no coincidence given my claims about the imagined readership of *Country Living*. Just as much as this reader is directly implicated in the more conventional and routine signs of its pages on 'Food and Drink', or 'House and Garden', so do they begin to reclaim and reassert that vision when it is assaulted.

The television format: *Peak Practice* and rural lifestyles

The ambulance drives through the countryside which is shot through a golden glow. It's a strange hybrid really.

I now wish to compare this reading of *Country Living* with a short account of Carlton Television's *Peak Practice,* until recently a long-running UK drama series developed around the lives of a group of doctors living in a fictitious Peak District village known as Cardale, and part of a tradition of British rural dramas including Yorkshire Television's *Heartbeat* (1992–present) and *Darling Buds of May* (1991-3), BBC Television's *Down to Earth* (2001–present), *Hamish Macbeth* (1995-7), *Ballykissangel* (1996-2001), *Dangerfield* (1995-9), and perhaps most notably, *All Creatures Great and Small* (1978-89). Like *Country Living*, *Peak Practice* has been a strong performer in its marketplace, regularly reaching audiences over 14 million people, and one continuing to have its rights sold abroad. It also shares and extends the magazine's conception of audiencehood. Viewers of *Peak Practice* were, for instance, variously claimed to be 'middle-aged women' and 'middle-aged mothers', 'city folk' and 'townies', as well as people who had 'given up and moved into [the] countryside'. Unlike *Country Living* though, class iterations of audience were generally more scrambled. While viewers were regularly alluded to as 'middle-class', so too were they described in tacit working-class terms: 'people in *flats* without any green space' and 'people like my *ironing* lady'.

The textual themes at work in this countryside format, as well as the notions of audience that they were designed to serve, lend themselves to a similar kind of analysis as above. *Peak Practice* takes place, for instance, in a story world that is visually affirmative for those who gaze upon it, consistently dwelling upon a mixture of open and uninterrupted landscapes, scenes of the nucleated village and an embellished sense of nature. Regularly beset in light and warmth, *Peak Practice* shares with the magazine an elevated sense of cultural and natural heritage, an unashamedly affirmative construct of what it means to inhabit a rural space. As one practitioner put it:

> The show has a look which is a slightly romantic, rather lush image in terms of our lighting and directing style. But it's based around showing off the area. The show's always been about the countryside in terms of the hills, the landscape, the geography. It's terribly important to the show, it's another character . . . We shoot Derbyshire at its best. We never shoot on a flat if we can shoot on a hill.

Further, *Peak Practice*'s story world is peopled with central protagonists who function like enactments of the *Country Living* vision. In a related study, for instance, Phillips et al. (2001) show how the drama's main protagonists are constructed around middle-class incomer identities, ones shaped to a significant degree around ownership of commodities and patterns of consumption. Questions of taste and competency therefore have their provenance in the actions of these protagonists; an aspirational world of designed and gentrified interiors, country-smart fashions, stripped down furniture and fresh food. And like *Country Living*, it rests on an active process of audience self-identification. *Peak Practice*, it was consistently suggested, functioned as a site of projection, a way of realizing ideals. For the urban middle-class, the production evoked a feeling of 'how nice it would be to have a country retreat'. For the urban working classes it was a way of taking flight from the inevitability of their lived relations. It allowed them to compensate for their conditions of existence. As one practitioner put it: 'The urban working class . . . They've got no chance of having a weekend cottage. They've got no chance of going out there because unemployment is huge, but they use it as escapism'.

However, the practice of linking text and audience in this way has to be squared with issues of form, for what we can also say about this production is that it encounters the world as drama: a mode of representation that has, at its imaginative centre, the production and negotiation of conflict (Mamet 1998). To speak of *Peak Practice* as drama is to speak of it as a series of events, occurrences and happenings around which dilemmas unfold. It is to understand the rural world not so much as a perfected and unchanging state, but rather as a site of antagonisms and complicating factors. Like other examples of the genre, *Peak Practice* does this by developing a combination of classical and serial narratives, a system of meaning that unfolds conflicts within and across individual episodes (Corner 1999). Interpreted this way, we might therefore begin to suggest something of a difference between the idea of rural lifestyle produced in a magazine format such as *Country Living* and that at work in a television format such as *Peak Practice*. Whereas *Country Living* is a didactic narrative preaching the virtues of rural life and denying, playing down and inverting conflict, it would appear that *Peak Practice* must, at a dramatic level, seek to contravene the affirmative vision. As one practitioner explains:

> You've got to say we can only afford that lyricalness, we can only afford that nice slow pace with all those pretty pictures, if we are going to be brave, and I think when you start to get soft stories and keep all that, it all falls apart and you sort of end up watching television thinking, 'What am I watching?'

Such a claim would appear to gain further credence if we were to consider the narrative themes that have been regularly played out by *Peak Practice*. For *Country Living*'s 'Health and Beauty' section, read a panoply of illness, accidents and addictions, both fatal and not so fatal: heart attacks, leukaemia, brain tumours, blackouts, nausea, drug abuse. For *Country Living*'s celebratory matchmaking campaign 'The Farmer Wants a Wife', read a litany of divorces, separations and eternally doomed romances. For *Country Living*'s business 'success stories', read a GP practice that constantly straddles bankruptcy.

And yet, while it is undoubtedly true that *Peak Practice* must generate conflicts, so too will it actively seek to resolve them. After all, the narrative logic of this production is overwhelmingly classical in form, in the sense that its chief signifying logic is to build episodes around a single principal theme that will then be overcome over the course of the telling (Bordwell and Thompson 1993; Lowe 2000). Or to put this in the terms I expressed earlier, *Peak Practice* is interested too in the *inversion* of conflict. It builds up dilemmas in order for those dilemmas to be progressively turned into an affirmative outcome. How different, for instance, is *Peak Practice*'s episode 'The Price' (series 5) – a narrative that develops around the threat of closure to Cardale's village school and results in that school being saved – from *Country Living*'s account of the embattled village school being taken over and rescued by the community? I would argue no different at all. As one practitioner suggested, while *Peak Practice* was always 'stepping out' out of its idyllic world, so too did it inevitability 'step back in'. In the final assessment, *Peak Practice* was seen to be a 'Brigadoon' world, a community where 'everyone loves everyone else' and to which the viewer could return and be 'reassured'. Like *Country Living*, it places middle-class and/or incomer identities at the centre of these negotiations. The lives of the drama's main protagonists are not only sites through which matters of rural taste and affluence can be claimed and expressed, but also the means by which affirmative social relations are constantly (re)secured. Again, there seems little difference between *Country Living*'s efforts to gradually frame the foot and mouth epidemic as a story of hope, one undertaken through the exemplary work of the middle-class incomer, and the epidemiological narratives of *Peak Practice* with its high-minded, problem-solving main protagonists. As one practitioner put it, the drama created a recurring scenario in which 'the village is basically idiotic ... [and the] ... professionals are basically very bright and intelligent and they all come and live there ... I think there's a degree to which the doctors do tend to solve problems in the community'. While *Peak Practice* arguably entertains greater ambivalence in its vision than a format such as *Country Living*, these dramatic processes are often motivated around the same techniques and to the same effect. They are about the active inversion of conflict in which affirmative social identities of the incoming classes often come to the fore.

Rural lifestyles: the ordinary in spite of itself

In the introduction to this analysis I suggested that popular ideas of the ordinary and the rural, while seemingly antithetical, could be reconciled through the category of lifestyle. I explained that, as matters of lifestyle, ideas of rurality enter ordinary experience as an aspirational discourse: one designed to elevate, rework and transform its supposedly containing and limiting terms. Contemporary countryside texts such as the lifestyle magazine and the television drama offer, I suggest, formal expressions of this process, and in light of this analysis bear a similar kind of critical scrutiny. While it may be accurate, in one significant sense, to read these texts as the means for active and creative transformation of identity and experience, as sites of projection against which real and imagined ideas can be played out, we should caution that their ways of 'knowing rurality' are also highly conventional (Cloke 2003). When it is possible to speak of the countryside format in terms of compensatory urban working-class discourses and affirmative incoming middle-class discourses, or of narrative styles that seek to banish and invert rural conflict through the high-mindedness of the urban incomer, or of affirmative rural social relations marked out by particular distinctions of taste, commodity and competency – when it is possible to say all of these things of countryside formats – then we know, for all their appeals to a finished and perfected rural experience, we are encountering very ordinary worlds indeed. To all intents and purposes, these formats cast their affirmative versions of English countryside within a long-standing and recognizable cultural politics and reveal a system of contemporary cultural (re)production that understands its terms clearly. Such is the way the underlying politics of the rural lifestyle text must, in the final assessment, be understood and engaged: as much the ordinary in spite of itself as the ordinary in flight from or to itself.

Notes

1. For other accounts of *Country Living*, see Little (2003) and Bunce (2003).
2. A related treatment of *Peak Practice* can be found in Phillips et al. (2001) and Fish (2005).
3. By which I mean analogous with more pessimistic accounts of an ordinary life: one shot through with ongoing and irresolvable dilemmas, as opposed to being somehow conflict free.
4. These premises are taken from comments made in interviews, and an unpublished marketing plan made available to the author.
5. The official strap-line for *Country Living*.

Part IV
Learning lifestyles

12 It's a girl thing
Teenage magazines, lifestyle and consumer culture

Fan Carter

Launched in November 1994, the British teenage girls' magazine *Sugar* offered its readers a new twist on the staple format of fashion, beauty, pop and advice. A monthly publication produced on good quality paper in a perfect-bound edition, *Sugar* claimed it was offering its discerning readers 'something new' (*Sugar*, November 1994: 4). Beyond these immediate signifiers towards the grown-up world of the 'glossies', the launch and subsequent success of the magazine signalled a set of deeper shifts in the period which saw the increasing significance of lifestyle strategies in the organization and management of the teen magazine market.

Justified with the authoritative claim that the industry was giving teenagers what they wanted, the marketing puffs of teenage magazines declaimed the status of 'style bible' (*J-17* 1997) and 'best friend[s]' (*Sugar* 1997) for the teenage girl reader. As such, these magazines operated in terms of producing and legitimizing particular forms of knowledge about being a teenage girl and offering specific tutoring in appropriate feminine practices. Indeed, teenage magazines have long been considered to act as guides or instruction manuals in the operations of femininity and have been examined as such in feminist media and cultural research (Alderson 1968; McRobbie 1982, 1991, 1996; Tinkler 1995; Currie 1997).

In some ways the developments in the teenage magazine industry during the 1990s can be seen as an intensification of the processes that Angela McRobbie (1991) has termed the 'logics of consumption'. Increasingly editorial and promotional features have tied the making of adolescent feminine selves to the acquisition and deployment of appropriate products and celebrated shopping and consumption as specifically feminine pleasures. However, the changes in the 1990s were also shaped by the increasing circulation of lifestyle discourses both in the magazine editorials and also, significantly, in the industry's own narratives. Woven into these accounts of market development and expansion are particular images and imaginings of the teenage girl. Central to these formulations is the notion that adolescence constitutes a significant moment of identity formation, as both a teenage girl and a consumer. Indeed across industry accounts and the magazine pages themselves, the motif of 'becoming' best characterizes the mode and model of feminine consumption and identity imagined therein. These representations of 'becoming' are explored below with particular attention to ways that the teenage girl is configured as an active and burgeoning consumer framed by discourses of developmental psychology, consumerism and postfeminism. Across these discursive sites, the concept of 'becoming' is mobilized in an attempt to account for the particularity of adolescent femininity and also to legitimize attempts to manage this process through strategies for market regulation, the proliferation of lifestyle expertise and inculcation into particular taste cultures and consumer practices.

Becoming a girl: lifestyle magazines and technologies of the self

The approach taken towards the analysis of these commercial constructions of femininity in this chapter draws on recent mobilizations of Foucault's concept of 'technologies of the self' (1988) in relation to consumer discourses and practices of gendered selfhood (see in particular Nava 1992; Entwistle 1997; Nixon 1997; Rose 1999). Above all, these analyses have explored the tensions and ambiguities in the work of consumption to engage new identities, skills and competencies while at the same time operating as forms of self-regulation. While the discourses of lifestyle consumption productively mobilize notions of consumer sovereignty and conceptualize selfhood in terms of an 'autonomous subject of choice and self-realisation' (Rose 1999: xviii), they also draw increasing aspects of personal and everyday life with such 'technicizing' frameworks of self-regulation (Nava 1992). The relationship of lifestyle discourses to youth cultures of consumption has been particularly interesting in this respect and commentators have noted the ways in which youthful lifestyles are often celebrated as particularly desirable in relation to fashion, music and leisure (Miles 2000). The suggestion is sometimes made that 'youth' has become an increasingly shifting and fluid signifier, indicative of specific taste cultures rather than chronological age (Miles 2000). However, what is missing from these accounts is a sense of the ways in which such discourses are gender specific. The youthful lifestyles celebrated are predominantly masculine and urban. Instead, this chapter focuses attention on the more 'ordinary' lifestyles associated with young teenage girls as configured within discourses of magazine culture. These commercial constructions of teenage femininities articulate a central motif of 'becoming' in their imaginings and images of the teenage girl. This notion of 'becoming' plays both to traditional narratives of adolescence as a critical, and importantly natural, stage in the development of mature gendered identity (Erikson 1968; Heaven 2001) and also to the fluid narratives of postmodern consumer culture where 'becoming' is envisioned as a continuous process of desire and deferral (Clark 1987). While commercial discourses attempt to manage these different perspectives through the alignment of discourses of lifestyle with those of 'life-stage' tensions remain. In examining commercial constructions of 'becoming', this chapter draws attention to the specificities of gender and generation in discourses of lifestyle marketing.

The making of girls: the teenage magazine market

The teenage magazine market in Britain underwent a period of rapid expansion and development in the mid-1990s. The growing cluster of titles and rising circulation figures for teenage girls' publications pointed to a degree of confidence and buoyancy in the market. While the development of teenage publications in the 1990s was economically driven, reliant on growing advertising spends and publishing strategies of increasing market expansion and segmentation (Braithwaite 1997), it was also culturally informed and produced by particular understandings of femininity and adolescence. Industry accounts of these developments were suggestive of particular professionally inflected knowledges that shaped the industry's understanding and construction of its target consumer, the teenage girl. The organization and development of the teenage magazine market was reliant on, and in turn productive in, the construction of specific commercial articulations of femininity. Marketing directors and publishers were particularly active in constructing the figure of the teenage girl to meet the logic of consumer capitalism (McRobbie 1991), and in so doing creating a 'natural fit' between the desires and demands of the teenage girl as an adolescent and a consumer with the solutions provided by the magazine product.

The development and growth of the teenage market in the 1990s was underpinned by the increasing confidence of advertisers in the teenage market (Cook 1997). Teenagers were believed to have rising disposable incomes, achieved through greater allowances and part-time employment (Mintel 1998), and magazines were considered an 'essential purchase' for this relatively affluent group, with 93 per cent of teenage girls buying regularly (*Sugar* 1997). In addition, teenage girls were perceived as a market for future investment, leading financial services, among others, to advertise now with the hope of building brand loyalty for the future. As Neil Raaschou, then managing director of Attic Futura, noted: 'advertisers are realizing how important it is to speak to this group early, perhaps even before they are in a position to be really big consumers' (cited in Cook 1997: 33). Furthermore, the rapid turnover of readers, as they progressed to more 'grown-up' titles, meant that the market constantly renewed itself, which helped to offset any anxieties of saturation. However, while the market was constructed in optimistic and buoyant terms, it was also perceived as unstable, dependent on the fickle tastes of the teenage girl who, while a voracious consumer, was not always or necessarily a loyal one. This quirk of the market was perceived both to require careful management on the part of publishers and cultural intermediaries to forestall any potential disruption (*Campaign* 1997) and to necessitate diversification of product lines within publishing groups.

The launch of *Sugar* in 1994 as a joint publishing venture between Attic Futura, a subsidiary of News Corporation, and North South Publishing, caused a considerable shake-up in the teenage market. *Sugar* challenged many of the conventions of teen publishing that had become established since the launch and growth of *Just Seventeen* (*J-17*) in 1984. Unlike the existing titles, *Sugar* was produced on a monthly basis with better paper quality and in a perfect-bound edition (rather than the stapled pages of *Just Seventeen* at the time). Borrowing the signifiers of quality and 'grown-upness' from the older 'glossy' market offered *Sugar* an immediate style advantage. This 'grown-up' quality was considered by industry insiders to have contributed to the rapid and sustained growth in its circulation figures, which came at a cost to the other titles in the market (*Marketing* 1997). The challenge made by *Sugar* was noted by its main competitor, Emap Élan, which responded by launching a similar monthly *It's Bliss* in 1995,[1] and relaunching its former market leader, *Just Seventeen,* as *J-17* with a monthly bound edition in March 1997. '*Sugar* has raised the game considerably, in the same way that *J-17* did when it was first launched', remarked Sue Hawkin, then managing director of Emap Élan (cited in Cook 1997: 32). Its content was considered to 'reflect the confidence and the independence of an increasingly savvy target market', according to Caroline Simpson, head of press at Zenith Media (cited in Lee 2000: 6).

The teenage girls' magazine market at this time was marked not only in terms of overall growth in the sector but also by a move towards increased niche segmentation. By the mid-1990s publishers had begun to subdivide the teenage market into specific sectors, 'entertainment' (focusing on pop, media and celebrities) and 'lifestyle', which encompassed fashion, beauty, advice and 'real life' stories (*Campaign* 1997, 1999; *Sugar* 1997). The deployment of lifestyle as a structuring mechanism in this sector echoed the widespread take-up of such marketing discourses in the women's market more generally (Gough-Yates 2003). The move towards making and managing youth markets in terms of lifestyle rather than age has been noted by Osgerby (1998), and is suggestive of the increasing success of marketing in terms of 'taste cultures' organized for instance in terms of music, leisure and fashion (Miles 2000). However, while the marketing of teenage magazines has drawn on the discursive registers of lifestyle, it has not abandoned the more traditional ones of generation. Indeed, 'lifestyling' the teenage girl has necessitated a particular, and at times perhaps precarious, synthesis of the rhetorical codes of taste and style with those of gendered adolescent development. The teenage girls' magazine industry of the 1990s produced an astute profile of its ideal consumer market that linked the registers of lifestyle to those of 'life stage'. This is most clearly evidenced in the marketing pack produced by *Sugar* (1997), which identified three magazine 'life stages' for teenage girls, dovetailing these with specific publication titles. Each 'life stage' was accompanied by a sketch of the teenage girl where imagined attitudes and dispositions together with specific developmental needs were linked to particular demands as media consumers. Within such a framework magazines become both desirable products and indispensable guides to life for the developing teenage girl. The first of these 'life stages' is 'adolescence', which targets 11 to 14 year olds and is characterized as the 'pre-boyfriend years' where, according to the industry narrative, girls' interests circulate around media celebrities, television soap stars and posters of pop performers. This is followed by, and overlaps with, 'the teenage years' which targets 13 to 17 year olds and is distinguished as 'traumatic':

> Here relationships with parents and other authority figures are strained and boys have emerged as a major obsession. If girls within this life stage aren't already having sex they're certainly thinking about it. Appearance is also incredibly important and a spot could mean days locked behind the bedroom door. They are looking for support, guidance and friendship from their magazines – a best friend really.
>
> (*Sugar* 1997: np)

Magazines are presented as central to the successful management of this potentially troubled time, ensuring that readers emerge at the other end as confident and assertive 'young women'. This last stage covers the age range 17 to 20, by which time readers will have developed a 'strong sense of their own identity' and be looking to titles such as *More!* and *19* to confirm this (*Sugar* 1997).

The pattern of teenage consumer development sketched above draws on popular notions of adolescence as a significant period in which separating from parents and adopting accepted gender roles are viewed as central to successful 'growing up'. These understandings draw tacitly on developmental models of psychology and accounts of adolescence that characterize life stages in terms of specific tasks and challenges to be met in the quest to achieve a stable and coherent adult identity (Havighurst 1972; Newman and Newman 1987, both cited in Heaven 2001). Notions of the developmental role of consumption in such tasks intimated in these industry accounts can also be found in academic approaches (see Miles 2000). However, while academic debates often centre on questions of consumer autonomy versus commercial control, no such tensions emerge in industry narratives of teenage 'consumer sovereignty' (Bowlby 1993; Slater 1997; McGuigan 1998), with their celebrations of a 'postfeminist' sensibility marked by a sassy assertiveness and knowing pleasure (Brunsdon 1997; Winship 2000; Arthurs 2003). The image of the teenage girl constructed in these narratives of market expansion is one of a nascent consumer who can be encouraged to discipline her fickle habits and so 'build brand loyalty' for a lifetime's consumption of goods and services. Adolescent femininity is emphasized as both a natural stage of development and, at the same time, in need of careful management and training on the part of an informed editorial which steers her towards successful adult femininity through the practices of personal lifestyle consumption.

'It's what being a girl is all about': textual formats and lifestyle expertise

In his discussion of consumer culture, Don Slater (1997: 86) notes that forms of expert knowledge and guidance increasingly manage and mediate the relationship between 'consumer goods, services and experiences and the project of maintaining a self'. Teenage girls' magazines clearly position themselves within this culture of expertise and advise their readers on the task of 'becoming a girl' in specifically consumerist terms. Guiding their readers through a limited range of consumer goods, such as cosmetics and fashion, as well as mainstream media goods, such as chart CDs and DVDs, may seem minor league when compared to the consumer possibilities of the adult women's glossy market, but it is important to remember that these too produce '"discourses through and about objects" which allow us to orientate ourselves to the social meanings of things in a commercial world' (Slater 1997: 86). Such discourses of expertise are increasingly couched within the rhetoric of lifestyle, establishing particular and distinct taste cultures, sensibilities and dispositions (Featherstone 1991a). Teenage magazines in the 1990s made particular use of lifestyle signifiers in their attempt to signal their distinctiveness from previous formats and formations of adolescent commercial femininity:

> Hairy legs and hols don't mix. But if you're going ape about gorilla legs, don't fret. Just choose you ideal way to defuzz here.
>
> (*Bliss*, August 1997)

> Swanky stuff for less dosh alert! J17 loves this new 'Revolution' range of body sprays from Tesco.
>
> (*Just Seventeen*, 26 February 1997)

> Cheekbones. Kate Moss uses cream blushers, so nuff said really! They're great for a 'dewy look' – just rub into the apples of your cheeks with your finger tips ...
>
> (*J-17*, May 1997)

Personal consumer products such as cosmetics and toiletries feature highly across the contents of teenage magazines, both in the busy pages of consumer information that are interspersed throughout the contents and in longer features on make-up and grooming. Incitements to consume leap from almost every page and address the readership in terms of an imagined community of feminine shoppers (Talbot 1992). However, this assertive consumer address is somewhat tempered by the more ironic tone employed in magazines, which has become a dominant mode within contemporary magazines (McRobbie 1996), and which undercuts the more emphatic appeals in a playful way. Nevertheless, the emphasis given to product information, useful tips and solutions which make up the short and bitty copy of beauty features positions consumption as central to the work of femininity and instrumental in the process of 'becoming' a teenage girl. Advice and consumer information is conveyed using an upbeat and irreverent style, which emphasizes the pleasures of consumption and equates this work of femininity with fun. Magazine editorials position themselves as imparters of specific knowledges, instructors in feminine disciplines and authoritative consumer guides. While the language of these features is playful and the mode of address often knowing and irreverent, beauty advice still offers products as solutions to the problems of adolescent femininity.[2] Dissatisfactions of physical appearance are remedied through careful consumer choices and the reader is invited to look upon her self, and in particular her body, as a set of attributes that can be emphasized or managed, rather than as a whole. While such a discourse positions the feminine subject as active and assertive in her ability to 'manage' herself, the adolescent body is still configured as potentially unruly and in need of vigilant management to achieve a stable, mature femininity. As such, while the discursive mode of contemporary cosmetics features articulates a postfeminist and knowing address, this continues to draw on, albeit implicitly, more traditional models of femininity marked by insecurity and self-regulation (Ferguson 1983; Ballaster et al. 1991).

While the textual address used in editorial formats may produce an adolescent feminine subject in need of expert guidance, the visual display of products highlights the sensual pleasures of products and the fun associated with practices of self-beautification rituals. The cluttered, busy layouts of beauty pages with photographs of products laid against white backgrounds, or arranged in tasteful heaps, both signify an excess of consumption and invite an appreciative gaze from the viewer. The practice of displaying cosmetics, crumbling powders and spilling bottles across the page layout emphasizes the elemental qualities of the product and is suggestive of the tactile and sensual pleasures associated with making up and the ritualistic care of the self. Such incitements to pleasure are, perhaps, not wholly recoupable within the dominant discourses of consumer capitalism and heterosexuality, not least because at one level they operate in terms of visual pleasures through the sumptuous and sensual enjoyment of simply looking (Radner 1989). However, at the same time these visual appeals are productive of a particularly style-conscious feminine subject whose consumer skills extend towards aesthetic discernment as well as shopping know-how.

'*Sugar* coated love': fashioning the feminine self

From the outset, fashion coverage was a key element in *Sugar*'s efforts to differentiate itself from existing titles and to reshape the format of the teenage lifestyle magazine. The magazine carried more fashion pages than its competitors and was the first teenage title to invest in foreign shoots (*PPA* 2001). Unlike established titles of the time, spreads in *Sugar* ran to several pages and played with narrative and location in order to convey more complex imaginary and imaginative settings coupled with a greater emphasis on design and layout composition. Borrowing design features which echoed those associated with glossy publications lent a degree of authority and cultural capital (Bourdieu 1984) to the teenage title, connoting a sense of 'up-to-dateness' for both the clothes featured and the magazine itself. Specific signifiers of 'good design' such as the use of white space around text and photograph worked with a specific design directive to avoid clutter and emphasized the formal aspects of the images displayed. This was augmented by the use of close-ups and cropped images in which details such as a shoe lacing or bag clasp were pictured. Together, these stylistic devices pointed to an awareness of the conventions of fashion photography in older 'glossies' such as *Elle*, with its reputation as a style leader in the mainstream fashion press (Usherwood 1997; Jobling 1999; Gough-Yates 2003), and lent a degree of sophistication to this younger title.

The narratives of youthful femininity circulating in teenage fashion spreads employ specific signifiers to construct a set of representations of youth as 'fun'. This is a world of sun-filled shots of pleasure, leisure and romance located on beaches, pools and outdoor spaces. While the narrative spaces of teenage fashion spreads share something with the archetypes of fashion narrative identified by Barthes (1983), with their emphasis on leisure and luxurious consumption, within the sphere of adolescent femininity these spaces stand distinct from the everyday world of the teenager and work to convey a sense of excitement and out-of-the-ordinary-ness. This sense of anticipation is often framed within a discourse of heterosexual romance and the loose narrative structure of 'the date'. Linguistic codes draw equivalencies between the clothes features and the heightened emotions of romance, while visual codes ape the conventions of personal photography (Holland and Spence 1991) and layout and design schemes echo the collages associated with teen bedroom culture (Steele and Brown 1995) and handwritten diary entries.[3] The cultural signifiers employed in teen fashion spreads construct a generationally specific taste culture in which the fashioning of a feminine self entails particular modes of 'becoming'.

In addition to codes of romance, fashion spreads often make use of 'retro' styles and period detailing. These casual borrowings of 1950s and 1960s styling, and the loose references to historical period, can be seen as attempts to place contemporary youth within a continuum of adolescent experience organized in terms of post-war consumer culture. Appealing to a mythic construction of adolescence in terms of fun, consumption and (heterosexual) romance addresses the readership in terms of a postmodern knowing consumer well equipped with the cultural competencies of intertextuality and consumer savvy (McRobbie 1996). The props of the retro style shoot – painted black eyeliner, bubble cars and psychedelia – work as floating signifiers mobilizing sets of meanings that play across different historical periods. Recognition of them serves to construct an imagined community of teenagers across different historical and geographic locales and naturalizes the consumer logic of adolescence that circulates in magazines.

'Welcome to Snogsville': disciplining desire and the expertise of lovin'

The publishers of teenage magazines justify their features on sex and relationships in terms of meeting the specific emotional and developmental needs of their readerships. Bound by regulatory concerns and, since 1996, specific mechanisms (TMAP 1996; Wellings 1996), together with a sense of what will appeal to readers, the magazines maintain strict editorial guidelines on what will be covered (Baker 1997). Features tend to focus on mapping out a set of preparatory stages to heterosexual romantic relationships, rather than the technicalities of sex, and emphasize a developmental approach to adolescent sexuality more generally. While teen magazines tend not to cover the mechanics of sexual intercourse in great detail, unlike titles aimed at the older market such as *More!* (Kehily 1999), they share a specifically 'technicizing' approach in their discursive construction of adolescent sexuality. 'Becoming' a (heterosexual) girl is bound up with the acquisition and practice of specific knowledges, skills and aptitudes and is characterized by a specifically reflexive approach to the feminine self.

In keeping with their general upbeat and irreverent style, magazines often approach features on heterosexual relationships in a similarly light-hearted and humorous manner. However, this is limited to items that deal with the etiquette of relationships, rather than matters of sexual health and intercourse. Common to this format are articles which detail the social and technical aspects of romance, such as kissing, being 'asked out' and 'ditching'. These items take the form of light-hearted anthropological guides to sexual and social practices emphasizing the new and potentially unsettling world of heterosexuality which readers are assumed to be entering. Positioning themselves as authoritative guides, different scenarios are discussed and techniques evaluated. The irreverent and informal style of such articles positions romance as an entertaining aspect of 'becoming' a girl. The adolescent feminine subject is addressed as a quick learner who will soon utilize her newly acquired skills for pleasure. At the same time, however, these work to produce and maintain normative models of social and sexual behaviour and invite a mode of engagement based upon self-regulation wherein both bodily and emotional practices need to be checked and performed appropriately in order to 'become' a girl successfully. While the style of these articles is colloquial and humorous, it also suggests that the magazine editorial has a role to play in demystifying the complexities of romance for the reader. Heterosexual dating is constructed as both a natural developmental stage, and as potentially hazardous and unsettling.

Consistent with popular discourses of self-help literature, the adolescent masculinities circulating in the pages of teen magazines are generally constructed as naturally fixed and stable in their attributes and flaws.[4] Girls are encouraged to learn and understand these masculine types, tics and foibles in an effort to manage their relationships successfully. As such femininity is conceived of as a reflexive project of the self, attuned and responsive to the actions of others. This is by no means a new discursive strategy (Ehrenreich and English 1979; Coward 1984); however, it is updated and reinvigorated by reference to a specifically postfeminist disposition where knowledge means power – over boys.

The figure of the 'postfeminist girlie', epitomized in the UK by the Channel 4 television production *The Girlie Show* (1996) and the advertising campaign for Rimmel cosmetics ('It's not make-up – it's ammunition'), conveyed a specific feminine identity which blurred the signifiers of traditional feminine attractiveness with the flaunting of some more feminist sensibilities. This postfeminist girlie was attractive, determined and resolutely heterosexual, championing her desire while critiquing certain aspects of masculine behaviour and culture. Her positive citation in teen magazine features on sex and relationships produced an assertive configuring of heterosexual relations wherein dubious masculine strategies required tactical outsmarting both linguistically and practically. Readers were advised to manage boys through sassy quips and respond with a snappy retort or 'girl power put-down' (*J-17*, May 1997). Within the pages of magazines, 'becoming' a (hetero-) sexually smart teenage girl required accomplishing developmental tasks and solving gendered problems through the careful deployment of knowledge and learnt expertise.

Life and style beyond the pages: extending the brand

While magazine formats circulate particular configurations of adolescent commercial femininity, the meanings of the 'brand' and its particular version of adolescent femininity increasingly find life beyond the pages of the magazine. *Sugar* magazine has been at the forefront of branding opportunities in the teenage sector and is considered to be second only to *Cosmopolitan* in offering a wide range of brand extensions, according to the publisher's managing director Vivien Cotterill (*Media Week* 2001). 'It was immediately apparent to *Sugar* publisher Lara Watkins, that the "baby glossy exist[ed] beyond its pages"' (Bainbridge and Lake 2001), and its publishers were quick to capitalize on this, offering a compilation album in 1997 and launching a clothing and lingerie line through

Littlewoods catalogues the following year. Brand extension is viewed by the industry as a risky but potentially lucrative venture for magazines to embark on. Getting the balance between core qualities of the brand and the associated product can mean harnessing extra revenues, while misadventure can spell financial ruin (Wilkinson 1998). *Sugar*'s enthusiasm to capitalize on such opportunities signals a detailed knowledge of the spending habits of its target readership and a commitment to extending lifestyle as a marketing concept in this sector. The marketing buzz surrounding the launch of *Sugar* 'lifestyle environments' in leading Debenhams department stores in 2000 was indicative of the optimism surrounding the brand's development at the time (Brech 2000). This ambitious scheme linked magazine brand style to retail environment with the commissioning of specific 'lifestyle environments' that would 'aim to recreate the magazine's "Pick 'n' Mix" fashion spreads' (Brech 2000: 5). Synergies between the brand and retailer would also include feature advertising in the store's magazine, again adopting the *Sugar* house style, as well as coverage of the range in *Sugar*.

Opportunities for 'tie-ups', linking other brands and products with the magazine, are also part of the magazine's wider promotional strategy. The '*Sugar* Show', launched in 2000 offered 'heavyweight' brands such as Procter & Gamble the chance to 'target teens directly' (*Media Week* 2001), while the Rimmel-sponsored *Sugar* model competition 2002 linked particularly consumerist teen fantasies of 'becoming' a model with guaranteed future editorial and the well known high street cosmetic brand.[5]

Branding opportunities have focused on products already associated with the teenage market – fashion, clothing, accessories and stationery – as well as attempting to secure inroads into various digital media platforms: *Sugar* launched the '*Sugar* Virtual Makeover' CD-Rom in 2001 (Bainbridge and Lake 2001) as well as offering a text messaging (SMS) service to readers (PPA 2001). Marketing industry papers have for several years posted news of imminent digital television launches for various teen titles. At the time of writing, *Sugar* is set to feature in four MTV-branded television shows while featuring 'MTV branded editorial' in its pages (*The Guardian* 2004). This cross-promotional venture is viewed positively by brand consultancy executive Jez Frampton, who asserts that in a rapidly changing marketing environment where teen consumers change allegiances and interests almost continually, this 'provides greater depth of content and the instant feed from a publishing point of view as to what is going on. It will help MTV continue from global brand to local relevance' (cited in *The Guardian* 2004).

In economic terms, successful brand extension offers publishers ways of further harnessing advertising revenues, offering clients multiplatform packages and so helping to stave off competition in an unpredictable market (Bainbridge and Lake 2001). Brand developments also represent attempts by 'cultural intermediaries' to manage the consumption practices of their 'fickle' market through extending the rhetoric of lifestyle further.

The narrative presented here might at first seem to present a story of ever-increasing brand colonization and controlled teen consumption, an example perhaps of the ways that discourses of lifestyle inevitably organize the project of the self in consumerist terms. However, it is worth noting how short-lived and often unsuccessful many of these ventures are. The *Sugar* clothing range has long since disappeared from Debenhams' rails and the 'Makeover' CD-Roms can be found in the discounted bins at PC stores. The unpredictable teenage consumer both drives this market and haunts it, failed projects a constant reminder of her capricious and unruly tastes.

Conclusion

In this chapter I have explored some of the developments in the British teenage magazine market in the mid-1990s in relation to discourses of lifestyle and consumer culture. I have argued that during this period attempts were made to interweave discourses of lifestyle with more traditional notions of adolescence as a significant developmental 'life stage'. This produced a particular imagining of teenage femininity as a process of 'becoming'. This notion of 'becoming' was mobilized in an attempt to capture distinct, and potentially contradictory, understandings of adolescent femininity as, on the one hand, a natural stage of development and, on the other, a consumer project of the self. 'Becoming' a teenage girl necessitates a careful consumer operation to successfully manage the 'natural' self. Across the editorial formats of beauty, fashion and relationships advice, teenage magazines impart instruction and advice in the development of appropriate consumer tastes and also the care and management of the self, which is constructed as a site of both physical and emotional labour. Training in the particular lifestyle cultures of adolescent femininity is not simply a matter of acquiring knowledge of appropriate taste cultures (which product? what band? which shop?) but extends to the interior landscape of the self as well. Magazine texts focus on the bodies, minds and thoughts of the imagined teenage girl. Such representations of femininity offer not only stylized models for the construction of self, but also practical and technical knowledge that can be enacted in various practices of shopping, grooming and self-reflection.

Recent feminist research in media and cultural studies has drawn attention to the complexity of women's and girls' relationship with discourses and practices of consumption as a potentially productive site for the constitution of new feminine identities and also a mechanism of self-regulation (Nava 1992; Macdonald 1995; Andrews and Talbot 2000; Hollows 2000). While this chapter has focused on the ways in which commercial industries and discourses mobilized particular images of 'becoming' as a means of capturing and managing a potentially 'fickle' market, it should not be assumed that the consumption of teenage magazines mirrors these narratives of gender formation. The relationship between teenage girls and the magazines they read cannot simply be assumed or 'read off' from the texts themselves and instead requires careful mapping and reflection.

Notes

1. Relaunched as *Bliss* in 1996.
2. See also Ostermann and Keller-Cohen's (1998) discussion of the 'problem-solution' structure of quizzes in teenage magazines.
3. In the example 'Sugar coated love' (*Bliss*, November 1997), mock Polaroid shots of the couple are annotated in freehand with the interior thoughts of the girl pictured: 'He really makes me laugh – I think I'm falling ...' 'she' muses, setting up the narrative sequence that follows. The theme of romance is further conveyed through a variety of visual signifiers. The models' poses conform to those expected of the romantic couple with the pair leaning in towards one another and the boy's arm drawn protectively around the girl's shoulder. The use of a star filter in this shot also works to enhance the connotations of romance, bathing the couple in an orange glow that ties them visually to the orange of the word 'love' in the title.
4. See, for example, Gray's (1992) sociobiological approach to gender relations and also Cameron (2000) for a critical discussion on consumption of this genre.
5. See Lumby's (2001) discussion of narratives of modeling in Australian teenage magazines.

13 Gender, childhood and consumer culture

Melissa Tyler and Rachel Russell

In this chapter we consider the relationship between gender and consumer culture with specific reference to what Allisa Quart (2003: xxvi) has described as 'the unbearable commercialization of youth'. The research on which the chapter is based began in 2000, and focused initially on a UK-based chain of retail outlets called Girl Heaven (Russell and Tyler 2002), aimed primarily at 3 to 13-year-old girls and described variously as 'a piece of retail folklore' (Lumsden 1999) and as 'Guardian Wimmin Hell' (Kettle 1999). In 2003, we followed up this study with a broader focus on the relationship between young girls' lived experiences of consumer culture and gender acquisition. The aim of this second phase of the research was to reflect on the transition from childhood to teenage status for the same group of teenage girls who took part in the initial research, to consider, with particular reference to their experience of consumer culture, both continuities and changes in their under-standing of gender, and to examine the role of media culture in shaping their lived experience of gender and consumer culture.

Our discussion here argues that while on the one hand retail environments such as Girl Heaven appear to provide a celebratory social space in which girls can affirm their femininity, they also seem to epitomize the commercial appropriation of childhood and the transition into young adulthood. As a way into exploring these two alternatives, our focus is concerned initially with what it means to 'do' feminine childhood and young adulthood against the backdrop of contemporary consumer culture. It then outlines the methodological approach that we took to researching Girl Heaven, and the ways in which we explored young girls' lived experience of consumer culture and gender acquisition more generally in the second phase of our research. Our analysis culminates in an attempt to reflect critically on the complex relationship between consumer culture and the process of becoming a young woman, highlighting the ways in which this is mediated, at least in part, by consumer culture. We reflect on retail formats such as Girl Heaven – with which, our research suggests, young girls themselves are acutely aware of having a relationship that is far from straightforward – as a notable manifestation of this complexity.

Gender and consumer culture

There is a growing body of literature that explores the relationship between gender and consumption (McRobbie 1994, 1996; Lury 1995; Radner 1995), much of which emphasizes that shopping occupies a pivotal place both in shaping and manifesting this relationship (Falk and Campbell 1997). Much of this material has focused on commodification, but it has also drawn attention to the social significance of 'girlie' culture; to the ability of young women to challenge, resist, parody and ultimately undermine hegemonic representations of what it means to be, or rather become, a woman through various aspects of consumer culture, and particularly shopping as a quintessentially 'girlie' pastime. The term 'girl' is clearly a marker of status, denoting both a positioning within childhood but also a relatively passive designation within a gender hierarchy, one that the (now seemingly defunct) theme of 'girl power' attempted to rearticulate.

Callum Lumsden (1999), who designed the concept of Girl Heaven, states that girl power was the starting point for its design and development. The idea was to develop a chain of retail outlets in the UK specifically for 3 to 13-year-old girls that not only stocked a range of (largely dressing up and party) clothes, hair styling products, cosmetics and accessories, but also provided the opportunity for girls to have a makeover – 'to be transformed into a princess' – in-store. This theme is fundamental to Girl Heaven's self-presentation as something of a gynocentric retail space in which femininity is able to celebrate itself; 'where a little girl's dreams would come true' – 'glittery but not tacky . . . it could not be stereotypical, but neither could it be demure and bashful', as Lumsden (1999) puts it. Girl Heaven, he emphasizes, therefore took its inspiration from girl power and its cultural celebration of what it means to be 'girlie'.

That Girl Heaven should take girl power, with its emphasis on the cultural celebration of femininity through consumption, as the aesthetic starting point for its stores, seemed to make it a particularly appropriate focus for our analysis. In the case of young girls particularly, the capacity to function as effective consumers seems to be honed largely through the pursuit of an ideal femininity that we consider here with reference to Girl Heaven and the (relatively neglected) relationship specifically between childhood, consumer culture and gender. In focusing on the intersection between these three dimensions of what it means to be a young girl in contemporary consumer society – to be a child, to be a consumer, and to be feminine – our aim here is primarily to explicate something of the complexity and ambiguity of young girls' perceptions of Girl Heaven as a particular example of the relationship between feminine childhood and consumption, and of their engagement with consumer culture and the process of becoming a woman more generally.

Researching Girl Heaven, gender and consumer culture

What we aimed to produce was a kind of 'ethnographic confrontation' with the seemingly normal, taken for granted aspects of femininity and consumer culture encountered in the everyday lives of the girls who took part. Yet as Dorothy Smith (1988) has argued, a methodological focus on everyday experience cannot deliver a critical understanding of the conditions which produce that lived experience, particularly those that place structural limitations on it. With this in mind, our initial research focused on Girl Heaven specifically, but also involved a broader analysis of the relationship between childhood, femininity and consumer culture. During this stage we focused on customers and staff, and particularly, on the aesthetic dimension of Girl Heaven as a text. We were concerned to get a 'feel' for Girl Heaven, paying attention to lighting, music, frontage, layout and space in its stores. We were also concerned with how femininity was defined within Girl Heaven, reflecting, to put it simply, on what the store seemed to be saying about what it means to be a 'Girl' and to be in 'Heaven'. As well as participant observation, this initial research focused on representations of femininity in marketing and sales literature, on the company website and in the stores themselves. We also accompanied eight girls – all 10 and 11 year-olds (who were already known to each other socially, and thus had an established rapport) – on a store visit to Girl Heaven. We observed them while shopping in the store and carried out a group interview immediately afterwards. In this way, the store visit served as a stimulus in the group discussion. The girls could provide vivid interpretations of their perceptions of the store and used their purchases, as well as their time with each other, to strengthen descriptions of their experiences of Girl Heaven.

At the end of the group interview, we invited them to draw a picture of Girl Heaven (and to return it to us at a later date). This added to the aesthetic dimension of the research methodology, focusing on the girls' own perceptions of what Girl Heaven feels and looks like, and also responds to the findings of previous methodological research on childhood that, while acknowledging some of the potential difficulties of such an approach (Backett and Alexander 1991; Harden et al. 2000), emphasizes the importance of giving children the opportunity to reflect on their own interpretations of the social world (James and Prout 1997).

The follow-up research, carried out some three years later, involved arranging a shopping trip for six of the girls who took part in the first phase of the study (now aged 14 and 15), and issuing them with disposable cameras to make a photo diary of their day together. We then subjected these photographs to textual analysis and used this data, as well as visual displays of the images, to underpin a follow-up group discussion, the transcript of which we analysed in light of our previous findings.

Our account, then, is something of a mosaic from which we hope it might be possible to discern an overall picture of Girl Heaven, and of what it suggests to us about the relationship between consumer culture and gender. Our analysis attempts to reflect critically on the ways in which a number of girls understand the mediated images of femininity targeted at them and examines how the discourse of femininity, in Girl Heaven particularly and in contemporary consumer culture more generally, is played out in these girls' consciousness of gender. Following Corarso (1997), our concern is with children as active agents in the construction of their 'everyday' social world yet constrained by the structures and relations of this world.

Mediating children's lifestyles

As sociologists such as Giddens (1991) and Jenks (1996) have noted, contemporary life is marked by a relatively high degree of uncertainty and confusion, especially for those facing the prospect of leaving the relatively safe environment of childhood and entering the unknown world of young adulthood. As Jenks (1996: 104) puts it, contemporary society 'calls for a constant, reflexive re-presentation of self ... critical to the experience of being a child'. This means that 'tweenies' in particular want to ensure as much as possible that they will fit in and seek external confirmation that this is likely to be the case, often through 'branding' (Quart 2003).

Girl Heaven is described by Callum Lumsden (1999) as a retail format that lets little girls 'live a dream'. He goes on to assert that Girl Heaven sums up the spirit of an evolution towards stores as places to do more than just shop. This is clearly reflected in the look and feel of the shopping centres in which the Girl Heaven stores are located, as well as the stores themselves. They are sanitized, carefully regulated spaces in which the boundaries between consumption and leisure are seemingly conflated. Embracing this 'consumption as leisure' format, Girl Heaven tends to be clearly distinguishable from other retails outlets occupying the same commercial space largely due to its aesthetic – it is loud, bright and has a discernible colour and style theme that serves to differentiate it from other stores in the vicinity.

During our initial research, the girls involved seemed very aware that their attention (and their purchasing power) was being competed for, and noted that Girl Heaven could be distinguished from its competitors largely on the basis of its look and feel, its background music and particularly its colour scheme. Indeed, colour was considered to be a vital component of the design and the design team decided that 'everything should be in pink . . . and glittery, with lots of hearts'. This provided the 'style theme' throughout the project and, as Lumsden puts it, helped to bring to life the idea that the presentation of the products should be a 'magical' experience' (Lumsden 1999). Once the concept of Girl Heaven had been established, inspired by the theme of girl power, an experiential conflation of consumption and leisure and a strong 'girlie' aesthetic characterized by an abundance of pink, glitter and heart shapes, 'Girl Heaven could start to *take design ownership of some of the icons* which were to be employed within the concept' (Lumsden 1999, emphasis added).

Indeed, customers are enticed into the stores by the glittery theatricality of what it has to offer. What makes Girl Heaven distinct, we noted from our own fieldnotes, is a kind of 'sensory overload' or what Welsch (1996: 18) calls a 'hyperaestheticization'. This is experienced through a combination of music, abundant use of glitter, bright white lighting and flooring, combined with chrome fittings, pink lettering and iconography (hearts and stars), as well as rows of sparkly costumes and make-up. In addition to the various aesthetic signifiers of Girl Heaven, sales staff perform dance routines regularly at the front of the stores, creating 'an atmosphere of excitement' (Lumsden 1999). This reflects a much broader performance ethos underpinning the organization as a whole and, at least in part, differentiating Girl Heaven from similar retail organizations.

In this respect, the marketing team developed a number of other features designed to differentiate the Girl Heaven brand from other retail 'experiences'. As Lumsden (1999) describes it: 'Not only does Girl Heaven stock all things feminine and girly [sic], it provides its young customers with the opportunity to be transformed into a princess in the store'. At the front of the stores are located spaces called the Princess Studios – hair styling and make-up areas where customers can have their hair and nails done, as well as a range of themed makeovers. Once they have been 'made over', girls can have their photographs taken on a pink velvet 'throne' wearing a 'jewelled' cloak. Shop assistants and customers alike are then able to observe the girl's 'special' treatment, performing as an appreciative audience and paying homage to her aesthetic femininity.

Surrounded by three-way mirrors, the girls thus sit on their pink velvet thrones as objects of vision who 'watch themselves being looked at' (Berger 1972: 46).

Crucially, Lumsden (1999) stresses: 'This shop was not to be seen as an exploitation of children: it had to represent their dreams, and every girl who visited Girl Heaven had to feel as though she had walked into a shop which was there just for her'. In respect of the 'just for her' ethos, Lumsden emphasizes how the concept of Girl Heaven, which he describes as 'a piece of retail theatre', reflects the extent to which

> customers are no longer willing to accept that the shops they visit are just places to buy goods. They demand drama and deserve to be delighted by the experience. Shops have become destinations in themselves – not only a place to purchase, but a place to be entertained, inspired and, in the case of Girl Heaven, to have loads of fun.
>
> (Lumsden 1999: 6)

The commercial perception seems to be that girls are never too young to be self-conscious about their bodily appearance and to define their identity in relation to a relatively narrow set of social and cultural reference points, but also to be 'inspired' and 'have loads of fun' in the process. The various layers of text that constitute Girl Heaven are made up of largely aesthetic citations of 'little girls', heaven, angels, stars, hearts, flowers and glitter. It seems to us at least that a clear performance imperative underpins Girl Heaven's definition of femininity, one that is continually reinscribed through repetition of these idiomatic themes and images. This performative element resonates well with Judith Butler's (1993: 232) contention:

> To the extent that the naming of the 'girl' is transitive, that is, initiates the process by which a certain 'girling' is compelled, the term, or rather, its symbolic power, governs the formation of a corporeally enacted femininity that never fully approximates the norm.

What this means, Butler argues, is that a 'girl' is compelled to continually cite particular gender norms in order to qualify as feminine to the extent that 'femininity is ... not the product of a choice, but the forcible citation of a norm' (Butler 1993: 232). In the case of femininity, Butler argues that these norms are largely aesthetic and corporeal. As she puts it, however, 'femininity is often cast as the spectacular gender' (p. 235), and as one that can never fully achieve a subjective realization of the endlessly cited norms pursued. It was particularly interesting, in this respect, to discover how our respondents engaged with these norms and with the construction of femininity in Girl Heaven.

The main topic of our initial post-shopping group discussion was the spectacular nature of femininity on show in Girl Heaven. The girls told us that it would be easy to identify Girl Heaven as a girl's shop even if it wasn't called 'Girl Heaven' because of the hearts, glitter, bright lights and make-up, its 'pinkness' and 'girlie colours'. These were not, they concluded, 'a boy thing'. They emphasized that 'girlie things' would dominate a girl heaven because 'girls like shopping', it 'is in their nature' and it is a 'girlie thing'. This, many of them argued, served to differentiate them from boys – boys shop 'when they have to', girls shop 'because they like it'. To be feminine, in this respect, seemed very much to be defined according to the two aesthetic dimensions outlined earlier – that to be feminine means to conform to an aesthetic ideal of femininity, and that femininity itself is an aesthetic phenomenon. To be a girl, and to be in heaven, means to be surrounded by lots of 'lovely', 'girlie' things – concrete, aesthetic objectifications of femininity – but also to have an abundance of products that assist in the pursuit of an ideal feminine 'look'. The notion that it was specific products and artefacts that defined 'girlieness' could also be seen in their drawings, which tended to be based on literal representations of the commodification of femininity. Some of the more popular consumable objects cited, both in the group discussion and in the drawings, were glitter make-up and hair styling products that came in teddy bear or flower, heart or bow shaped packaging. They were (feminized) aesthetic products in themselves (effectively toys), but also products designed for the pursuit of an ideal feminine appearance.

Their constant repetition of the term 'girlie' intrigued us. We were told that 'Buffy the Vampire Slayer' – a character in a television series they had previously identified as their hero (because 'she appears stronger than boys, and girls are not really stronger than boys') – would not shop at Girl Heaven because it was for 'girlie girls': 'Buffy doesn't do glitter'. We responded by asking them if they were 'girlie girls', a question met by a resounding 'NO' – largely due it seems to their affection for and skill at lunchtime football games. 'Girlie girls', we were told, do not like dirt, they are 'clean and shiny' and 'they wear nice things that might get dirty'. However, following this rather swift dismissal of a 'girlie' identity, one by one they started making comments like 'well, I'm a bit girlie', 'I like hair stuff', until they had collectively decided that they were in fact 'half girlie' and 'half [their terminology] normal'. Their definition of 'normal' as being 'not girlie' seemed, to us at least, to be a poignant articulation of femininity as Otherness. As one particular girl put it, 'Half girlie means to be different, to do things that only girls do ... like go shopping, do your hair, ... not get dirty, but being normal is ... well, just normal, it doesn't mean not being girlie, just normal'.

With regard to what it meant to them to be 'girlie', the girls we interviewed were particularly concerned with the Princess Studio – another area in which their engagement with Girl Heaven appeared complex and contradictory. At first they described this as 'a totally bad idea', it was 'too over the top' and the Girl Heaven 'beauty experts' were 'much too young' to know what they were doing. It transpired, however, that what they objected to was the idea of being made up into a specific character. They did not want to be a princess or a fairy. They wanted eye shadow, rainbow nails and glitter – to be 'made up' rather than 'made over'. The distinction seemed to be one of degrees of hyper-femininity. Being 'made up' would be okay because it was 'over the top', whereas being 'made over' would be 'too over the top'. They seemed to be very conscious that femininity can easily become 'excessive' and is, therefore, something that needs to be kept in check. But this feeling did not seem to sit comfortably with their objection to the specific, prescribed makeovers that Girl Heaven had on offer. They were aware of the need to contain a feminine appearance, it seemed, but objected to Girl Heaven's imposition of particular characters on their appearance – keeping their own femininity from going 'over the top' appeared to be something that the girls wanted to take on themselves. They seemed to identify this taking responsibility for controlling their own gender, and for managing its aesthetic dimension, as something of a rite of passage, as a subjective experience important to being a young woman concerned with appearance rather than a child engaged in play.

In our follow-up research the purchasing and consumer behaviour of those who took part in the study appeared to reflect the precarious status of young girls immersed in the transition from childhood to teenage status. Several 'aspirational' objects, spaces and practices (Edwards 2000; Cook 2003) featured in the photographic element of the research, for instance, including photos of adult make-up and clothing. These were contrasted with photos of 'make-up as sweets' (cosmetic products that look 'chewy' and which are effectively packaged as toys – see Quart 2003). Much of this merchandising of course positions young girls as both the subjects and the objects of consumption. Photos of little girls' handbags, of baby clothes and also of teddy bears that appeared to reinforce the girls' occupation of what Cook (2003) calls 'proprietary spaces' – spaces to which the girls felt they belonged, and objects that signified this – also featured.

Many of the consumer goods that featured in the photographic element of the research were what we might call 'aesthetic artefacts' – carrier bags featuring teen brands were particularly popular; cosmetics, hair accessories, handbags and other articles implicated in the pursuit of an ideal feminine appearance were also apparent. Branding was a strong theme in this particular part of the research. There were several photos of store frontages, shops that the post-shopping discussion revealed were important to the girls' consumer cultural map. Again suggesting transition, this map featured a mix of 'proprietary' and 'aspirational' spaces.

As well as in relation to the consumption of objects and spaces, this transitional theme was also articulated in terms of the framing of consumer practices – often in terms of risk, confusion and in the apparent need for a parallel sense of identification and differentiation (the post-shopping interview in particular, as well as the photo diaries, emphasized a need to fit in and stand out simultaneously). Simultaneous processes of socialization (reflecting various themes in contemporary social theory such as sociability and proximity, for instance), and also individualization (a sense of competition, performance and pressure in relation to consumer culture and gender) were also apparent in this respect:

> It's like when you are walking down the street and you don't want other girls looking at you and thinking 'oh God, what's she wearing?' You want other girls to respect you and think you look good or whatever. Girls can be bitchy towards you because with boys it's more important, like how you play football, but with girls you are judged by how you look.
>
> (Group interview, November 2003)

The girls that took part in the research reported a sense of being targeted and 'branded' (Quart 2003) by increasingly sophisticated and prevalent commercial and marketing interests; a theme that manifested itself in various ways such as performance anxiety, choice as confusion, and an awareness of 'tweenagers' as a market segment. Several of the girls had seemingly sought to convey this theme visually, through taking photographs of queues for cash dispensers outside high street banks, for instance: 'It's a nightmare … you have to spend such a lot of time in queues at cash machines just to keep up with all the stuff you are supposed to buy' (Group interview, November 2003).

A related theme to emerge from our follow-up research, one that echoed the findings of our earlier work, was an ambivalent experience of gender, as the girls referred variously to both the pleasures and the pressures of femininity as it is experienced in and through consumer culture. Shopping, at least for the girls that took part in our research, is clearly a communal activity, but one in which, as several of the girls noted, they are ultimately alone: 'It's really hard, there's just so much pressure to buy stuff and to look good' (Group interview, November 2003). The post-shopping group discussion was shaped by recollections of shopping together, sharing advice and particularly by the communal experience of 'choosing': 'It is good to be together ... when you're shopping on your own it's less fun ... you feel kind of lonely' (Group interview, November 2003). However, major purchases (perhaps coats or shoes) were framed as occasions when girls would go alone or with parents. A sense of isolation also marked the discussion of ineffective consumption practices (and objects) – making mistakes and returning goods was discussed largely as a shameful activity, a form of inconspicuous consumption best carried out alone, or better still not done at all. In fact, in our group discussion, references to inappropriate purchases and to 'taking things back' was the only time when the girls looked uncomfortable, so much so that ineffective consumption almost became a taboo subject: 'I'd never take things back, never do it. I just get my Mum to buy me another thing' (Group interview, November 2003).

In both the initial research and the follow-up study, the girls seemed only too aware of the extent to which they are continually presented with images of perfect beauty in the pages of teen magazines and various other media forms (such as television and cinema as well as pop music), and that in many ways this serves to differentiate them from boys of their own age. Accompanying these images are articles and, increasingly, what have come to be known as 'advertorials', that specify the components of this perfection – perfect skin, hair, body size, shape and so on. Such textual messages, as Duke and Kreshel (1998: 64) note, often draw attention to flaws and imperfections that girls might not otherwise have been conscious of. The female body – dissected – becomes in need of constant reparation and transformation (or make-over); all this while organizations such as Girl Heaven simultaneously encourage girls to 'be themselves' and to 'have loads of fun'.

Girls are invited to participate in a shared, clean, safe, bright and glittery atmosphere divorced from the messiness and apprehensions of the world outside. Yet at a superficial level, entry into heaven presupposes a shared cultural experience of 'girlhood'. Divisions disappear, girls are girls, they are the same. While girls do seem to shop together as a social experience in Girl Heaven (and our participant observation of girls shopping together confirms this), 'choosing' being rather more fun when carried out with friends, this choosing in company, as Bauman (1998: 30) notes, only highlights the nature of consumption as a thoroughly individual act – a testimony to the 'individuality of choice' at the heart of consumer culture (see also Bauman 1988). This is echoed by Smith (2000: 6), who argues that the 'approach is made to them collectively, but they must then make the same purchasing decision individually, millions of times over'. Here the gender/consumption relationship is perhaps at its most visible. 'Little angels' are engaged in the competitive process of consumption in order to 'become'. Becoming, a collective, intersubjective and embodied experience, is rationalized (reduced to a series of rational principles such as the purchasing and 'correct' application of particular products) and homogenized. The endlessly repetitive themes pursued mean that femininity is reduced to a conception of the aesthetic as superficial and monotonous; girls are positioned as perpetual consumers of objects, rather than as creators of their own lived experience. Contra Giddens (1991), the proliferation of choice in this respect seems to operate as a constraint – girls are never far away from the notion that, by definition, they must continually consume. Hence, this complex positioning is further compounded because the little angel is encouraged to engage, for a fee, the services of an expert for advice on the ultimate in feminine transformations (paving the way for her future engagement of a range of hair, face and body 'experts' throughout her adult life) and mapping out her route through the abundance of options with which she is continually presented.

It seems that in this respect the processes we have identified at work in Girl Heaven are embedded within the more general norms, values, attitudes and expectations that shape girls' and young women's engagement with consumer culture, in which the relationship between power and play is complex and often contradictory. This complexity was expressed by the girls we interviewed in their apparent ambivalence towards a 'girlie' identity, as they veered between conceiving of being 'girlie' as something to be denied, almost ashamed of, and emphasizing that being 'girlie' was to be celebrated and affirmed. In this respect they expressed, quite incisively, both their ambiguous ontological status as children and their ambivalence towards becoming a woman. In a sense, both conceiving of themselves as 'girlie' *and* recognizing their complex relationship with this particular aspect of their identity seemed (somewhat ironically) to be something that bound the girls we interviewed into a collective sense of belonging together. However, what they also shared in common was an aesthetic conception of a 'girlie' identity – for them, to be 'girlie' meant to appear as, or to look, hyper-feminine. During our discussion, they tended to conflate a feminine identity with various aesthetic artefacts identified in the product range at Girl Heaven as exclusively feminine – jewellery, hair accessories, make-up and fashion items, for instance. Many of these have traditionally been conceived of as icons of hyper-femininity, such as feather boas. While they considered the staff at Girl Heaven too young to be able to give 'expert' advice to them about the process of transforming these artefacts into an appropriate 'feminine look', they did not question the fact that as girls they needed this advice. As they said, 'girls are more conscious of their appearance. As there is more on offer for them to choose from, girls feel they have to be'. In the simplicity of its formula, Girl Heaven seems to commodify this complexity – this ambivalence towards being 'girlie' and the ambiguous ontological status of childhood – very effectively.

Conclusions

Because of this complexity, the intended meanings of the producers of texts such as Girl Heaven seem to have only a partial impact on girls' actual engagement with practices of consumption, childhood and femininity. Our research also emphasizes, however, that girls seem to be less willing or able to negotiate the idea of a 'standard' of physical beauty inherent in the images directed at them. This seems to suggest that the ironic distance McRobbie's (1994) work highlights – the idea that girls and women are now able to reflect more critically on aesthetic standards of what it means to be feminine than was the case previously – does indeed appear to be present in girls' perceptions of dominant prescriptions on how to 'do' gender but *not* in their conception that an ideal way of doing gender exists. Girl Heaven seems to instil in girls and young women, then, not a step-by-step guide to becoming feminine, but the idea that they should be body conscious; that they should analyse their bodies and identify ways in which they deviate from the ideal. The girls that contributed to our research were extremely conscious of the importance of looking feminine to their social acceptability, but resented the imposition of being transformed into commercially defined characters (they wanted to be made up rather than made over).

Although the findings of our research suggest the extent to which girls actively engage, as they 'do' gender, in making meaning through their everyday interaction with texts such as Girl Heaven, they seem to do so albeit 'knowingly' (McRobbie 1994), but also bearing in mind that society has very clear expectations of their gender performance. They do gender, it seems, at a critical time in their lives when an appreciative audience, one willing to applaud the authenticity of their act, is particularly important to them. This means that although they appear to have a wide range of options available to them in terms of *how* to become feminine, the compulsion is always to do so in such a way as to pursue both an externally imposed feminine aesthetic, and a notion of femininity itself as an aesthetic phenomenon.

Acknowledgements

We would like to thank those girls who gave up valuable shopping time (twice!) to take part in our research. An earlier version of this chapter was published as 'Thank heaven for little girls: "Girl Heaven" and the commercial context of feminine childhood', *Sociology* 36(3): 619–37.

14 A taste for science
Inventing the young in the national interest

Johannah Fahey, Elizabeth Bullen and Jane Kenway

The atmosphere inside the exhibition room of P.T. Barnum's American Museum is charged to a fevered pitch as a captivated public scrutinize his form of popular anthropology. Chang and Eng the Siamese twins, Madame Clofullia the bearded woman, and Jo-Jo the Dog-faced Boy, so-called 'freaks of nature', are a spectacle on display for the masses. A century later, the BBC's *Tomorrow's World* is beamed into the homes of an equally captivated British television audience enthralled by the new inventions driving the media age. As science and the media converge, the scientist becomes a compelling personality popularizing science. Attenborough speaks in a whisper while crouched in the depths of a verdant forest, Bronowski traces the ascent of man while overshadowed by the Sphinx, Suzuki ponders the nature of things, and Julius Sumner Miller asks 'Why is it so?'

By and large, scientific collections assembled in museums were not open to the general public before the end of the eighteenth century. Those few that were tended to be accessible only to those with the right social connections (Macdonald 2004). For the common folk, information about natural science was more likely to be presented as entertainment than education. During the nineteenth century, the wonders of the natural world and contemporary science constituted part of the entertainments at Bartholomew's Fair in London and the American Museum in New York City. These days science is still being packaged as entertainment, however, science and technology centres have taken over from the museums of old, as hands-on exhibits entice curious onlookers with their brand of edutainment. And the media have become the predominate vehicles for popularizing science, with print, radio and television all presenting their own amusing versions. Furthermore, science as entertainment and reinventing the young as scientifically literate has become serious business for the nation.

Why has science become serious business for national governments? Why have the young become the focus of attention? How are various popular media deployed as means of developing a taste for science in the young? Are such mediations likely to produce them as scientifically literate subjects who not only consume but also produce science? This chapter seeks to answer these questions. We begin with an explanation of the economic pressures on nation-states to produce a scientific culture and scientific subjects. To assist us to explain why attempts to engage the young as scientific subjects have taken the particular forms that they have, we consider the primary identifications of the young people of today. Our discussion then focuses on two strategies within national systems of innovation: interactive science and technology centres (a global phenomenon), and the *Sleek Geeks* radio and theatre shows (a phenomenon particular to Australia). Both employ popular pedagogies to appeal to young audiences in the hope that they may be inspired to pursue science careers and eventually become knowledge workers in the knowledge-based economy.

Advanced economies and advancing scientific lifestyles

Advanced economies are moving towards knowledge (knowledge-driven, or knowledge-based) economies 'which are directly based on the production, distribution and use of knowledge and information' (OECD 1996: 7). When Bell (1973: x) theorized 'postindustrial society', he did so with regard to the emergent and transitional changes of the times and with a focus on technological change, particularly information and communication technologies (ICTs). Others who followed in his wake saw ICTs as the basis of economic growth. That said, the 1990s brought the realization that a focus on the information technology industries as the basis of economic growth was far too narrow.

This view was articulated by the Organization for Economic Co-operation and Development (OECD) in the mid-1990s when it published *The Knowledge-based Economy*. In this document economic growth is explicitly linked to science and technology more broadly. Science is equated with new knowledge generated though basic research, and technology with knowledge generated through applied or commercial research. Moreover, science is mainly understood as an economic resource to be deployed in the national interest. Indeed, national systems of innovation have been designed to 'support the advance and use of knowledge in the economy' (OECD 1996: 24). This model of national innovation is now widespread. It involves knowledge transactions between 'market' and 'non-market' entities, that is, between research and education institutions and industry and business. These are collectively guided by government innovation policies with the aim of facilitating economic growth.

Knowledge here is understood as a commodity and its commodification is seen to have specific implications for formal education systems. The pre-eminence of scientific knowledge means that education must serve a new role in supplying knowledge workers with the right scientific credentials. The nation's schools must invent particular sorts of subjects if the nation is to have sufficient knowledge workers to sustain wealth creation (Robb et al. 2003). But nations are also seeking other lifestyle-based ways to encourage young people's engagement with science and technology and to enhance popular conceptions of science more broadly. The knowledge economy not only needs scientists, but a society in which science is well understood as a feature of ordinary life, particularly by the young. National governments implicitly acknowledge that schools alone are unable to achieve this and that they are competing with consumer-media culture for young people's identifications. They have thus turned to 'lifestyle media' to help them to invent youthful scientific subjects.

Youthful consumers

It is often argued that as a generation the young people of today are characterized by their command of ICTs. They have been variously labelled 'the computer generation' (Papert 1993: x), 'the Nintendo generation', 'techno-kids' (Green et al. 1998: 19, 21) and 'cyberkids' (Sefton-Green 1998: 2). Yet, this generation's fascination with technology is not necessarily translating into a broader interest in the sciences more generally. The level of enrolments in science in higher secondary and tertiary education is a cause of concern in many countries. It is for this reason that Australian innovation policy (2001) made provision for extra funding for university science places, and the US House of Representatives passed the Technology Talent Act of 2001, a bill to help increase the number of people holding engineering, mathematics, science and technology degrees.

But of course there is more to youthful consumers than their links to ICTs and their patterns of enrolment in education. The Y Generation, a term used to refer to today's children and youth, for example, is regarded as being 'highly consumption oriented and sophisticated in terms of their tastes, aspirations and shopping skills' (Schneiderman 2000). Marketers seeking to target this generation are already recognizing the imperative of reaching them through existing and new media forms. Older generations understand employment as the key to independence and identity building. However, because steady employment is not as readily gained as it was for previous generations, for the Y Generation identity (both 'individualized' and 'standardized', see Beck et al. 1994) is asserted through style, image and the screen, much of it derived from media-consumer culture.

Importantly, this all suggests that national efforts to develop a 'taste for science' among the young must attend to consumer-media culture, diversity and issues of youthful pleasure and agency. In other words, they must blend education, entertainment and, to a certain extent, advertising (see Kenway and Bullen 2001). So, what are such national efforts, and how do they seek to harness pleasure and agency as a way of reshaping young people's taste cultures in the national interest? As we will now show, pleasure is deployed as a central resource in the cultural mediations designed to reinvent the young.

Interactive science and technology centres: 'family fun'

'There are currently more Science and Technology Centres being built around the world than museums and art galleries combined', states a press release issued by the science and technology centre in South Australia. This statement could be simply read as indicating a diminishing interest in other more traditional cultural institutions. However, it also speaks to the fact that governments globally are investing in national systems of innovation, with science and technology centres representing one strategy for raising awareness about science and technology. The British Association for the Advancement of Science is a national programme promoting the 'understanding and development of science, engineering and technology' as a means to 'illuminate and enhance their contributions to cultural, economic and social life' (Gascoigne and Metcalfe 2001). The National System of Innovation (NSI) in South Africa seeks to produce 'a society that understands and values science, engineering and technology ... thereby ensuring national prosperity and [a] sustainable environment' (Gascoigne and Metcalfe 2001). A government initiative in Australia called *Backing Australia's Ability: Building our Future through Science and Innovation 2004* has 'a commitment to pursue excellence in research, science and technology' (Backing Australia's Ability 2004) through the generation of new ideas which will lead to commercial application, and will ultimately sustain economic growth in a knowledge-based economy. One aspect of the *Backing Australia's Ability* initiative is the expansion of Questacon (the National Interactive Science and Technology Centre) Smart Moves Programme that funds interactive and high-energy, in-school face-to-face presentations by young science communicators in rural and regional secondary schools.

Interactive science and technology centres (ISTCs) 'support the advance and use of [scientific] knowledge in the economy' (OECD 1996: 24) by making science accessible to the general public, and therefore raising public awareness and understanding of science. These centres place an emphasis on interactive exhibitions in order to attract young audiences who relate to ICTs and equate science with entertainment. According to Friedman, 'ISTCs bridge the many, often conflicting, domains which have been characterized as *edutainment*' (1996: 16, emphasis in original). Edutainment can be understood as the point 'where formal, informal, and non-formal education is found within the context of the leisure industry' (Walton 2000: 49).

At science and technology centres, visitors are encouraged to physically engage with the exhibits in order to discover principles of science and technology themselves. This 'idea is founded on the premise that first-hand experience with scientific phenomena will captivate ordinary people' (Cossons 1999: 10). This hands-on approach contrasts with a more traditional view of scientific knowledge where it remains in the hands of scientists. In this scenario, scientists are positioned as authority figures removed from the rest of society, diligently carrying out experiments behind the closed doors of the laboratory. The interactive model of exhibits used at science and technology centres also operates against a more traditional approach to the display of objects in science museums, where glass cases protect specimens and artefacts from over-curious onlookers, and a detached model of observation at a distance is created. Public access to science at ISTCs, in contrast, is manifest in a literal sense as physical contact that not only 'captivates ordinary people' but also attempts to promote public participation by placing scientific knowledge, however limited, in the public's hands.

There is a further significant rationale for ISTCs' promotion of interactivity. Hands-on entertainment is 'fun', and 'fun' is connected to the family where it becomes an inclusive activity involving both parents and children. Hughes (2001) maintains ' "family fun" is a discourse of science that is prominent and widespread'. He uses a range of examples to support his claims, such as the Ontario Science Centre's website which promotes 'fun stuff for the whole family' and includes a navigation button titled 'Family Fun' (Ontario Science Centre 2004).

The notion of 'family fun' at ISTCs is of particular relevance when discussing the promotion of science and technology to young audiences. The 'family fun' of interactive exhibits at science and technology centres may reassure and build confidence in children who are encouraged to participate under a parent's watchful eye. However, for adolescents keen to establish an independent identity by breaking away from their parents, their parents' hands-on involvement in interactive exhibitions may discourage them from participating, despite the attempts of ISTCs to attract these audiences by focusing on pleasure and using screen technologies. Children may accept 'family fun' primarily as science as entertainment. As the director of one Australian science centre says, 'Because it's interactive, *kids* come here, they have fun. First and foremost, they have fun. They have no idea that they're learning and if they did, they probably wouldn't enjoy it' (quoted in Hughes 2001, our emphasis). On the other hand, adolescent audiences may view 'family fun' primarily as 'fun' with a distinctly educational purpose, a form of pedagogy popularized through its promotion as pleasurable entertainment. This may not be to their taste.

One way to conceptualize the pleasure of 'fun with a purpose' experienced at ISTCs is by using Barthes' terminology which defines different orders of pleasures in terms of *jouissance* and *plaisir*. Grace and Tobin (1997: 177) clarify the distinction between these two types of pleasure, explaining that whereas 'plaisir produces the pleasures of relating to the social order; jouissance produces the pleasures of evading it'. As *plaisir* thrives within the social order it is positioned as a particularly adult conception of pleasure at odds with the *jouissance* of adolescent pleasure. Therefore, because ISTCs promote this adult conception of pleasure (the 'family fun' of interactive exhibits), the young audiences they attract are more likely to be children willingly guided by their parents rather than adolescents, the more immediate target group for the burgeoning knowledge economy. We may further ask whether ISTCs succeed in building the scientific literacy that national innovations systems are seeking to promote.

A taste for scientific obedience

One way to establish the difference between traditional museums and hands-on science and technology centres is by suggesting the latter are concerned with 'the transmission of scientific ideas and concepts rather than the contemplation of scientific objects' (McManus 1992: 163). It is not simply the ways in which science is promoted at ISTCs, but also the promotion of particular scientific ideas and concepts within the science-as-fun interactive model that is problematic. Hughes argues that 'for all their alleged novelty, interactives often express and reinforce a traditional (modernist) Enlightenment model of science' (2001). Therefore, while ISTCs seek to attract young audiences through their use of new technologies, this apparently innovative strategy is subverted by a retrogressive epistemology: 'Many interactives embody and express a linear relationship between cause and effect recalling ... the determinism of nineteenth century positivism' (Hughes 2001). Csikszentmihalyi's (1987: 85) description of a visit to the Exploratorium in San Francisco, Oppenheimer's pioneering model for all subsequent ISTCs, reinforces this perspective: 'Most of the problems were already structured, presented, and all I had to do was follow the lead given by the card on the display, and most of it was not much fun'. Within this strictly teleological model, the individual who obediently presses a button and activates the digital cogs and wheels of an exhibition demonstrates a science based on definite beginnings and definitive endings. He or she is placed at a critical distance from the science of the new millennium which, by contrast, is based on 'paradigms of indeterminacy, such as quantum mechanics, relativity, fractal geometry, chaos theory and complexity theory' (Hughes 2001).

Macdonald (2004) reiterates Hughes's claims about the deterministic nature of the scientific knowledge promoted at ISTCs when she suggests 'science centers, and science center type exhibits, by their very form, tend to present science as a set of natural laws and principles about which there is a single truth'. Chambers and Faggetter (1992) support Macdonald's claim concerning the reductionist approach to the presentation of science at ISTCs when they identify the 'science-as-progress' model as the primary scientific principle promoted at the Powerhouse Museum in Sydney, Australia. They say 'the familiar simplistic formulas (technical change equals technical advance, technological progress equals social progress) are everywhere implicit and often explicit' (Chambers and Faggetter 1992: 555). Postman (1990) provides another example of science reduced to the 'single truth' when he describes the Experimental Prototype Community of Tomorrow (EPCOT) in Orlando, Florida. He says that 'in every exhibit, in every conceivable way, EPCOT proclaims that paradise is to be achieved through technological progress, and only through technological progress. The message includes the idea that new is better than old, that fast is better than slow, that simple is better than complex' (Postman 1990: 56-7, cited in Hughes 2001).

As ISTCs' exhibits are focused primarily on celebrating the achievements of science and technology according to this vision, they 'prevent visitors from contemplating alternative visions of their society' (Postman 1990: 59, cited in Hughes 2001). They obscure the 'messy controversial areas' (Macdonald 2004) that are an integral part of scientific application, where trial and error is the norm, and where gains in knowledge are so incremental they could hardly be referred to as progress. Macdonald (2004) further suggests that when science centre exhibitions demonstrate these seemingly 'eternal truths', they become removed from both the realm of technological application, and the experience of everyday life. Paradoxically, while the interactive mode of delivery at ISTCs attempts to make science less abstract and more tangible, the actual scientific principles promoted by these exhibits are removed from the reality of scientific application and everyday experience. As Walton (2000: 52) suggests, these scientific or technological principles 'exist only within the culture and context of the ISTC'.

The connection between science and ordinary life is of particular relevance when discussing young audiences. Science and technology centres package science as interactive entertainment and use new technologies to appeal to young audiences focused on the pursuit of pleasure in their everyday lives. However, these attempts are simultaneously undermined as the scientific knowledge promoted at the ISTC is decontextualized, disconnected from young audiences' everyday lives and therefore not considered personally relevant. In a radio interview, Stocklmayer, who runs the National Centre for the Public Awareness of Science at the Australian National University, said: 'Whilst the general public takes a great interest and feels excited by science, they don't really own it, it's not in their lives exactly' (O'Regan 2000). If young audiences are to develop the sorts of scientific sensibilities that are in demand, if they are to 'own' science and as a consequence create a scientific culture, then the scientific knowledge promoted by ISTCs must be connected to their ordinary lives. While family fun may produce the pleasures of consuming safe 'science' for children, and while ordered fun may be comforting for parents, adolescents are likely to have a taste for being differently pleasured, and national efforts to provoke the scientific imagination need to attend to this. Fun is still serious business here, but it is also linked to everyday comedy.

Sleek Geeks: science, comedy and the everyday

Triple J is the youth radio network (aimed at an 18- to 24-year-old demographic) of the Australian national public broadcaster, ABC. ABC has traditionally positioned itself as devil's advocate to incumbent governments on either side of the political divide. As a result, Triple J has a reputation for being hip and subversive, and represents itself as a radio station that 'strives to be an entertaining, innovative and accessible voice for young Australians' (Triple J 2004). *Sleek Geeks*, presented by Dr Karl Kruszelnicki and Adam Spencer, was one of the programmes featured on Triple J in 2001. Although Kruszelnicki and Spencer now fill different radio timeslots, they continue to present live shows with the support of the National Innovation Awareness Strategy, an initiative funded under *Backing Australia's Ability* (2001).

Sleek Geeks demonstrates the convergence of an innovation strategy (aimed at raising science and technology awareness) and media-consumer culture, as the government uses popular cultural forms to disseminate information about science and technology to youth audiences. From the government's perspective, it is believed that raising youth audiences' awareness of science and technology will lead to an interest in science and technology at secondary and tertiary levels of education that will ultimately produce knowledge workers, proficient in science and technology, for a knowledge-based economy. In this respect, the *Sleek Geeks* show is a government-funded popular pedagogy produced in the public interest.

The presenters of *Sleek Geeks* both have a strong science background. Kruszelnicki has degrees in physics and mathematics, biomedical engineering, and medicine and surgery, and Adam Spencer is a mathematician. However, they are also consummate comedians who 'coerce comedy into science' (*Theatre of Science* 2002). Commenting on their 'Mike the Headless Chicken' sketch, Kruszelnicki says: 'We have some fun and then sneak in a bit of knowledge' (quoted in Walker 2002).

The *Sleek Geeks* team transform humourless scientific discourse into public knowledge by forging a seamless connection between science and comedy and by creating a compelling form of scientific humour that is entertaining, but more importantly makes sense to most people. As one listener says: 'I think Dr Karl and Adam actually bring a bit of brightness to [science] and sort of – not dumb it down exactly, but pitch it at a level that you can understand' (O'Brien 2000). As humour becomes the driving force behind what is usually thought of as a serious and staid discipline, and as science is discussed on a popular medium such as radio, it becomes popular science, a form of enticing edutainment that bridges the gap between education and entertainment and makes science more accessible to a predominantly youth audience. As another listener states: 'You learn more things because, like, you are actually listening because they put humour into it, but at school it's just, like, dragged out ... it's a bit crazy, a bit zany, but you do learn something at the same time' (O'Brien 2000).

Scientists 'don't know how to communicate with the public. We don't understand our audience well enough', says Dr Neal Lane, head of the National Science Foundation in America (quoted in Hartz and Chappell 1997: 38). However, Kruszelnicki and Spencer's connection with a youth radio station with the objective of 'leading and contributing to the expansion of youth culture' (Triple J 2004) means that they *do* understand their listeners, and are therefore able to communicate with them. They remain in touch with issues that interest youth audiences, particularly forms of media-consumer culture that are a contributing factor to the assertion of youthful identity. As Kruszelnicki's and Spencer's expertise extends beyond the bounds of scientific knowledge to encompass media-consumer culture, they are able to connect with a significant part of youth audiences' everyday lives. Conversely, these audiences are then more inclined to tune into Kruszelnicki and Spencer's radio show on the basis of this mutual interest.

Lane believes that scientists 'don't know the language and we haven't practiced it enough' (quoted in Hartz and Chappell 1997: 38). However, when Spencer was interviewed on a television programme about the changing perception of science and technology, he said:

> The way I think of it is, 20 years ago, if, as a 15-year-old, you sat home and programmed computers on the weekend you were thought to be a bit of a dork. These days, if you can make web pages and home pages and do stuff on the Internet, you're thought to be fairly *cool*.
>
> (O'Brien 2000, our emphasis)

Spencer makes knowledge about new technologies more attractive to youth audiences by redefining the image of authority and by suggesting that individuals who possess this knowledge will also acquire status that positions them as 'cool', at a distance from the pejorative 'dork' of old – a position reinforced by Kruszelnicki's and Spencer's own status as 'sleek geeks'. By using the term 'cool' to describe an interest in technology, Spencer shows he is in touch with 'the majority attitude among young people' because he uses 'the favoured language of popular culture and, in particular, youth culture' (Pountain and Robins 2000: 21). If youth audiences are a demographic whose very identity is constructed around notions of style and image, then Spencer's ability to speak to his audience in a contemporary vernacular they respect and understand and to give technological authority a 'cool' edge will be more appealing to them than the outdated language belonging to another generation whose idea of 'family fun' promoted by ISTCs leaves adolescents cold.

In a radio broadcast discussing the resonance between science and the media, cultural commentator and academic McKenzie Wark argued that if science is to become 'a legitimate and valuable part of the community', then rather than positioning the scientist as an 'infallible source of authority' – the so-called 'men in white coats' model of the scientist – scientists need to create and maintain 'an ongoing presence' within the broader community (O'Regan 2000). Kruszelnicki and Spencer maintain this 'ongoing presence' by communicating about science using youth culture's vernacular, showing they understand their audience and ensuring their audience can also understand them. This presence is upheld by breaking down the barrier that separates Spencer and Kruszelnicki, as authoritative scientists, from less informed ordinary people. Rather than exploiting their scientific background and positioning themselves as authority figures, Kruszelnicki and Spencer use the talkback format of the *Sleek Geeks* radio show to create an ongoing dialogue between themselves and their listening audience that places both parties on an apparently equal footing. In this way, Kruszelnicki and Spencer not only speak to the public (using a language they understand), but the public is also given the opportunity to speak back to them. In the context of a talkback conversation, speaking about science becomes a spontaneous process connected with issues that affect people in their daily lives, in opposition to the single, decontextualized truth of deterministic scientific principles that are promoted at ISTCs. For example, one listener asked: 'Why, after you boil your water in the microwave, and then you put your tea bag in it goes a bit crazy, then if you add sugar it goes really crazy?' (Triple J 2004).

Kruszelnicki's and Spencer's theatre version of the *Sleek Geeks* show also contributes to their 'ongoing presence' in the community as they engage with their audience in the flesh rather than remaining disconnected voices broadcast on the radio. The *Sleek Geeks* theatre show is presented as part of National Science Week in Australia and the National Innovation Awareness Strategy outreach programme, with performances in schools and universities throughout Australia. The show has also been performed at the Soho Theatre in London in conjunction with the *Theatre of Science*. The live show follows the same format as the radio show with Kruszelnicki and Spencer. The comedy is the result of applying scientific principles to apparent trivia rather than the profound questions usually addressed by scientists. As a press release for the *Sleek Geeks* comedy theatre show says:

> Dr Karl and Adam Spencer will drag you by the brain through their fast-talking, roller-coaster ride of fabulous facts and sensational stories ... Together they'll tell you about the Science of Nose-Picking, Belly Button Lint, home accidents in the UK and Punching Glass.
>
> (*Theatre of Science* 2004)

The *Sleek Geeks* show contributes to the creation of a scientific culture, defined by Solomon (1996: 157) as 'the public's attitude towards science, and their understanding of it', as Kruszelnicki and Spencer 'spin the web which knits science into its [ordinary everyday] human application, a situation which is rarely recognized as a part of the nature of science' (Solomon 1996: 162).

This is in strong contrast to the hands-on but out-of-touch scientific knowledge disseminated by interactive exhibits at science and technology centres. While these exhibits attempt to raise community awareness about science by making scientific knowledge more accessible, literally placing it in the hands of the general public that visit these centres, the 'single knowledge culture' (Solomon 1996: 162) remains disconnected from the other equally significant areas of knowledge and experience that influence the general public. When discussing youth audiences more specifically, it is important to acknowledge that media-consumer culture, based around a multitude of different mediums including film, radio and television, is a significant area of knowledge and experience in their everyday lives (Mackay 1997).

As adolescents tune into a range of different media within media-consumer culture, such as the Internet, the Playstation, the sound system and the television – preferably all switched on at the same time – they become 'active individuals' who are able to occupy a 'multiplicity of positions' where 'different meanings, experiences, powers, interests and identities can be articulated together' (Grossberg 1994: 16). As ISTCs currently promote science and technology as a 'single knowledge culture', their pedagogical strategies remain unattractive for young 'active individuals'. One way ISTCs can address this issue is by adopting Grossberg's pedagogy of 'articulation and risk', where educators are 'willing to take the risk of making connections, drawing lines, mapping articulations, between different domains, discourses, and practices, to see what will work' (p. 18). In this respect, it is worth speculating that the *Sleek Geeks* show is appealing to young 'active' audiences partly because Kruszelnicki and Spencer already make connections between different media by working across radio, television (where they both make occasional appearances) and theatre.

We have previously suggested that the connections which Kruszelnicki and Spencer make between science and everyday experience are in the interests of making science more accessible to a broader audience. However, another factor influencing this everyday science is the fact that radio is a domestic medium requiring a particular mode of address. As radio (and television) are entertainment technologies broadcast into the private realm of the home, when Kruszelnicki and Spencer address their audiences they use a form of language that is inclusive and 'personalized' (Langer 1981: 352). Science is discussed in relation to everyday examples and broadcast into an everyday domestic context, creating an intimate relationship with listeners and their personal world. In terms of Grossberg's pedagogy of 'articulation and risk', it is not simply that Kruszelnicki and Spencer work across radio, television and theatre and therefore make connections between different media, but also the fact that by doing so Kruszelnicki and Spencer make a connection between private (domestic) and public (communal) domains.

Is celebrity science in the national interest?

The domestic focus of radio and television and the intimate mode of address used on these media also create a particular type of personality. 'Whereas the film celebrity plays with aura through the construction of distance' says Marshall, the radio and 'television celebrity is configured around *conceptions of familiarity*' (1997: 119, our emphasis). Therefore, in terms of the *Sleek Geeks* radio show, youth audiences' access to scientific knowledge is also based on the accessibility of the 'celebrities' that present it. One of the possible consequences of articulating education and entertainment in this way is that when the scientist is constructed as an accessible celebrity, not an inaccessible authority, it is celebrities themselves, rather than the science, that becomes the force attracting youth audiences. When Spencer says 'science is sexy' (in O'Brien 2000) he may be unwittingly acknowledging his own appeal to gendered and sexualized adolescents as a desirable celebrity, rather than the increased popularity of scientific knowledge. As the lure of celebrity becomes a captivating force for youth audiences, they may well develop into knowledge workers with an entrepreneurial sensibility directed towards entertainment, not science.

When talking about 'making science sexy' it is also important to acknowledge gender. Dr Simon Singh, a BBC broadcaster, author and physicist, is a presenter in the *Theatre of Science*, a comedy theatre show with an emphasis on science inspired in part by Kruszelnicki and Spencer, and funded by the British National Endowment for Science, Technology and the Arts (NESTA). He locates the *Theatre of Science* within a tradition dating back to the nineteenth century:

> The notion of holding a 'science show' isn't as strange as it may seem. After all, in the nineteenth century, lectures by the top scientists of the day, such as Michael Faraday and Humphrey Davy, were among the hottest tickets in town. Victorian science lectures drew huge crowds, all sorts of people went – princes, dukes, people like Dickens.
>
> (NESTA 2002)

Here Singh reveals as much about the history of science as an exclusively male domain as he does about the history of popularizing science. Although the *Sleek Geeks* shows (both radio and theatre) attract both male and female audience members, we cannot ignore the fact that

Kruszelnicki and Spencer are part of this continuing tradition. They may therefore reinforce the belief that science is still dominated by men, and discourage girls from pursuing science careers.

The *Sleek Geeks* team makes science more accessible, and therefore raises public awareness about science, by bringing science out from behind the closed doors of the laboratory and into the public domain. Kruszelnicki and Spencer attract youth audiences as they not only place scientific knowledge in an everyday context and make it funny, but they are also familiar celebrities within youth audiences' everyday lives. When commenting on Kruszelnicki and Spencer's popularization of science, Professor George Stewart said: 'When you're trying to teach students, you try to make it interesting and make it relevant to them, and I think that's what they're doing here' (in O'Brien 2000). In this respect, Kruszelnicki and Spencer's approach to science edutainment is in keeping with the official EU recommendations that urge 'teachers to pay more attention to the relevance to everyday life of the science that they teach' (Solomon 1996: 162).

Conclusion

Seeking to propagate a taste for science among the young, governments have turned to entertaining lifestyle media to assist them. Their long-term aim is to produce scientifically literate youthful subjects who will be drawn to science, who will continue to study it as part of their educational lifecourse, and who will eventually become producers of scientific knowledge in the interest of national knowledge economies. As we have shown, governments have pursued this popular pedagogical agenda via a range of media and through the deployment of various forms of pleasure. They have mobilized family fun, comedy and celebrity to enhance the appeal of science and to attract young audiences to it. In so doing, they have tried to demystify science and the scientist; in a sense normalizing science as ordinary life. We have outlined the key features of such modes of address and also pondered the extent to which they are likely to achieve their aims. While innovative, they will not necessarily lead to the production of innovative scientific sensibilities for, as we have shown, media culture 'invites a fascination, rather than a contemplation, of its contents; it celebrates surfaces and exteriors rather than looking for or claiming to embody depth' (Lee 1993: 143). It also 'transforms all cultural content into objects for immediate consumption rather than texts of contemplative reception or detached and intellectual interpretation' – and therefore the young are more likely to become consumers, as opposed to producers, of innovative science.

Part V
Work/life balancing

15 Sabotage, slack and the zinester search for non-alienated labour

Stephen Duncombe

Taking work seriously

I've got a problem with work. I HATE IT! ... Yet millions of people, including me, participate in the 9 to 5 death march each and every day. Ants carrying crumbs into a life long deathhouse so that a measly 1 to 2% of the rich fuckers in the world have all the good things in life. Why do we do it?

(Keffo, *Welcome to the World of Insurance*)

That Keffo has a problem with work is not surprising; most of us probably do. What's remarkable is how much time and effort he expends ranting and writing about it. For 50 pages in his fanzine, *Welcome to the World of Insurance*, he exposes the parasitical practices of the insurance company he works for, ridicules the servility of his fellow workers and the stupidity of his bosses, reprints public relations booklets and advertisements (after 'doctoring' them), advocates sabotage and union organization, then, finally, recounts his day of working in the mailroom, doing absolutely nothing.

Keffo isn't the only zine writer who rants about work. For a medium born out of commentary upon leisure activities (science fiction, punk music and, especially in the UK, sport), fanzines contain an inordinate amount of writing about labour. This chapter explores how zine writers' personal discussion of their jobs is, in fact, a general critique of the nature of work under advanced capitalism as well as an assertion of a different model of labour and life. Promoting practices like sabotage and slacking off, zinesters share resistant strategies designed to restore a psychic sense of victory over their deadening and demeaning jobs. But this is not pure negation; what begins in rejection leads to an ideal of a life in which labour plays a meaningful and creative part, and where the sharp distinctions between work and play which hold sway in the world outside melt away. Identifying work under capitalism as inherently alienating, they valorize their own work creating a zine as an act of non-alienated labour. Through such critical and creative practices they sketch in an important part of a larger picture of an *authentic* lifestyle.

The critique of work as an alienating activity in which a person has little or no control over what is produced, how it is done, who it serves and who profits from it is hardly new. These have been recognized as standard features of the capitalist labour process since Karl Marx wrote his famous fragment on 'alienated labour' in 1844 (Marx 1975). But far from having improved over the past century and a half, the lack of control that most employees enjoy in their jobs has accelerated. The last vestiges of pre-industrial work traditions have withered or been eradicated, and organized labour – in the United States at least – has by and large exchanged workplace control for higher wages, or today, any wages at all. Zine writers, being primarily young people, have had their work experience defined by this reality.

The economic restructuring that began in the 1970s has only accelerated this process. Over the past two decades, in the effort to compete on a global scale, corporations have successfully fought to create what they call a 'flexible' environment. In terms of production this means breaking up large factories and subcontracting component parts all over the world. For consumption this means the abandonment of a stable mass market and the aggressive identification of specialty and niche markets. And for labour, the euphemism of 'flexibility' translates as increased part-time, temporary, and non-union work. Compounding this trend, over the same 20 years economic activity has shifted from industrial to cultural/information production and the service industry, sectors where this sort of 'flexibility' is more and more a given condition.

As a result of these changes, corporations have effectively regained competitive strength. But this edge has a social price, particularly for young people. The traditional industrial workforce – high-school educated, blue-collar working classes – has been made superfluous as many of the new information and service jobs that replaced the old industrial ones demand the cultural capital of a middle-class upbringing and a college education. At the same time, the bulk of these new jobs no longer hold the promise of income, stability and autonomy that was once the luxury of the middle-class. The outcome has been a decimation of the job opportunities for the traditional working class (particularly the non-white working class) and a 'proletarianization' of jobs open to the new middle-class. Young people today, in both income and job conditions, face the reality of downward mobility and declining aspirations.

When zinesters write about work they rarely discuss political economy; what they dwell upon is the psychic cost of the labour they do. For instance, in *The Olecatronical Scatologica Chronicle*, Jokie Wilson

(1991: n.p.) exposes the banality and degradation of his work as a convenience store clerk, writing down a list of '101 Annoying Things That Convenience Store Customers Do or Types of Annoying Customers'. These annoyances range from customers who 'take out their daily aggression on me because they know that they can', to those who 'think what a cool job this must be since we get to "drink free sodas all day long"', to those who 'take convenience stores seriously'.

While at one time working organizations rallied to preserve the 'Dignity of Labour', in the new deskilled service economy zine writers feel there's nothing left to preserve. In this context, Jokie's comment that one of the most annoying things a customer can do is to take his workplace 'seriously' makes sense. Keffo, writing in his later zine *Temp Slave*, describes a temp job in which he was sent an advance letter detailing his task of putting up shelves. The note ended with these words:

> THANK YOU for accepting this important assignment! We appreciate your willingness to take part in this project. The next time you walk through the paint department of this store you will realize how nice it looks and that your help made it this way!

At the job site Keffo meets the other workers:

> At starting time, a huge group ... gathered around their bosses and listened to their orders for the day. Suddenly, one of the bosses began yelling 'OK what's No.1?' The workers screamed back their answer, 'CUSTOMER SERVICE' ... I couldn't believe this kind of feel good crap went on.
>
> (Keffo, *Temp Slave* #4, 1994: 22)

The day turned out well for Keffo as his boss never showed up and he and the other temps got to go home with pay. But what holds the reader's attention is not this limited victory, but Keffo's description and ridicule of the management's bid to get their workers to care passionately about what is basically scut work.

Factories have always been adorned with posters of happy workers and motivational phrases, but the insincerity of this tactic is more apparent today than ever. At the same time that companies – through downsizing, eradication of benefits, and use of part-time labour – are making it quite evident that they don't care about workers, they are also pushing propaganda about quality circles and worker participation, and demanding that workers give their moral commitment to the job. It is this disjuncture between the actual workings of these businesses and the image foisted on the employees and the public that enrages zine writers. Unlike industrial exposés in history past – Upton Sinclair's disclosure of the horrid working conditions in Chicago's stockyards and packing houses at the turn of the century, for example – zines speak less of the actual conditions of the workplace and more about the hypocritical social and economic relationships that surround their work.

This emphasis grows out of the ideal of an *authentic* life so crucial to the underground. Nearly every day in the workplace zinesters are confronted with a contradiction. On the one hand, raised within the middle-class, they've internalized a middle-class ideal of work: work is not just a simple job that demands physical and mental exertion, but a meaningful vocation that requires moral commitment. Work is part of the self. Dumped into the contemporary labour market, however, zinesters soon realize that most work in our society is done for, directed by, and benefits someone else. The disjuncture between these two definitions of work – the former being self-affirming labour, the latter, alienating work – prompts zine writers to first identify the source of this dissonance in the social relations which make up their work experience, then devise ways to fight it and reassert a life of authenticity. In *Welcome to the World of Insurance*, Keffo (n.d.: 1) puts it well: 'Most people are confused about the meaning of work and life, frequently assuming that both are the same. How wrong they are'.

Sabotage

The Sabot Times is a zine produced, in their own words, by 'a band of renegade reporters and photographers dedicated to sabotaging Journalism from within'. In the editorial of their first issue they explain that they are:

> tired of being fucked over by small-minded, vicious editors and publishers whose only pleasure in life is making journalists squirm in fear and sweat for their lousy jobs, which are ruled by these unbreakable commandments: Do it cheap, do it quick and don't offend any advertisers. We say it's time to fight back. We're going to show you how.
>
> (*Sabot Times* #1, 1992: 1)

The editor – calling herself Lois Lane – and her compatriots go on in *The Sabot Times* to tell tales of fabricating quotes, getting paid by sources for favourable stories, and writing sloppy stories full of known errors. Besides their goal of expending as little effort as possible for the editors, their justification for these decidedly unprofessional acts is that mainstream newspapers do this anyway; but whereas the newspapers do it hypocritically, they want to be 'honest' about their deception. And maybe, they write, *Sabot Times* will offer 'a way for the average newspaper reader to find out what's *really* going on down at the local paper' (Johnson, *Sabot Times* #1, 1992: 2).

Besides the intrinsic joy that one gets from harming the very thing that harms you, sabotage has a constructive side. Not only can you strike back at the place you work for, but you can also 'redistribute' some of the goodies every workplace has to offer. Brendan writes of working the graveyard shift selling coffee at the Phoenix airport. She calls it a 'very neat job situation' as 'the inventory at this place is pretty loose and easy to adjust, so I give a lot of stuff away for free'. Only half tongue-in-cheek, Brendan applauds

> this opportunity to carry out direct redistribution of wealth. The company I work for charges customers too much (remember airport prices?) and doesn't pay its employees enough (trust me), and this way both inequities are resolved, since people just 'pay' me whatever they feel like paying, and my income is supplemented.
>
> (Brendan, *Temp Slave* #4, 1994: 6)

In addition to screwing her employers and helping out herself, her sabotage gives Brendan a way to work on something that *she* feels is important: creating her 'own free underground cafe, right under the nose of the mega-corporation that employs me!'

Tales of sabotage and theft are not just represented *in* zines, but often *by* them. Stealing the material and 'borrowing' the technology necessary to produce zines is considered part and parcel of making zines. Joe, of *JOEnews*, brags that his zine 'didn't cost me a dime. I totally ripped off my employers, which is a big, big, part of it. I did it on my office copy machine. I used their postage meter. I used their PO box'. And when I asked Missy Lavalee, editor of *Bushwacker, Gaybee,* and *Kittums,* how she puts out her zines, she responded matter of factly that 'my roommate . . . works the night shift at Kinko's. She's been copying for people for free for years. In some ways I would say that she keeps the Bay Area zine scene going' (pers. comm.).

Stealing from the workplace is nothing new. Anyone who has worked in a factory or office can testify to the amazing amount of pilfering that goes on. But neither is it a very fruitful strategy to hurt the corporate world. But for zinesters sabotage is about psychic victories, given that they have little hope of taking control of the production process in their workplace, never mind society at large.

But if the system is too big and too entrenched to conquer, zine writers can at least make sure the system doesn't conquer them. The surest way to do so is to distance themselves from the work, the company, and the boss, if not physically, then mentally and morally. Sabotage is a way to stake out their identity as *other*, as not part of the system.

Slack

> Purposely, early on in my life, I saw my dad chase that pot of gold, you know, at the end of the rainbow. It took him seventy years of his life until he could retire, when he could stop working [and] get to sit around. And I just figured I'm not going to waste the next fifty years of my life when I can sit around right now.
>
> (Dishwasher Pete, pers. comm.)

'REPENT! Quit your JOB! SLACK OFF!' *SubGenius Pamphlet #1* (1981) enjoins on its first page. The popularization of 'slack' as a lifestyle and 'slacker' as a role aspiration within the modern underground has its roots in this tongue-in-cheek religion/conspiracy started in the early 1980s. The goal of the elect of the *SubGenius* is to attain slack. What this beatific state actually is, as with all religions, is somewhat hazy, but the path is clear: devotion to the pipe-smoking figurehead Bob, a path charted outside of the evil suburban, normal and 'pink' lifestyle, and most important to our discussion here, a life of perpetual leisure ... of perfect slack.

Slacking is a time-honoured tradition of those kept at the bottom of society. The rejection of the ethic of hard work and determination makes sense if you know that it will make no difference anyhow, but why zinesters raised within the middle-class would adopt the ideal of slack is a bit more puzzling. Part of the answer is bohemian tradition. Being on permanent vacation within a society that stresses work has always appealed to the cultural underground. Even Karl Marx's own son-in-law, Paul Lafargue, wrote a spirited defence of slack entitled *The Right to be Lazy* in the 1880s, arguing that 'the proletariat must trample under foot the prejudices of Christian ethics, economic ethics and free-thought ethics. It must return to its natural instincts, it must proclaim the Rights of Laziness' (Lafargue 1989/1883: 41). Bohemians, villagers, beats, hippies, almost every modern underground has celebrated leisure.

With roots in the past, the slacker as role aspiration fits perfectly with what zinesters know about the economy of the present and their prospects for the future. But people don't merely react to the environment which surrounds them; instead, they invest their decisions with meaning. What slack offers to zinesters is a philosophy of laziness as a positive attribute. Turning the tables on definitions of who and what you are and making a negative into positive is a subculture's way of taking the sting out of being limited in possibilities and labelled as such. Faced with diminished career opportunities, labelled as an apathetic generation by the mainstream press, the members of this underground have made apathy and a lack of career options something to cheer.

In rebellion against a culture that glorifies the work ethic with silly football coach aphorisms like 'Winners don't quit and quitters don't win', then offers up meaningless work with an unsure future, zine writers celebrate quitting. The *Quitter Quarterly*, edited by Shelly Ross and Evan Harris, gives advice to the prospective quitter, not only to quit things yourself but to feel good about it and revel in it:

> Tell everyone you know that you have quit. Because of the stigma attached to quitting, many quitters deny themselves the pride and gratification of quitting ... Send reminders, call [friends] to discuss the circumstances of your quitting, invite people to your house and dwell on whatever you quit.
>
> (quoted in *Harper's Magazine* 1994: 28)

If you yourself have difficulty quitting, they counsel, then, 'Encourage someone else to quit', as 'Even vicarious quitting is better than no quitting at all'.

Sooner or later circumstances force one back to work, but the goal is to get a job in which quitting, not showing up, or goofing off won't take much of an effort. 'I always like a job without responsibility and such', Dishwasher Pete explains when I ask why he only washes dishes. 'And I don't mind if other people think it's lowly. Because then I can have the job without responsibilities and they won't mind if I walk off the job' (pers. comm.).

As with sabotage, there is a certain political logic to this philosophy of slack. Withdrawal from economic, social and political production makes sense as a (partially unconscious) strategy of resistance in our (post)modern world. In the past people struggled to become subjects of history, demanding what was denied to them: the right to act upon the world. As Jean Baudrillard (1988: 219) writes: 'To a system whose argument is oppression and repression, the strategic response is to demand the liberation rights of the subject'. But this sort of simple repression, while certainly still inflicted upon those at the bottom of our society, is no longer the dominant logic of control in the West. Instead, Baudrillard argues: 'The present argument of the system is to maximize speech, to maximize the production of meaning, of participation. And so the strategic resistance is the refusal of meaning and the refusal of speech'.

In other words, strategies of social control have changed. Whereas once suppression of information and political activity was the design of the ruling powers, now a veritable flood of information drowns citizens, and exaltations to 'get involved' in your community or be part of the workplace 'quality circle' bombard them. Still, citizens and employees know they have no real power. How do you rebel against this injustice? When they won't let you participate in society, you fight for that right. When they force you to engage, you slip into slack. Revolution – the fight for the right to be a subject of history – is a strategy of the past, dead and buried. Today's resistance can be found in 'devolution' (Baudrillard 1988: 215). In a very zinester-like move, Baudrillard takes what has traditionally been considered revolutionary deficits – apathy, passivity, ironic detachment – and turns them on their head, making these traits attributes instead of faults. And he may be right. In the developed world, with its sophisticated security apparatus and its democratic patina, violent revolution as a tactic for overarching social change is not viable at present, while the simple withdrawal of consent may be an effective tactic.[1]

The underground politics of dropping out finds an advocate in Mickey Z, creator of *Flaming Crescent* and *The Reality Manifesto*. In the latter pamphlet he concludes:

> There is only one course of action if we are not part of the economic ruling class: Play the 'game' just enough to get by, stop wasting energy in futile efforts to change the world, and set up your own little world in your own time and space in which you can experience the revolutionary pleasure of thinking for yourself.
>
> (Mickey Z 1993: n.p.)

At first read, Mickey's rant seems simply a justification for retreating from politics and society, a politics of pure 'devolution'. While there is some truth to this interpretation, Mickey himself refutes it, claiming that slack is a conscious political act and stance, a 'passionate indifference' he calls it. And there may be some truth here too, for as these last few lines of his manifesto suggest, *withdrawal* from the greater world is accompanied by *engagement* in something else: setting up 'your own little world . . . in which you can experience the revolutionary pleasure of thinking for yourself'.

This is what distinguishes the underground philosophy of slack from simple disengagement. What slackers – and perhaps the larger, apathetic population as well – are rebelling against is not participation per se, but social, economic and political participation as it is defined by the powers that be. Is it any wonder that workers look askance at 'employee participation' if they are hired as temps? Is it a mystery that people refuse to vote when politicians respond to the interests of PACs instead of citizens? What others might see as a fatalistic rejection of interest may be reconsidered as a rejection of phony activity, leaving the possibility of an assertion of 'authentic' engagement wide open. For slackers are not just dropping out, they are also turning on and tuning in to the possibilities of another culture and society – whether that be 'your own little world' or, as the fact that Mickey Z cares to distribute his zine suggests, the larger underground community. As one of the characters in the Richard Linklater's 1991 film *Slacker* states: 'Withdrawing in disgust is not the same as apathy'.

What starts out in negation can lead to revitalization. Rejecting the 'rat race' allows for time and mental space to rethink what matters in work, in leisure, in life. Missy Lavalee, for example, told me about her anti-career trajectory:

> I finished high school and dabbled in college for three and a half years. I decided to drop out and move to San Francisco . . . I have a lot of reasons for this, but the main one is that I think [college] prepares you for the rat race, then you get out of college, jump into the rat race, and end up losing . . . I am trying to reject the lifestyle that is expected of this generation, to go to school and be successful. I am trying to change my definitions of successful.
>
> (pers. comm.)

Missy's life strategy is one of withdrawal, but also engagement, as her new definition of success includes putting out her own zines and working with others in Blacklist Mailorder, a co-operative, networking organization that distributes underground zines and records worldwide.

On a more intimate plain, slacking is about rediscovering experiences that are lost in the pace of modern life. Dishwasher Pete told me that his slacker lifestyle leaves time to meander:

> I took a walk around town today and I did all kinds of stuff. Like I made my way into this abandoned building and found all this neat stuff, and was watching these turtles swim around and got into some pretty cool stores and talked to some people.
>
> (pers. comm.)

Pete and other zine writers live then to write about their life outside the bourgeois ideals of hard work, material success and boundless consumption, implicitly setting up an alternative model of the good life. As a counter model to mainstream society, however, slacking is problematic. Like Henry David Thoreau at Walden Pond, slackers rely upon the privilege of the better off. As Thoreau relied upon the kindness of his friend Ralph Waldo Emerson for the property on which his 'isolated' cabin stood, and had food delivered to him regularly by friends, slackers depend upon the affluent society they reject for a backdrop of sustenance. As long as the rest of the world isn't made up of slackers, slacking is made easier. This doesn't mean slacking is a scam, merely that it embodies a contradiction: like so many other features of the underground, this strategy of resistance depends on the very society it resists. As the SubGenius Foundation (1987: 64) gleefully admits: 'Slack is like freedom, but unlike freedom it brings no responsibility'.

There is another problem with slacking as a resistance strategy: the celebration of leisure poses no challenge to the dominant system. While the ideologues and practitioners of early and middle capitalism extolled the virtues of hard work, sacrifice and vocation, since the 1920s at least consumption has been recognized as capitalism's driving force. And consumption takes place primarily in the realm of leisure. Far from being in direct opposition to advanced capitalism, slack – as the leisure time necessary to consume goods, or as a reward for the sacrifice of a life spent in toil – is an integral part of it. As Dishwasher Pete declares in the quotation that opened this section, he is merely taking a shortcut to what his non-bohemian father always desired.

But slackers are asking for something else as well. Slacking is not about doing no work and waiting for a Buick in the carport and a pop-up toaster in the kitchen. It is also a philosophy which promotes doing more with less; finding enjoyment less in Nintendo and Disneyland and more in contemplating turtles swimming, exploring old buildings, talking to others and creating one's own culture.

There is an important exception to the zinester ethic of zero work, for the zines which carry these articulate arguments against work are themselves products of intense labour. In conversation, I pressed Pete on his dislike for work and responsibility. I brought up the fact that his zine *Dishwasher* is lovingly created and designed and must have taken an immense amount of time and effort to create. He immediately outlined the difference between two types of work. The former, work for money and for someone else, was taxing, boring, degrading and to be avoided at all costs. The latter, making zines, was work too, but 'it's fun and it's for myself, and it's not for the buck' (pers. comm.). As Pete points out, there is another ideal of work operating in the zine world, in a word: non-alienated labour.

For love, not money

> What do you do?
> I find things out.
> You don't make any money
> out of your work?
> No, I don't work in the way
> that people usually
> understand the expression.
>
> (C. Nash, *Queer Magnolia*)

Zines, as *Factsheet Five* founder Mike Gunderloy likes to say, are produced for 'love, not money'. This hardly seems like a radical or even important ideal, but its implications are grand. For the oft-repeated statement about a separation between money and love is really a stand-in for another argument: the type of work that is done for money versus the type of work done for love. For at the crux of the zine ethic is a definition of creation and work that is truly fulfilling: work in which you have complete control over what you are creating, how you are doing it, and whom you are doing it for; that is, *authentic* work. As with other characteristics of the zine world, this ideal of a non-alienating creation is not born by immaculate conception. It has its roots in rejection; in particular, rejection of their day-in, day-out experience of work.

To understand the importance of zines as an antidote to the workaday world one need look no further than their subject matter. Popular music, science fiction and other leisure pursuits which make up the bulk of zines' subject matter have traditionally been those very 'spaces' in society where a person could escape from work and create their own world. As rock critic Simon Frith (1981: 77) has pointed out, one of the things that makes popular music so attractive – particularly to young people – is that the musician represents a life free from work, a person whose work is their play, an individual, in short, who 'did it their way'. As popular music has become integrally tied to big business this may be more fantasy than reality; still, the ideal of popular music as respite from work has a strong hold.

But unlike most employment, working on a zine is *fun*. 'It's fun as hell', writes Lois Lane about putting out *Sabot Times*; and in reply to the question 'Why Publish?' J. C. Coleman of *Life on Planet Earth* explains simply, 'Because it's fun'. 'Fun' is an answer I've heard many times from zine writers justifying why they do what they do, and it is meaningless in itself – even JC acknowledges it's 'very clichéd'. But the reasons JC gives for why 'it's fun' reveal a bit more complexity and hint at where the pleasure one gets from producing a zine comes from. 'The only restrictions are those I put on myself', he writes, 'That's what makes it fun, the freedom to just do it' (Coleman 1988: 54). That zines are a place where the creator has only his or her own restrictions to heed is key in understanding what they offer their makers.[2]

This issue of control shapes the very aesthetics of zines. To begin with zines, as a material medium, have form; and this form becomes part of the message from zine creators to their audience. The physical form of zines often complements their personal nature, and being handmade the hands of the creator are clearly visible in the publication. Aaron Cometbus, for example, carefully hand-letters each of the 82 pages that make up issue #31 of *Cometbus*. This intimate quality reinforces Aaron's personal narrative as he takes the reader on his journeys across the United States. He ends his zine by sharing with the reader *his* completion of the zine: alone in a room in Richmond, VA:

> where I am now and where I've been every night, working on this issue midnight to 6:30 am, with a half hour lunch and two smoke breaks. Writing. It's taken me six weeks just to do the damn handwriting. But tonight I'm finishing this little book, and tomorrow I'm gonna take my piles of notes out into the alley and have one hell of a bonfire.
>
> (*Cometbus* #31, n.d.: 82)

Concluding like this, Aaron brings the *Cometbus* reader into his very process of creation.

Most publishers don't hand-letter their zines, using typewriters, word processors, and computers instead. But even here, emphasis is placed on physically demonstrating the control of individuals over their technological tools. The editor of *Slut Utopia*, Lizzard Amazon, writes in her second issue (n.d.: inside cover): 'OK OK … it is not so hard to use pagemaker and i've got access so here is a slightly (slightly …) less scuzzy looking zine than #1. But I am still going to write all over this thing in pen at the last minute' – which is exactly what she does.

Zine aesthetics not only reflect who the individual creator is, but also delineate what the zine is not. 'The scruffier the better', as Michael Carr, one of the creators of *Ben is Dead*, argues in describing what makes a zine look like a zine. He continues: 'Photocopied ones particularly appeal to readers, because they have a more homespun or real feel to them … they look as if no corporation, big business or advertisers had anything to do with them' (quoted in Carter 1993: 1). In other words, the zines *look* as if they are controlled by no one other than their producer.

This issue of control crosses over from aesthetics into the production and distribution of zines as well. Scott Cunningham, a co-editor of *World War III,* once worked for what he calls a 'mega-corporate' commercial publishing concern, housed in a tall building whose floors were divided into different divisions: art, editorial, advertising, business and distribution. In all the time he worked there he never spoke to anyone in the different departments, though they were all working on the same projects. He juxtaposes this fragmented organizational model to the lack of hierarchy and division of labour at *WWIII,* where 'the same person doing a major piece is pasting down the page numbers' and he himself is closely involved in every facet, large and small, of creating and putting out the comic (pers. comm.).

Dan Werle, the sole editor of *Manumission,* defines this involvement as 'one of the greater aspects' of putting out his zine in that 'I can control who gets copies, where it goes, how much it costs'. 'Why is that so important?' he asks rhetorically, then answers:

> I think it's ... a means of empowerment, a means of keeping things small and personal and personable and more intimate. The people who distribute my zine I can call and talk to them, and I talk directly to them instead of having to go through a long chain of never-ending bourgeoisie [he laughs].
>
> (pers. comm.)

One might argue that zinesters are only doing what non-bohemians do when they build birdhouses, knit sweaters, or engage in any one of a thousand hobbies. There's some truth to this. Like zinesters, hobbyists too are fleeing their own alienating work experiences by creating their own products and sharing that experience with others. But there the similarities end. For unlike hobbyists, the creators of zines *consciously* bestow their activity with adversarial meaning. It is this adversarial intent which elevates what might be considered just a variation on a common practice into a political proposal. Yet the fact that millions of 'normal' people share the basics of a practice which distinguishes work done for money from work done for love, holds out the promise that such critiques of alienated labour are not the sole possession of underground malcontents.

With all their contradictions and all their limitations, zines testify powerfully to the underground culture's unwillingness to accept the definitions of work that reign supreme in our society. They are the vernacular evidence of a radically different way to define and act upon the productive and creative urge that runs through every one, a definition that backs up C. Nash when he states simply in *Queer Magnolia*, 'No, I don't work in the way that people usually understand the expression'. And most importantly, zines are not just idle preaching, but the fruits of a practice. At a time when many are resigned to bitter acceptance of things as they are, an unrepentant idealism bubbles up through the cracks, finding its voice in the words of those like Steven 'Hardcory' Cervantes, editor of *Hardcry*, who writes in his premier issue's editorial (1990: inside cover): 'Yo, Hardcory here, just to let you know that this is a first time publication. It's not the most professional thing in the world, but when you do it to do it; well to me that's all that matters'.

Acknowledgement

This chapter is a revised version of the chapter 'Work' in *Notes from Underground: Zines and the Politics of Alternative Culture* (Duncombe 1997, London: Verso).

Notes

1. 'If you don't want bombs, don't pay for them', J.R. Molloy, the editor of *Alligator Grundy*, writes; '[t]he Pentagon gets more revenue from idle class peace marchers than from all the poets living on welfare. The way to break the back of the arms business is to quit your job, give up your Mercedes and your Laser Printer'. The accusation that peace marchers own Mercedes may be foolish, but Molloy's overall point is valid: the liberal democratic state is threatened as much by private withdrawal of financial and moral support as public petition of anger (Molloy 1991: 8).
2. In his study of (mostly) science fiction and fantasy zines in the early 1970s, Frederick Werham (1973: 71) notes this, arguing that this freedom from exterior constraints and controls was 'no mere formal matter; [but] goes to the heart of what fanzines are'.

16 The worst things in the world
Life events checklists in popular stress management texts

Steven D. Brown

Preamble

In a notorious scene from the closing sections of George Orwell's *Nineteen Eighty-four*, O'Brien explains to Winston Smith that there is no real purpose to his 'interrogation'. The point of this practice, O' Brien states, is neither the extraction of information nor punishment, but simply the systematic destruction of Winston as rational individual – 'the object of torture is torture' (Orwell 1949: 212). Winston's pain is the object – there is no other point. Richard Rorty (1989) notes that this message has presented commentators with considerable difficulties. O'Brien is undoubtedly a monstrous creation, and the vision he offers of the future as 'a boot stamping on a human face – for ever' (Orwell 1949: 215) is as puzzling as it is repugnant. Yet O'Brien neither conceals nor avoids the true object of the practice. In Room 101, Winston will be forced to confront the worst thing in the world because it will destroy him, such that he will be 'forced to realize that he has become incoherent, realize that he is no longer able to use a language or be a self' (Rorty 1989: 179).

This description is based on Elaine Scarry's (1985) analysis of torture as 'unmaking'. Scarry also argues, based on a wide variety of cases, that torture has no other object than the inflicting of pain. This is its sole truth, albeit one that is often obfuscated within the practice itself. However, Scarry points to the peculiar domesticity that often characterizes the inflicting of pain. The objects used are typically mundane, commonplace items – chairs, telephones, doors, baths. Scarry argues that the use of these items both narrows the 'world' of the victim and objectifies their pain in such a way that agency is dissolved, language is defeated. The sole reality is that of the overwhelming pain which is written large into every contour of the world.

What Scarry and Rorty describe is the structure of a mundane cultural logic and technical practice that robs the victim of the ability to meaningfully articulate their world or to grasp any agency therein. In confronting the worst thing in the world, the victim becomes incoherent to themselves and finds their ability to name and even describe their experience rendered utterly without meaning. To have one's world 'unmade' in this fashion is to find oneself amenable to reconstruction, to give oneself over to the language of those who perpetrate and prolong the practice.

Problem

The commonplace, taken-for-granted world that serves as the backdrop for ordinary lifestyles can often take on the appearance of a hostile environment, populated with terrifying threats, some nameless, some all too familiar. Managing the personal impact of these threats, from local contingencies like unhealthy foods and unsafe streets, to global horrors such as climate change and transnational terrorism, constitutes, for most of us, a mundane ongoing project. Such a project becomes all the more complex when the local and the global are collapsed into one another. For instance, the 'politics of fear' which are self-evident in recent Western Anglo-American public rhetoric tends to create a seamless web of insecurity where threat and terror is omnipresent. Such rhetoric clearly relies on effacing the differences between heterogeneous fears. It depends on a logic that is capable of converting literally everything into a potential object of suspicion and concern.

One such logic is to be found in the discourse of 'stress'. In a comparatively short space of time, stress has become the pre-eminent term for describing a huge range of experiences and conditions. In common usage, stress is something that arises from life experiences that can be both trivial (for example, missing a bus) and highly significant (for example, traumatic incidents such as violent assaults). It covers the routine and predictable (for example, changing jobs, overworking) and the unusual and unpredictable (for example, redundancy, industrial accidents). Stress itself can be transitory and relatively benign (for example, the stress of preparing for a party) or long-term and life altering (for example, the stress of adapting to serious illness or injury). As a condition, stress may be characterized as relatively low-level (for example, backaches, 'tension') or as completely overwhelming (for example, myocardial infarction, 'burnout').

It seems to me that a concept which is doing this kind of everyday descriptive work is a concept that deserves closer inspection. This is not to argue, as some have done, that stress itself is a 'myth' (Pollack 1988), or that it is an ideologically laden term (Young 1980). Merely that it is not self-evident why these varied life experiences and circumstances ought to be described in terms of stress, and that since there are numerous other kinds of concepts drawn from different sorts of discourses (for example, oppression, injustice, hopelessness, neurosis, frustration) that might equally well be applied in each case, there is something to be understood in the apparent 'naturalness' and ease with which stress is typically invoked.

Indeed one might go so far as to argue that it is now entirely normative to use the language of stress to describe certain sorts of activities, notably work-related practices. For example, a number of trades unions in the UK have surveyed their members to assess the levels of stress typically experienced in the workplace (see Hepburn and Brown 2001 for the case of secondary school teachers). The point of these exercises appears to be to generate an evidential base for criticizing current working arrangements by demonstrating how such arrangements directly impact on the health of employees. While there are doubtless many direct and indirect links to be made here, coupled with some moderate success in using the notion of stress-related illness in litigation against employers, the effectiveness of systematically redescribing legitimate complaints in the language of stress is far from proven. In fact, there are reasonably compelling instances where entirely the opposite has been shown to be the case (Tesh 1984).

The difficulty is with managing the self-evidency of the experiences that are marked as 'stressful'. We all know that particular working or domestic arrangements can induce distress, and ultimately may prove deleterious to physical or mental health. We all know that certain kinds of experience, such as the trauma of loss or witnessing the suffering of others, have long-term effects – one does not walk away unaffected. We all know that there are ways of living and types of life experiences that are painful, tough and sometimes tragic. All of this is self-evident. It then seems appropriate to adopt a common language wherein all of these forms of experience can be plainly described under a single rubric that will make the pain and distress of these experiences clearly visible. This is the promise of the discourse of stress.

But this is not the case. For example, occupational groups who are clearly and self-evidently doing 'stressful' jobs do not always appear to differ from other groups on technical measures (see Cobb and Rose 1973 for the classic case of air traffic controllers). Even if it is possible to unambiguously state that a particular group of individuals are routinely 'stressed' – and even then much turns on the status of the instrument used to produce the measures – it is rarely clear exactly why this is so. For instance, one would expect a study of stress and burnout amongst nurses to come up with a fairly straightforward account of just what is difficult about the job nurses do. But a typical study, such as Anderson's (1991), involves measures of 13 separate variables (ranging from 'training' to 'role conflict' to 'depersonalization') which are interrelated in a complex statistical pattern. What is more, it is rarely the case that these relationships can be disentangled in any satisfying way. One case in point is 'social support'. For over 30 years, stress researchers have studied the apparently self-evident fact that having other people around helps when one is stressed, without arriving at a clear sense of how and why this should be so. Models in this area (see, for example, Hobfoll 1989) emphasize that social support acts as a 'moderating' variable – that is, it conditions the relationship between two or more other variables, which may themselves be intertwined with other moderating relationships. And so on.

The point I am trying to make is that redescribing self-evidently distressing and fearful experiences in the language of stress tends to either complexify or even undermine what it is we think we all know about these experiences. That is not to say that the end results are not helpful, that the findings of stress research are without use. Clearly, under certain circumstances, they have considerable pragmatic value. But it does beg the question of how and why the concept of stress has become such a compelling notion. Or, put in slightly different terms, how is it that personal experience becomes recruited into the discourse of stress, and how does such recruitment allow personal distress to be reconfigured?

Thesis

My argument is that the concept of stress has been popularized through a series of narratives, metaphors and other tropes which render the 'stressed individual' as an object of technical concern (see Brown 1999). For instance, one common metaphor often used in relation to stress is that of 'heat'. This constructs the complex physiological processes that are thought to occur during 'stress reactions' in terms of a movement from 'cooler' to 'hotter'. Around this basic core metaphor, a whole series of descriptions of persons (for example, 'hot reactors'), conditions (for example, 'burnout') and interventions (for example, 'cooling down') can be arranged. What is more, this crude rendering of the physical experience of stress is given its own mythology through narratives which emphasize, for instance, that this physiological reaction is an biological remnant from the deep past of human evolution (a Stone Age 'primitive response syndrome' adapted to more hostile times).

This work of popularizing the language of stress occurs across a number of media. It is most readily recognizable within the genre of self-help literature, in texts such as the intriguingly titled *60-second Stress Management* or *Stress Control: How to Cope with Anxiety*. In looking at these texts, it becomes readily apparent that there is considerable variation in the kinds of advice offered and in the particular way in which stress itself is understood. However, what all these texts appear to share, beyond a vision of a world where stress is an omnipresent and pressing threat, is the notion that distress can be reduced to a series of technical decisions based on the allocation of personal resources. The most commonly discussed resource is 'energy'. Persons are seen as endowed with a limited stockpile of energy that must be wisely managed and directed in such a way as to maximize individual goods, such as 'health', 'happiness' or 'success'. Stress is seen as fundamentally corrosive of such personal resources, and as further arising from their poor management.

What I think is gained by adopting the language of stress is the ability to render distress as part of a semi-abstract calculus of resource allocation. Distress is shorn of its dilemmatic qualities. For example, divorce is transformed from an experience involving a set of moral choices and legal decisions to an event which may be quantified in terms of its impact on one's health and ability to function effectively. It may then appear that stress is a means of reducing moral or emotional complexity into a straightforward calculus of the supposed impact of the experience in question upon the individual. However, as I have noted, on closer inspection this calculus is endowed with its own forms of complexity which may prove to be no less tractable for the individual than the dilemmatic features of the original experience.

In this chapter I do not want to dwell on the paradox of exchanging one form of complex description for another. Instead I want to concentrate on the initial question of how it is that personal experience is initially recruited into the discourse of stress. In order to do this, I will focus on what might initially appear to a purely stylistic matter: how stress is typically introduced in popular literature.

Lists

Lists are a common feature of most popular texts around stress. These lists may map out sets of 'symptoms' that are commonly associated with stress related conditions. These can include physical symptoms, such as appetite loss, fatigue or high blood pressure, along with behavioural symptoms such as irritability, anxiety or insomnia. Irrespective of their precise contents or particular use of categories, the common feature of these lists is their relative length and comprehensiveness. Physical symptoms, for instance, will usually include all the major categories of human activity, from eating to sleeping, and will make reference to all of the major organ systems (from headaches to stomach aches) and muscular-skeletal divisions (backaches to sweaty hands). It would take a fairly determined reader to deny recognizing at least some of these symptoms as a routine part of their everyday experience.

The lists which interest me most, however, are those which outline a series of common 'life events'. These invariably include the following events:

- Death of a spouse
- Divorce
- Marital separation
- Jail term
- Death of a close family member
- Personal injury or illness
- Marriage
- Fired at work

At first glance this seems to be reasonably good summary of the worst things in the world. Losing one's life partner, going to prison, the death of a child or parent, suffering some form of debilitating illness or injury – these must all figure in any private catalogue of nightmares. What is initially jarring is to see events of this magnitude laid out in such a clearly defined and abstract manner. Moreover, most texts will also assign a relative value to each event by indicating a hierarchical ordering and a numerical value. For instance:

- Death of a spouse   100
- Marriage   50
- Change in living conditions   25
- Christmas   12

These values are designed to guide the reader through the list in a number of ways. They are meant to act as a direct indication of the relative magnitude of the experience involved. Thus the 'death of a spouse' is roughly twice as stressful an experience as 'marriage', which is in turn equivalent to about two 'changes in living conditions' and so on. This assigning of values creates paradoxes of value. For instance, eight successively stressful family Christmases will be held to generally equate with 'death of a spouse'. It also creates some interesting myths, such as the one that 'moving house' is one of the most stressful events in one's life (it turns out it's actually the thirty-second). Readers are typically asked to summate these values to obtain a total 'score' which indicates the likelihood of suffering from stress-related ill health in the future. Some versions of the list state that 300 is the threshold figure for events occurring in the past two years, but it is not uncommon for a figure as low as 50 to be mentioned (a score which is rather easily achieved).

Readers are then explicitly instructed to construct a general equivalence between the past experiences described in the list. As with physical symptoms, because of the comprehensive nature of the list, practically all readers will be able to locate some categories that have biographical meaning. Consider the following:

- Outstanding personal achievement   28
- Change in recreation patterns   19
- Change in eating habits   15

These categories are so broad, so inclusive, that it requires very little effort on the part of the reader to fit each category to some aspect of past experience. 'Change in eating habits', for instance, could refer to anything from dieting to eating rather more/less than usual to changing where and when one eats. In this way the list acts something of an open text – a set of statements structured in such a way to avail themselves of utterly diverse reading strategies and interpretations. Which means in turn that most readers will not only be able to reconstruct their immediate past in terms of the structure of the list, but will moreover in all likelihood be able to calculate a 'score' which will place them in the 'at risk' category of responses.

What, then, are these lists seeking to achieve? They are clearly not providing a unique vocabulary for the reader to reflect upon their own distress, since the categories used are mundane and overly broad descriptive statements. They are certainly not providing a means to differentiate between respondents, since most readers will be able to arrive at remarkably similar scores (generally around 200+) through the summation of lower items on the list. And whatever else they may be doing, these lists are most definitely not entertaining any relation to some higher or more powerful truth, since to complete such a list is to discover simply that you are the sort of person for whom the notion of stress has some purchase. That is, you are a reader who may be interested in stress. Or, crudely put, the object of completing the list is to complete the list. There is no other object.

Origins

Looking to the origins of this kind of list proves instructive. The story begins with an epistemic turn in psychiatry in the early twentieth century. Adolf Meyer argued that psychiatric categories were relatively

insensitive to the everyday demands of adapting to mundane contingencies. For Meyer, mental health problems are best described in
terms of more general 'disorders' of adaptation ('egasias'), as the person
struggles to match their routine activities with the vicissitudes of the
local environment (see Lief 1948). In order to understand how such
disorders occur, it is necessary to produce exhaustive descriptions of
precisely what kinds of activities and experiences a given individual is
engaged in. These descriptions would be recorded as a 'life chart'.

Meyer then developed both a philosophical orientation to mental
health as grounded in the business of adapting to life demands, and a
technology to render this conceptual link visible. The term 'life stress'
was added later to this epistemic configuration by Harold Wolff. Life
stress describes the state within the individual that is created by the
demands of adaptation – 'inadequate' or disorganized responses increase
the overall level of stress. Wolff, like Meyer, emphasized that in order to
understand the particular genesis of a given episode of illness, it would
be necessary to map out the idiosyncratic pattern of events and
responses that the individual had undergone (Wolff et al. 1950). This
means not merely understanding what has happened, in some abstract
manner, but also the significance of the event for the individual. In this
respect, Wolff drew upon existing psychosomatic paradigms to claim
that symptom patterns may involve a displacement of biologically
appropriate responses (for example, a 'runny nose' serves the direct
biological purpose of clearing the nasal passage, but it may come to take
on a symbolic importance for the individual such that it becomes an
object in its own right).

It was within this general framework that the first version of the list
we have discussed appears. Known as the Schedule of Recent Events
(SRE), it was designed to ascertain the prior life experiences of a group of
patients suffering from respiratory illnesses (Hawkins et al. 1957). The
aim, entirely in line with Meyer and Wolff's approach, was to emphasize
the 'psycho-social' contribution to physical illness. That is, how the
broader patterning of life experience disposes an individual toward
respiratory problems. This is a fairly challenging claim to make in a
biomedical context. The SRE was originally based around Meyer's life
chart technique, but subsequent versions sought to standardize the
procedure in terms of generic 'life changes', which could in turn be
quantified in a purely arbitrary sense to create 'life change units' (LCUs).
It is noteworthy that the original scaling of values was performed by
participants themselves (Rahe 1974), resulting in list of 42 items (or 'life
events') with corresponding values ranging from 17 to 100.

From the early 1960s onwards, the SRE was used in retrospective
studies with US Navy enlisted sailors and former Marine Corps soldiers

discharged on psychiatric grounds. In each case, respondents were asked to complete the SRE, and resulting scores were then correlated against recorded episodes of ill health. During the course of these studies, it appears that the conceptual basis of the instrument changed somewhat. What had initially been a means of making visible the otherwise invisible contribution of wider social and psychological variables to physical ill health, understood in terms of distinct individual life patterns, became instead an objective measure of a set of standardized items, which were evaluated irrespective of any subjective value a given participant might accord to them. Moreover, since the size of the samples increased significantly (around 2500 'subjects' in some studies), the sensitivity to biographical detail which featured in the original Meyer 'life chart' was lost. We might go as far as to cynically observe that the instrument was ideally fitted to its contexts of use as a managerial tool to render visible all aspects of the private lives of enlisted service personnel.

In any case, Holmes and Rahe published a further refinement of the instrument – now called the Social Readjustment Rating Scale (SRRS) – with one additional item, in 1967. It is this version that in one form or another appears in practically every popular text on stress. The SRRS is by no means widely accepted in stress research, however. Numerous critiques of the tool have been published, dealing with issues ranging from the representation of items included (which render the particular life experiences of, for instance, women, the elderly, lower socio-economic status groups, invisible – see Thoits 1983), the possible confounding of 'events' with 'symptoms' (Dohrenwend et al. 1982), and even the very logic of summating LCU scores (Brown and Harris 1978). One well known critique even takes issue with the correlation of LCUs with ill health, pointing to extremely low correlations given the large sample sizes (Rabkin and Struening 1976). Whatever the merits of these critiques, what is certainly the case is that the SRRS departs entirely from the goal of making context visible – it tends instead to render 'life experience' as utterly decontextualized and stripped of all subjective meaning.

Unmaking

If we now restore the relationship of the lists in popular texts to their original sources, a number of peculiarities emerge. First of all, there is no obvious relationship to truth. For more or less obvious reasons, popular texts typically omit reference to any of the critiques of the SRRS. What is regarded within stress research as a somewhat dubious and problematic instrument, which certainly does not deliver on its promise to provide clear and unambiguous evidence of the likelihood of stress-related illness, is treated in these texts as a robust and straightforward means for learning the 'truth' of one's personal distress. You have suffered and you will become ill.

Second, while the SRRS has its roots in a medical tradition which takes 'everyday life' as a conceptual object, and which moreover tries to make this otherwise invisible object a part of 'common sense' medical reasoning, popular uses of the instrument perform precisely the reverse operation. In the Meyerian epistemic configuration, the patient knows more than the doctor about the causes of their illness. The life chart is a device that enables that knowledge to be usefully elicited and clarified. Popular uses of the SRRS, by contrast, imply that the reader knows nothing of particular value about their own life, and require the instrument to authorize their own experience. Crudely put, there is something utterly ridiculous about a procedure which considers that a useful purpose is served by instructing the reader to assign a LCU score of 100 if they have suffered the personal catastrophe of the death of a life partner. One does not need to have this event 'certified' in this way to understand its significance and potentially devastating effect.

Third, inasmuch as popular use of the SRRS can be said to have any theoretical content, then the model of stress constructed is a crude 'economics of energy' (Brown 1999). This model, which can be reduced to the statement that 'life wears you out', has only a very tangential relationship to what has been understood for some time about the complex immunological and psychological interactions which characterize stress (see Weiner 1992 for a good summary). It has rather more to do with a contemporary cultural logic of 'flexibility' in the mobilization of resources, where what counts as a resource is fairly broad ranging (see Martin 1994). That is, the model is best treated as a piece of modern 'management speak' rather than an instance of 'popular science'.

Given all of this, I want to return to my original question: what purpose is served by asking readers to confront their worst fears? Because that is what popular versions of the SRRS amount to – a list of the worst things in the world gathered up all in one place. The object cannot be to construct a relationship to some more powerful truth, since, as we have just seen, there is no such relationship. The checklist will not tell you what you do not already know. In fact, its operation requires that you set aside or discount what you already know in order to arrive at an ill-structured and ultimately unhelpful general equivalence between a set of categories that are so broadly defined as to be rendered entirely without meaning.

No – the object of the checklist is the completion of the checklist.

But what happens when one finishes ticking the boxes and adding the scores? What does one feel after having confronted the worst things in the world? I want to argue that what one feels is 'unmade'. To read the SRRS and calculate one's LCU score is to arrive at the peculiar conclusion that life is, in the end, simply a matter of withstanding the pain of experience. Since the checklist demands that a general equivalence be formed amongst the items, given as the LCU score, any differentiation, any tone, any specificity between experiences is occluded. Each and every item is merely another source of pain. They differ solely in terms of the intensity. All one has to reflect upon is that pain.

Now I am not suggesting any direct comparison between the terrors described by Scarry and the relatively benign experience of idly reading a checklist. But I do want to suggest that they are both instances of the cultural technique of 'unmaking'. This involves the shrinking and narrowing of personal experience into a field of general equivalence. All there is to think about is suffering. Moreover, in displacing the features of ordinary life, in showing that everything can be a source of pain, the ability of the person to find an appropriate language to speak of experience is fundamentally compromised. Ordinary language goes on holiday when confronted with the profoundly dispiriting conclusion that life is just different intensities of suffering. And in its absence, the language of stress can come to seem quite compelling.

The point, then, of these checklists is to construct the conditions where the language of stress appears to be a powerful and natural way of lending meaning to the inevitably meaningless pain of experience. The checklist 'unmakes' the reader by discounting their personal experience, demanding general equivalence, and defeating ordinary language. It thereby creates the epistemic space where the peculiarly hybrid language of popular stress management appears to have some purchase. Who could otherwise believe that such an unusual set of narratives and tropes would have anything to say about their personal life? Well, me, you and anyone else with an LCU score of 320+.

Coda

What do we learn from checklists? Your spouse and your family may die. You may be fired, get divorced, have to leave town. Those arguments with your partner you had? They'll get worse. Your kids will come to hate you. And they'll leave you. Just like everyone else. You won't be able to sleep properly. The sex will go. You can't eat right anymore these days. You might go on holiday, but you can't get away from your same old damn self. You barely notice the seasons changing, and another year is eking itself out until the ritual of disappointment and tension that is Christmas comes around. Everything is a source of stress. And everyone's life is stressful. That stress will make you ill. That stress will, ultimately, kill you. You want to know your future? It's a boot stamping on your face. For ever.

17 Thinking habits and the ordering of life

Elspeth Probyn

A morning in the life of a chapter

Shortly after 7 a.m. the beloved's alarm goes off and she heads for the shower, stopping to put the kettle on. I pry myself from the bed and the cat and make coffee. Half a cup and a cig, sitting outside looking at the blowing jacaranda tree in the distance, serves to flush the night's labours of dream-work away. The day has started. The girlfriend leaves for work with kisses and exhortations to have a good day and drive safely.

Not quite 8 a.m. and the workday has started with a quick perusal of email. There are the usual 50 or so messages that have gathered since the night before. A lot of spam. I wonder at the ingenuity of spammers, who try to entice me to open their documents with messages about 'nice text, good effort'. It sounds like the comments students receive from us, or maybe the spammers got one too many anodyne comment from their university teachers before they turned to a life of piracy on the broadband highway.

I dodge the offers of hardcore porn, admiring the audacity of their headers: 'Anorexics get their protein', says one. Neatly deleted, there's still a heavy load of admin email. 'Read, respond or delete' is my new motto and in the space of 15 minutes I've cleared the inbox – for the moment.

Ah yes, that chapter on ordinary life. Time to get at it. So far I've tried a couple of different angles. The food media, a project I've been working on for three years would seem to offer scope, and in fact it's what I promised the editors whenever it was that I returned their invitation with an abstract, now long forgotten. I tried it out but I am so fed up with food right now that it quickly went nowhere.

At that dead end I then became obsessed in a rather paranoid fashion with the very idea of the ordinary. I fumed to myself, who'd want to be ordinary anyway? Certainly I never have. Flashes from school of being hauled in front of the headmaster and rebuked: 'You'll never be anything but an exhibitionist'. It didn't faze me. Of course I wanted to be extraordinary.

With the passing of time you realize that ordinary is not the equivalent of normal, nor is it indeed necessarily to be opposed to extraordinary. At a certain point of life perhaps one stops always looking and bounding forward to the next glittering event, and begins to appreciate the routines that pace out time. The direction of this chapter has now turned towards an investigation of the habits that mark out life – the ordinary things that give order to the day. Guided by Peirce's understanding of habits, and Bourdieu's ideas about habitus, let's think about the ordinary passing of time, the ordering of our lives.

But back to my morning as I try to write. Email duties done, for the moment at least, I'm sitting on the sofa as the early morning winter's sun streams in. The cat is playing in the corner; probably with one of those giant cockroaches you just have to live with in the southern hemisphere. My attention is supposed to be on an essay by Teresa de Lauretis. Called 'The Violence of Rhetoric', it is a complex argument that weaves from Nietzsche to Foucault, Eco and Pierce to attempt to account for gender. She concludes:

> [Gender] must be understood not as 'biological' difference that lies before or beyond signification, or as a culturally constructed object of masculine desire, but as semiotic difference – a different production of reference and meaning such as, not Derrida and not Foucault, but possibly Peirce's notion of semiosis may allow us to begin to chart.
>
> (1987: 48)

As I'm reading I can feel my brain beginning to work. It's a sort of pleasing irritation. Thought creaks as it once again tries to master reading complex and interesting arguments. Too long it has been fed with marking student papers, filling out the trivia of university memos and forms. I try to rush ahead, to plough through the text, but I keep getting derailed or more precisely slowed by passages. And because of the lack of momentum, other thoughts split off. I think what a smart writer de Lauretis is, and how this book, *Technologies of Gender*, hasn't received its full due. I use the title essay in one of my big introductory undergraduate classes and from years of teaching it, I've dumbed it down in my mind. I become snared on a passage she quotes from Peirce. It's that famous one I must have learned long ago when I was an undergraduate: 'A sign, or a representamen, is something that stands to somebody for something in some respect or capacity' (quoted in de Lauretis 1987: 39). De Lauretis glosses it:

> Thus, as we use signs or produce interpretants, their significant effects must pass through each of us, each body and each

consciousness, before they may produce an effect or an action upon the world. Finally, then, the individual's habit as a semiotic production is both the result and the condition of the social production of meaning.

(1987: 41)

I'm trying to get a handle on this. At some point in my training I must have veered onto the Barthesian track of semiotics. His idea of the mythological workings of signs is a well worn groove in my brain, again from too many students' analyses of advertising – a perennial favourite in undergrad courses on popular culture. But Peirce's habit tantalizes, just out of reach of my comprehension.

The phone rings: it's my colleague with whom I've put in for a big government funded grant on youth obesity. She's a hard social scientist and we've proposed to do a nationwide mapping of youth cultures of eating and obesity in Australia. The Australian Research Council is the government body which funds all social science research, and much like schemes in other countries (SSHRC in Canada, the ESRC in the UK) it is a long and demanding process. We're at a halfway point when the experts give us rejoinders. It's a nervy time because a lot rides on these grants. Increasingly in the cash-starved higher education sector, you're stuffed without them. Besides it took us about six weeks of our short summer break to write the thing. And it's a good project.

Jenny thinks the reports are better than I do. But I like my eggs hardboiled in my hands before I get my hopes up. We divide up the work of responding. She gets to handle the complaints about whether the instruments are validated or not. It's another language, another world. I will tackle the objection that we're too ambitious.

I decide I want to know more about Charles Sanders Peirce, and head to the computer to Google my way through too much information. No one is giving me a succinct explanation of habit but there's lots of interest. Avoiding the philosophical explanations of pragmatism and where and how Peirce fits in with William James and Dewy, I read about his life. It's an old habit that got me kicked out of physics. The details of the lives of the famous were always more intriguing than the mechanics of how their systems worked. 'Hmmn', I mutter as I read that he only had one academic appointment and that was terminated when it was discovered that his wife was a gypsy and that he'd had relations with her before they married. He was an academic brat and I wondered whether that made him ambivalent about fully joining into university life.

I pace around the house trying to get a sense of where I'm going. I look down. The kitchen floor is filthy. We've been trying to find a gay boy cleaner on the principle that you'd have a better than average chance of getting someone who'd actually clean. But to no avail. I mop the floor all the while chasing the notion of semiotic habit around the dusty corners of my mind. The floor looks good, a legacy of having been a commercial cleaner in my youth. I smile, thinking that my gal will notice. We're having a friend over for drinks later and she does like the house to look like two tidy girls inhabit it. Ann wouldn't have minded. She's a writer who appreciates the richness and messiness of ordinary life.[1]

I go back to the couch and the splayed copy of *Technologies of Gender*. The phone again interrupts. It's another colleague with whom I'm involved in trying to nail down a consultancy from the Australian Sports Commission. In Australia, as elsewhere, there's been a rash of athletes behaving badly. From a gender studies point of view it's fascinating. Players from the National Rugby League have recently been caught out having group sex with women. The rape allegations have slid off the front page but the spectacle has remained: big boofy footie players watching each other have sex with the same woman.[2] All those theories of scopophilia and homosociality have found front-page empirical proof. An offshoot has been that institutions that wouldn't have touched gender and cultural studies with a bargepole now want us to change the gendered culture of football. No problem, except they want the proposal by Monday and they only understand quantitative social science. They're sports types who like their statistics.

Catharine and I divvy up the work and agree to meet on the weekend. We will have to drastically cut back on the ethnographic, interview and focus group side of the project that might have had a chance of providing the Sports Commission with some insight. It costs too much and the blokes and gals with the purse don't get it.

By now Peirce seems far away and I turn to another essay in de Lauretis' book. It's a lovely one about the woman Gramsci was in love with. De Lauretis originally wrote about it for a non-academic publication and it's a romp of a read. A sad tale: Guilia ends up incarcerated in a mental institution in the Soviet Union, while her sister administers wifely care to Antonio in prison. De Lauretis reports how a collective of Italian feminists retrieved his love letters – the ones that didn't count as material for the famous *Letters from Prison*. In one, Gramsci writes to his wife:

> How many times have I asked myself whether it was possible to tie oneself to a mast without ever having loved anyone … whether one could love a collectivity if one hadn't deeply loved some single human beings … Wouldn't that have made barren my qualities as a revolutionary, wouldn't that have reduced

them to a pure intellectual fact, a pure mathematical calcula-
tion?

(quoted in de Lauretis 1987: 87)

Yes, Antonio, it would have. As I contemplate how deeply tragic, how
deeply human and sad this is, the mobile rings. It's one of the research
assistants at work and I've forgotten to sign her pay form. A complicated
manoeuvre around the fax – the cartridge is finished – requires several
more phone calls. I suggest she forge my scribbled signature 'just this
once', but eventually we work it out in a legal manner.

Starving, I eat the lunch I always eat since a pharmacist told me how
good Omega 3 is for the immune system. Tuna sandwiches five times a
week may sound dull, but if she is to be believed it'll stave off depression
and colds. I try not to think about what the fishing practices do to the
life of the ocean.

Thinking interruptus

I could go on, but I risk falling into the banal for its own sake. I love my
intellectual and everyday life but it is a constant challenge of multitasking. Rather than consider this an evil to be borne, I want to consider
how these ordinary everyday habits, interruptions and reminders of life
serve thinking. A line from Meaghan Morris's (1988) first book of essays
reverberates – something about feminist cultural criticism being as never-
ending as housework. That sounds fussy and totally unlike Morris's style,
which is incisive to the palpable point of acuteness. Her point is that the
rhythm, pace and spacing of everyday life constitute the stuff with which
we think. They are, of course, deeply gendered. I suppose it is possible,
but I find it hard to imagine one of my senior male colleagues mopping
the floor in the midst of writing a paper. I'm not quite sure why I do,
except it needed to be done and I like the feel of the old-fashioned mop as
I clean the kitchen floor that will be dirty again by the evening.

In much the same way, I feel the need to cook some tough pieces of
veal shin. It takes two ticks to brown them with a bit of flour, cook down
some onions, throw in bay leaves and flambé the whole thing with single
malt – no brandy left. I drown the flames with red wine and cover it. It's
your basic osso bucco except I want to make it into a kind of pie with a
biscuit topping. Later when my girl comes home the place will smell
richly. Even later when I experiment with the topping, I make a fatal
mistake, adding either too much baking powder or baking soda, and it's
a total flop – nearly inedible – which I find rather intriguing. We tried to
eat it and the fire burned brightly. We watched my favourite television

show: *ER*. I've finally got the girlfriend into it, or at least she's been partially captured by the narrative lines that continually weave and unravel. Occasionally I tell her the past of some of the characters – the nurse becoming doctor who has slept with the entire ward, the disabled doctor they turned into a lesbian only to kill off the girlfriend and take their son away. The cruelty of scriptwriters and the viewing pleasure of self-inflicted pain – I can't imagine anything worse than losing a love found later in life.

Thankfully it is only a show, and an hour at that. After the drama, putting the dishes away is calming. I leave my love to the sofa and if it's warm enough I read outside with the stars. Of all my various habits and addictions, reading fiction last thing at night has sustained me for years. It's a bit like television, only better – you can race along the plot or simply stare at the night sky, thinking how fine it all is.

PhD students often ask me with a tinge of despair – how do you manage to write? I tell them that in the past I did so at the expense of a life. How many relationships went down the gurgler because of my intense focus on work? Too many to count. So now I write with life, not despite it.

Habit-thought

So much has been written on embodied thinking. For years the feminist rationale was clear, a simple case of reversal – upending the Cartesian dualism on its head. And it's certainly true that the weight of philosophical history bore down on women, reminding us – as if we needed it – that we are body. But it's kind of funny that embodied thinking is now in vogue. Thinkers, who are men, try to do it, or more often they now talk about how to do it. The attention to the body and the desire to place it within circuits of thought is all over the place: men are trying to find bodies, sometimes their own, across a number of disciplines. They are variously successful in their quests, but the effort often seems extraordinary. The task of achieving an embodied thinking becomes epic, whereas for many women it is merely ordinary.

It is for this reason – the habitual linking of thinking to bodies – that I'm drawn to Peirce. In de Lauretis' framing of one part of Peirce's rather epic enterprise, she explains:

> When Peirce speaks of habit as the result of a process involving emotion, muscular and mental exertion, and some kind of conceptual representation … he is thinking of individual persons as the subject of such process. If the modification of

consciousness, the habit or habit-change, is indeed the meaning effect, the 'real and living' conclusion of each single process of semiosis, then where the 'game of semiosis' ends, time and time again, is ... a person's (subjective) disposition, a readiness (to action), a set of expectations.

(1987: 41)

In this strong definition of habit, we see that 'the individual's habit as a semiotic production is both the result and the condition of social production of meaning'. As is well known, Peirce loved threes. Habit is the third term that is linked relationally to belief, the irritation of doubt and habit. Thinking and habit are inextricably linked. 'As it appeases the irritation of doubt, which is the motive for thinking, thought relaxes, and comes to rest for a moment when belief is reached' (1878: 397–8).[3]

Peirce shakes up our understandings of thinking, and I think he makes it readily part of ordinary life. Doubt, in his sense, is normal and it acts as the grit, which gets thinking going again. But equally, habit is necessary, as is belief. Neither is a reactionary force that would get in the way of thinking. While the wording of his proposition could lead us to think that habit reinforces the status quo, it is better to understand it as equilibrium. So if belief is a habit of the mind, and as Peirce says, it is 'perfectly self-satisfied', it is inevitable that it will 'meet with some surprise that begins its dissolution' (1905: 417). In this equation, doubt is necessary but not comfortable. It is, in Peirce's terms, 'the privation of habit [which] in order to be anything at all, must be a condition of erratic activity that in some way must get superseded by a habit' (1905: 417).

It could be argued that my ordinary habits are not of the same order as Peirce's notion of habit. This would be fair enough if the idea were merely to place as a template a theoretical frame/explanation on top of an empirical phenomenon. But equally that would be a travesty of the spirit of his idea – where would the grit be if theory just served to prove the already existing? As Peirce argued: 'Whatever is truly general refers to the indefinite future ... It is a potentiality; and its mode of being is *esse in futuro*' (1902: 148). Doubt needs to creep in because it is the agent of change, the indicator and the grist for movement and future potential action. In other words, there is doubt as to whether my framing of interrupted thinking can produce other thoughts. There is even doubt about whether my ordinary habits have the same valence and charge that doubt provides in Peirce's model.

Habits in the habitus

Obviously doubt is attractive. It is described in appealing terms. It co-exists with that state Peirce calls 'thought relaxed', and it ensures that thought doesn't wear itself into a groove and become the same-old-same-old. In other words, it is as precious as the grit in an oyster, as annoying as the sand in your sandwich at the beach – which makes you move to the rocks for the next picnic. In more grandiose terms, wasn't it doubt that allowed Foucault (1973) to argue, in the conclusion to *The Order of Things*, that the face of man would be 'erased, like a face drawn in sand at the edge of the sea'? Doubt as the grit that inexorably will cause discursive formations to shift, bringing with them seismic changes in how, and what, we can think.

This discussion of change brings me to Bourdieu's formulation of the habitus.[4] I turn to it now primarily because, while it offers a convincing depiction of the ordering of life, it often seems resistant to any notion of change. To put it another way, habitus can describe and account for the habits of everyday life, but it seems to indicate that they are part of an inevitable future: a future which dead-ends itself. Or as Peirce might put it, with no future there is no thinking. To recall Bourdieu's definition:

> The habitus, a product of history produces individual and collective practices – more history – in accordance with the schemes generated by history . . . [the habitus] ensures the active presence of past experiences, which, deposited in each organism in the form of schemes of perception, thought and action, tend to guarantee the 'correctness' of practices . . . more reliably than all formal rules and explicit norms.
>
> (Bourdieu 1990b: 54)

Our bodies continually speak of their pasts in everyday actions – habits, gestures, manners and small ways of being and inhabiting social space. Habitus delimits how we can move and in which spaces we can move.

An example close to home is the habitus of the academic. In order to become an academic, it helps to have had a family background where education was valued. If early on, reading and being interested in ideas is inculcated, you will be more disposed to the (strange) idea of spending your life with abstractions. In more grounded ways, as you jump the various hoops – good grades, undergraduate to postgraduate – your body learns to focus in certain ways. It becomes used to navigating the spaces of thinking: finding its way around libraries, putting up with hours of concentrating on some arcane passage of text. The habitus tells the body how to speak and move in conferences, lecturing classes, talking to other academics. As the years go by, the habitus incorporates all the rules and the body moves easily in the spaces of academic life – what Bourdieu calls 'the field'. The habitus is the body's second nature – it wears often arbitrary rules like a glove.

There is, I think, something quite poignant about Bourdieu's insistence on how our histories haunt us. Social rules become inscribed in our dispositions: how we see ourselves, and the extent to which we are able to envision alternative outcomes to those histories. This is for me captured by the way the habitus delivers a history that is 'both original and inevitable' (Bourdieu 1990b: 57):

> Emotion ... is a (hallucinatory) 'presenting' of the impending future, which, as bodily reactions identical to those of the real situation bear witness, leads a person to live a still suspended future as already present, or even already past, and therefore necessary and inevitable – 'I'm a dead man'; 'I'm done for'.
>
> (1990b: 292fn)

Here, emotion projects the habitus' tendency to continually frame and adjust between the unlikely (possibility) and the likely (probability). This can be clearly heard in Bourdieu's description of how 'agents "cut their coats according to their cloth" and so to become the accomplices of the processes that tend to make the probable a reality' (1990b: 65). In this rather dour depiction of the workings of the habitus, emotion seems to presage the fact that aspirations are always severely tailored by reality. Either hallucinatory or fatalistic, emotion seems to be the body's way of registering its return to 'the present of the presumed world, the only one it can ever know' (1990b: 65). There are no flights of fancy possible here; emotion acts like the miner's canary, and hope is snuffed out.

This becomes more explicit in Bourdieu's discussion of belief and the body. 'Practical belief', he argues, 'is a state of the body' (1990b: 68). 'Enacted belief [is] instilled by the childhood learning that treats the body as a living memory pad'. This learning ensures that values are 'made body', and instills a 'whole cosmology'. Belief – what he calls 'the almost miraculous encounter between the habitus and the field' – is then crucially linked to emotion's role in animating the body. Emotion and bodily gymnastics are central to the fact that 'it is because agents never know completely what they are doing that what they do has more sense than they know' (1990b: 69). It is the simple act of 'replacing the body in an overall posture which recalls the associated thoughts and feelings'.

Habit and change: other ordinary orderings

From this encapsulated description of key elements in Bourdieu's theory we can see how hard it is to envision change within his articulation of the habitus. As both carrier and signification of the past – structural and individual – habits can only confirm, not initiate. To return to my own habits, they would in this sense be confirmation of everything that has made me. As such they might be slightly interesting. Mopping the floor, going off on tangents, cooking, all the while immersed in pretence of academic work – does this speak of my gender, my class and my general embodied history ill at ease in the field of academe? Well, perhaps. Perhaps it's an indication of how and why some of us feel like frauds within the world of thinking.

Obviously, this is not very satisfying. Beyond my own small example, it seems to forever demarcate between spheres of activity: on the one hand, the reproduction of daily life, in all of its gendered dimensions, on the other, the realm of thought as *'un monde à part'*, to coin Bourdieu's (1987) description of the otherliness of the academic world. The split is not surprising, but it doesn't move us forward; in fact, as it replays the familiar gender dichotomy, it radically disallows for the type of habit-change at the heart of Peirce's thought. Concomitantly, it also disavows other concerns – such as the potential of embodied thinking – which, while not contemporary with Peirce, are not incompatible, as I've indicated following de Lauretis' example.

To substantiate, let's return to *Technologies of Gender*. In the final essay, de Lauretis takes up the difficult question of whether there is a feminist aesthetic. The terms under which it is usually asked have tended to follow a split between the ordinary and the extraordinary, whereby women's artistic efforts are allied with the former. In Sylvia Bovenschen's 1976 tussle with the question, it seems that the ordinary can kill the aesthetic. Listen to this passage, a kind of post-hoc aestheticization of the ordinary – in this case the life of Sylvia Plath:

> The ambivalence once again: on the one hand we see aesthetic activity deformed, atrophied, but on the other we find, even within this restricted scope, socially creative impulses which, however, have no outlet for aesthetic development, no opportunities for growth ... [These activities] remained bound to everyday life, feeble attempts to make this sphere more aesthetically pleasing. But the price for this was narrowmindedness. The object could never leave the realm in which it came into being, it remained tied to the household, it could never break loose and initiate communication.
>
> (quoted in de Lauretis 1987: 129)

Here we have a description which, if we needed it, brings home the ensnared realm of women's lives. It's a world we know. It's a world that can be glimpsed reading older cookbooks, and amidst the frenzy of today's women's magazines. The depictions of the lives of the extraordinary make the articles on decoration and cooking seem so contained, so claustrophobic. How could you possibly freely choose the 'narrowmindedness', the being tied to the household? They are images which make us feel the dead-endedness of the feminine habitus, where there is literally no room for movement of thought, no incentive for thinking.

Within other feminist analyses, it is less a question of normatively deciding for or against the ordinary. Rather the juxtaposition of the ordinary and the aesthetic has given rise to a rethinking of women's cultural practices – as is the case in de Lauretis' essay, 'Rethinking Women's Cinema'. She returns to that extraordinarily loving depiction of a woman's ordinary life, Chantal Ackerman's *Jeanne Dielman*. Touted as one of the best ever made, the 1975 film probably lives better in the memory than it did in the viewing experience. Perhaps I was too young, but at the time the three-hour depiction of the ordinary life of a middle-class, middle-aged Belgian housewife struck me as a didactic exercise in showing everything I wanted to escape. I got the fact that it was one of the first filmic events that occurred in real time. What I didn't get was the profundity of what the film achieved. And it's only now, in considerable hindsight, that I realize how it perfectly portrays the grit which accompanies habit.

De Lauretis describes how narrative suspense 'is produced by the tiny slips in Jeanne's routine, the small forgettings, the hesitations between real-time gestures as common and "insignificant" as peeling the potatoes, washing dishes, or making coffee – and then not drinking it' (1987: 131). Here we have habit graphically depicted in its constant tension with the grit of slips, the forgettings, the tangents off. As de Lauretis argues, this is a pre-aesthetic rendered aesthetic. The stuff of ordinary life is rendered to the status of habit, through – in this case – Ackerman's desire to 'show a woman's gestures so precisely ... because you love them' (Ackerman, in de Lauretis 1987: 132).

De Lauretis begins her essay on 'The Violence of Rhetoric', which I have used as a basis and springboard for my own, with a quest to find an enunciative position that imbricates meaning with experience: 'with the mutually constitutive effects in semiosis of what Peirce called "the outer world" of social reality and the "inner world" of subjectivity' (de Lauretis 1987: 32). I want to end this chapter with a recasting of these terms. If we are to account properly for the creative function of the ordinary, if we are to squarely place it not as an adjunct but as the very stuff with which thought gets kick-started into thinking, we have to emphasize how the inner and the outer continually move through each other. This isn't the same as rendering the ordinary into an aesthetic object, or a homely decoration upon thinking. In the same spirit, if not *à la lettre*, as Peirce's conception of habit, washing the floor, cleaning the kitchen, cooking a meal, thinking a thousand thoughts of the loved one, are not distractions from thinking. They are, as Peirce describes it, moments when thought relaxes. Conducted with as much love as Ackerman accords to her representation of ordinary life, they also contain the grit that releases thought into action – into new thinking. That, at least, has been my wager. Now you try it.

Notes

1. For a very different take on some of the same questions I pursue here, see Game and Metcalf (1996, 2002).
2. 'Boofy' is a wonderful Australian term that captures some of the irony underlying the mythology of the iconic Australian bloke.
3. I have referenced Peirce in the text according to the date the essays were originally published. However, they are referenced in the bibliography according to the volume of the *Collected Papers* in which they were later published. In addition, I have used the online resources of the Commens Peirce Dictionary, www.helsinki.fi/science/commens (accessed 14 July 2004).
4. I am drawing on my argument in Probyn (2005), where I extend this discussion of the habitus, querying its ability to comprehend the physicality of the body – its thoughts, emotions and affects. I want to thanks Mandy Thomas for her reading of this argument and for insisting I think about the possibility of change within Bourdieu's work. As for juxtaposing Peirce and Bourdieu, at least if the Internet is to be believed it appears as a common exam question: for example, 'Compare Bourdieu's habitus and Peirce's habit and discuss'. I have tried not to look at the answers.

Bibliography

Adorno, T. (1974) *Minima Moralia*. London: Verso.

Adorno, T. (1978) On the fetish character in music and the regression in listening, in A. Arato and E. Gebhardt (eds) *The Essential Frankfurt School Reader*. New York: Urizen.

Alderson, C. (1968) *Magazines Teenagers Read*. London: Pergamon Press.

Aldrich, R. (1993) *The Seduction of the Mediterranean: Writing, Art and Homosexual Fantasy*. London: Routledge.

Aldrich, R. (2003) *Colonialism and Homosexuality*. London: Routledge.

Alexander, S. (1985) *Stephanie's Menus for Foodlovers*. Sydney: Methuen Haynes.

Alexander, S. (1988) *Stephanie's Feasts and Stories*. Sydney: Allen & Unwin.

Amazon, L. (n.d.) *Slut Utopia #2*. San Jose, CA: fanzine.

Anderson, J. (1991) Stress and burnout amongst nurses: a social network approach, in P. Perrewé (ed.) *Handbook on Job Stress*. Corte Madera: Select Press.

Andrews, M. and Talbot, M. (eds) (2000) *All the World and Her Husband: Women in Twentieth-century Consumer Culture*. London: Cassell.

Ang, I. (1996) *Living Room Wars: Rethinking Media Audiences in a Postmodern World*. London: Routledge.

Anthony, A. (2004) Watching brief: do you ever get that déjà viewed feeling about primetime television? *Observer Magazine*, 29 February.

Appadurai, A. (1988) How to make a national cuisine: cookbooks in contemporary India, *Comparative Studies in Society and History*, 30(1): 3–24.

Arthurs, J. (2003) *Sex and the City* and consumer culture: remediating postfeminist drama, *Feminist Media Studies*, 3(1): 83–98.

Ashley, B., Hollows, J., Jones, S. and Taylor, B. (2004) *Food and Cultural Studies*. London: Routledge.

Attfield, J. (1999) Bringing modernity home: open-plan in the British domestic interior, in I. Cieraad (ed.) *At Home: an Anthology of Domestic Space*. New York: Syracuse University Press.

Australian Family Circle (2000) *Family Circle Step-by-Step: Modern Australian Food*. Sydney: Murdoch Books.

Australian Women's Weekly (2000) *The Australian Women's Weekly Cookbooks: Modern Multicultural Dining: Easy Australian Style*. Sydney: ACP Publishing.

Backett, K. and Alexander, H. (1991) Talking to young children about health: methods and findings, *Health Education Journal*, 50(1): 34–8.

Bacon, F. (1974) *Of the Advancement of Learning and New Atlantis*. Oxford: Clarendon.

Bagnall, D. (2000) Born to be wired, *The Bulletin*, 15 August.

Bainbridge, J. and Lake, E. (2001) Brand extensions, *Mediaweek*, September 6: www.mediaweek.co.uk/ThisWeek.Features.View.aspx?ContentID=223 (accessed 21 Jan. 2004).

Baker, S. (1997) Interview with editor of *J-17*, April 24.

Ballaster. R., Beetham, M., Frazer, E. and Hebron, S. (1991) *Women's Worlds: Ideology, Femininity and the Woman's Magazine*. Basingstoke: Macmillan.

Bannerman, C. (1998) *Acquired Tastes: Celebrating Australia's Culinary History*. Canberra: National Library of Australia.

Barcan, R. (1998) Hansonism, 'caring' and the lament for modernity, *Meanjin*, 57(4): 748–58.

Barnes, A. and Assisting Committee (1936) *The C.W.A. Cookery Book and Household Hints*. Perth: E.S. Wigg & Son.

Barnes, A. and Assisting Committee (1963) *The C.W.A. Cookery Book and Household Hints*, 21st edn. Perth: E. S. Wigg & Son.

Barthes, R. (1973) *Mythologies*. London: Paladin.

Barthes, R. (1983) *The Fashion System*. New York: Hill & Way.

Baudrillard, J. (1988) The masses: the implosion of the social in the media, in M. Poster (ed.) *Jean Baudrillard: Selected Writings*. Stanford: Stanford University Press.

Bauman, Z. (1983) Industrialism, consumerism and power, *Theory, Culture and Society*, 1(3): 32–43.

Bauman, Z. (1987) *Legislators and Interpreters: On Modernity, Postmodernity and Intellectuals*. Cambridge: Polity Press.

Bauman, Z. (1988) *Freedom*. Milton Keynes: Open University Press.

Bauman Z. (1998) *Work, Consumerism and the New Poor*. Milton Keynes: Open University Press.

BBC News (2002) DIY boom set to continue. http://news.bbc.co.uk/1/hi/business/2265644.stm (accessed 8 Feb. 2005).

Beck, U., Giddens, A. and Lash, S. (1994) *Reflexive Modernization: Politics, Tradition and Aesthetics in the Modern Social Order*. Cambridge: Polity Press.

Beckett, B. (1999) *Australian Food: Recipes for Home Cooking by Leading Chefs and Food Writers*. Sydney: Lansdowne.

Bell, D. (1973) *The Coming of Post-Industrial Society: A Venture in Social Forecasting*. New York: Basic Books.

Bell, D. and Hollows, J. (eds) (forthcoming) *Historicizing Lifestyle:*

Mediating Taste, Consumption and Identity from the 1900s to 1970s. Aldershot: Ashgate.

Benjamin, W. (1978) *Reflections: Essays, Aphorisms, Autobiographical Writings.* New York: Harcourt Brace Jovanovich.

Bennett, T., Emmison, M. and Frow, J. (1999) *Accounting for Tastes: Australian Everyday Cultures.* Melbourne: Cambridge University Press.

Berger, J. (1972) *Ways of Seeing.* Harmondsworth: Penguin.

Berghoff, H. (2002) From privilege to commodity? Modern tourism and the rise of the consumer society, in H. Berghoff, B. Korte, R. Schneider and C. Harvie (eds) *The Making of Tourism: The Cultural History of the British Experience, 1600–2000.* Basingstoke: Palgrave.

Berman, M. (1988) *All That is Solid Melts into Air: The Experience of Modernity.* London: Verso.

Bernstein, B. (1990) *Class, Codes and Control, Volume 4: The Structuring of Pedagogic Discourse.* London: Routledge.

Binkley, S. (2004) Everybody's life is like a spiral: narrating post-Fordism in the lifestyle movement of the 1970s, *Cultural Studies – Critical Methodologies*, 4(1): 71–96.

Boddy, W. (1985) The shining centre of the home: ontologies of television in the 'golden age', in P. Drummond and R. Paterson (eds) *Television in Transition.* London: BFI.

Boddy, W. (2004) *New Media and Popular Imagination.* Oxford: Oxford University Press.

Bonner, F. (1994) Representations of the female cook, in K. Ferres (ed.) *Coastscripts: Gender Representations in the Arts.* Nathan, Queensland: Griffith University.

Bonner, F. (2003) *Ordinary Television.* London: Sage.

Bordwell, D. and Thompson, K. (1993) *Film Art: An Introduction.* New York: McGraw-Hill.

Bourdieu, P. (1984) *Distinction: A Social Critique of the Judgement of Taste.* London: Routledge.

Bourdieu, P. (1987) *Choses Dites.* Paris: Minuit.

Bourdieu, P. (1990a) *Photography: A Middle-brow Art?* Cambridge: Polity Press.

Bourdieu, P. (1990b) *The Logic of Practice.* Cambridge: Polity Press.

Bourdieu, P. and Passeron, J.-C. (1990) *Reproduction in Education, Society and Culture.* London: Sage.

Bowlby, R. (1993) *Shopping with Freud.* London: Routledge.

Brabazon, T. (2000) *Tracking the Jack: A Retracing of the Antipodes.* Sydney: UNSW Press.

Braithwaite, B. (1997) Magazines: the bulging bookstores, in A. Briggs and P. Cobley (eds) *The Media: An Introduction.* Harlow: Longman.

Brech, P. (2000) Debenhams to develop Sugar range, *Marketing*, 13 April.

Brendan (1994) Brendan's free café, *Temp Slave* #4, Madison, WI: fanzine.

Brett, J. (2004) The new liberalism, in R. Manne (ed.) *The Howard Years.* Melbourne: Black.

Brown, G. and Harris, T. (1978) *Social Origins of Depression: A Study of Psychiatric Disorder in Women.* London: Routledge.

Brown, S.D. (1999) Stress as regimen: discourse analysis and self-help literature, in C. Willig (ed.) *Applied Discourse Analysis: Social and Psychological Interventions.* Buckingham: Open University Press.

Bruneteau, J.-P. (1996) *Tukka: Real Australian Food.* Sydney: Angus & Robertson.

Brunsdon, C. (1997) *Screen Tastes: Soap Operas to Satellite Dishes.* London: Routledge.

Brunsdon, C. (2001) Once more on the insignificant, in C. Brunsdon, C. Johnson, R. Moseley and H. Wheatley (2001) Factual entertainment on British television: the Midlands TV Research group's '8–9 Project', *European Journal of Cultural Studies*, 4(1): 53–62.

Brunsdon, C. (2003) Lifestyling Britain: the 8–9 slot on British television, *International Journal of Cultural Studies*, 6(1): 5–23.

Brunsdon, C. (2004) Taste and time on television, *Screen*, 45(2): 115–29.

Brunsdon, C., Johnson, C., Moseley, R. and Wheatley, H. (2001) Factual entertainment on British television: the Midlands TV Research Group's '8–9 Project', *European Journal of Cultural Studies*, 4(1): 29–62.

Bunce, M. (1994) *The Countryside Ideal.* London: Routledge.

Bunce, M. (2003) Reproducing rural idylls, in P. Cloke (ed.) *Country Visions.* Harlow: Pearson.

Burke, A. (2001) *In Fear of Security.* Annandale, NSW: Pluto Press.

Burton, R. (1970) Terminal essay, in B. Reade (ed.) *Sexual Heretics: Male Homosexuality in English Literature from 1850 to 1900.* London: Routledge & Kegan Paul.

Butler, J. (1993) *Bodies that Matter: On the Discursive Limits of 'Sex'.* London: Routledge.

Buzard, J. (1993) *The Beaten Track: European Tourism, Literature, and the Ways to 'Culture'.* Oxford: Clarendon Press.

Byron, C. (2002) *Martha Inc: The Incredible Story of Martha Stewart Living Omnimedia.* New York: Wiley.

Cameron, D. (2000) A self off the shelf? Consuming women's empowerment, in M. Andrews and M. Talbot (eds) *All the World and Her Husband: Women in Twentieth-century Consumer Culture.* London: Cassell.

Campaign (1997) Sugar surges ahead as mature teens fall, 22 August.

Campaign (1999) Teen market in slump, 19 February.

Campbell, C. (1987) *The Romantic Ethic and the Spirit of Modern Consumerism.* Oxford: Blackwell.

Carter, M. (1993) The zine scene, *Cincinnati Enquirer*, 8 April.

Cervantes, S. (1990) *Hardcry . . . A Network Zine* #1, Whittier, CA: fanzine.

Chalker, J. (1969) *The English Georgic*. Baltimore: Johns Hopkins Press.

Chambers, W. and Faggetter, R. (1992) Australian Powerhouse Museum, exhibit review, *Technology and Culture*, 33(3): 548–60.

Chaney, D. (1996) *Lifestyles*. London: Routledge.

Chaney, D. (2001) From ways of life to lifestyle: rethinking culture as ideology and sensibility, in J. Lull (ed.) *Culture in the Communication Age*. London: Routledge.

Chaney, D. (2002a) *Cultural Change and Everyday Life*. Basingstoke: Palgrave.

Chaney, D. (2002b) The power of metaphors in tourist theory, in S. Coleman and M. Crang (eds) *Tourism, Between Place and Performance*. New York: Berghahn Books.

Clark, A. (1987) The girl: a rhetoric of desire, *Cultural Studies*, 1(2): 195–203.

Clarke, A. (2001) The aesthetics of social aspiration, in D. Miller (ed.) *Home Possessions: Material Culture Behind Closed Doors*. Oxford: Berg.

Cloke, P. (2003) Knowing ruralities, in P. Cloke (ed.) *Country Visions*. Harlow: Pearson.

Cobb, S. and Rose, R. (1973) Hypertension, peptic ulcer and diabetes in air traffic controllers, *Journal of the American Medical Association*, 224(4): 489–92.

Cobbett, W. (1996) *The English Gardener*. London: Bloomsbury.

Coleman, J. (1988) Why publish? *Factsheet Five* #27, Rensselaer, NY: fanzine.

Coleman, S. and Crang, M. (2002) Grounded tourists, travelling theory, in S. Coleman and M. Crang (eds) *Tourism, Between Place and Performance*. New York: Berghahn Books.

Cometbus, A. (n.d.) *Cometbus* #31, Berkely, CA: fanzine.

Commonwealth of Australia (2001) *Backing Australia's Ability: An Innovation Action Plan for the Future*. Canberra: Commonwealth of Australia.

Commonwealth of Australia (2004) *Backing Australia's Ability: Building our Future through Science and Innovation*. Canberra: Commonwealth of Australia.

Connor, S. (1989) *Postmodern Culture: An Introduction to Theories of the Contemporary*. Oxford: Blackwell.

Cook, D. (2003) Spatial biographies of children's consumption, *Journal of Consumer Culture*, 3(2): 147–69.

Cook, R. (1997) Teenage media grows up, *Campaign*, 5 September.

Corarso, W. (1997) *The Sociology of Childhood*. London: Pine Forge Press.

Corner, J. (1999) *Critical Ideas in Television Studies*. Oxford: Oxford University Press.

Corner, J. (2002) Performing the real: documentary diversions, *Television and New Media*, 3(3): 255–69.

Corner, J. (2004) Afterword: framing the new, in S. Holmes and D. Jermyn (eds) *Understanding Reality Television*. London: Routledge.

Corones, A. (1987) Multiculinarism and the emergence of gastronomy, in B. Santich and M. Symons (eds) *Proceedings of the Third Symposium of Australian Gastronomy*. Adelaide.

Cossons, N. (1999) *Museums of Modern Science*. Washington: Science History Publications.

Coveney, J. (1996) The government and ethics of nutrition. Unpublished PhD thesis, Murdoch University.

Coward, R. (1984) *Female Desire*. London: Paladin.

Crang, M. (1999) Knowing, tourism and practices of vision, in D. Crouch (ed.) *Leisure/Tourism Geographies: Practices and Geographical Knowledge*. London: Routledge.

Crissell, A. (2002) *An Introductory History of British Broadcasting*. London: Routledge.

Crouch, D. (2002) Surrounded by place: embodied encounters, in S. Coleman and M. Crang (eds) *Tourism, Between Place and Performance*. New York: Berghahn Books.

Csikszentmihalyi, M. (1987) *Human Behavior and the Science Center: Science Learning in the Informal Setting*. Chicago: Chicago Academy of Science.

Cunningham, S. and Jacka, E. (1996) *Australian Television and International Mediascapes*. Cambridge: Cambridge University Press.

Currie, D. (1997) Decoding femininity: advertisements and their teenage readers, *Gender and Society*, 11(4): 454–78.

Daily Telegraph (2004) Nation of media junkies spending £21 billion a year, 12 August.

David, E. (1951) *A Book of Mediterranean Food*. London: McDonald.

De Lauretis, T. (1987) *Technologies of Gender*. Bloomington: Indiana University Press.

Derrida, J. (1977) *Limited Inc*. Evanston, IL: Northwestern University Press.

Dittmar, H. (1992) *The Social Psychology of Material Possessions: To Have is to Be*. Hemel Hempstead: Harvester Wheatsheaf.

Dohrenwend, B., Pearlin, L., Clayton, P., Riley, M., Hamburg, B., Rose, R. and Dohrenwend, B. (1982) Report on stress and life illness, in G. Elliott and C. Eisdorfer (eds) *Stress and Human Health: Analysis and Implications of Research*. New York: Springer.

Don, M. (1997) Cider with the roses, *Observer Life*, 19 October.

Don, M. (1998) Cartoon characters, *Observer Life*, 6 September.

Donovan, M.K. (1955) *Continental Cookery in Australia*. Melbourne: William Heinemann.

Donovan, M.K. (1961) *The Far Eastern Epicure*. Melbourne: William Heinemann.

Dovey, J. (2000) *Freakshow: First Person Media and Factual Television*. London: Pluto.

Du Gay, P. (ed.) (1997) *Production of Culture/Cultures of Production*. London: Sage.

Duke, L. and Kreshel, P. (1998) Negotiating femininity: girls in early adolescence read teen magazines, *Journal of Communication Inquiry*, 22(1): 48–71.

Duncombe, S. (1997) *Notes from Underground: Zines and the Politics of Alternative Culture*. London: Verso.

Dunstan, D. (1976) *Don Dunstan's Cookbook*. Adelaide: Rigby.

Edensor, T. (2001) Performing tourism, staging tourism: (re)producing tourist space and practice, *Tourist Studies*, 1(1): 59–81.

Edwards, T. (2000) *Contradictions of Consumption: Concepts, Practices and Politics in Consumer Society*. Milton Keynes: Open University Press.

Ehrenreich, B. and English, D. (1979) *For Her Own Good: 150 Years of the Experts' Advice to Women*. London: Pluto.

Elias, N. (1994) *The Civilizing Process*. Oxford: Blackwell.

Elle Decoration (2002) Deco opinion, February.

Ellis, J. (2000a) Scheduling: the last creative act in television?, *Media, Culture and Society*, 22(1): 25–38.

Ellis, J. (2000b) *Seeing Things: Television in the Age of Uncertainty*. London: I.B. Tauris.

Entwistle, J. (1997) Power dressing and the fashioning of the career woman, in M. Nava, A. Blake, I. MacRury and B. Richards (eds) *Buy This Book: Studies in Advertising and Consumption*. London: Routledge.

Erikson, E.H. (1968) *Identity, Youth and Crisis*. New York: Norton.

Falk, P. (1994) *The Consuming Body*. London: Sage.

Falk, P. and Campbell, C. (1997) *The Shopping Experience*. London: Sage.

Featherstone, M. (1987) Lifestyle and consumer culture, *Theory, Culture and Society*, 4(1): 55–70.

Featherstone, M. (1991a) *Consumer Culture and Postmodernism*. London: Sage.

Featherstone, M. (1991b) The body in consumer culture, in B. Turner and M. Featherstone (eds) *The Body: Social Process and Cultural Theory*. London: Sage.

Felski, R. (2000) The invention of everyday life, *New Formations*, 39: 15–31.

Ferguson, M. (1983) *Forever Feminine: Women's Magazines and the Cult of Femininity*. London: Heinemann.

Ferrari, M. (ed.) (1996) *Ferrari Guides' Gay Travel A to Z*. Phoenix: Ferrari International.

Fish, R. (2005) Mobile viewers: media producers and the televisual tourist, in D. Crouch, R. Johnson and F. Thompson (eds) *Convergent Cultures: The Media and the Tourist Imagination*. London: Routledge.

Floch, J.-M. (2000) *Visual Identities*. London: Continuum.

Fornäs, J. (1995) *Cultural Theory and Late Modernity*. London: Sage.

Foucault, M. (1973) *The Order of Things: An Archaeology of the Human Sciences*. New York: Vintage.

Foucault, M. (1984) *The History of Sexuality: An Introduction*. Harmondsworth: Penguin.

Foucault, M. (1988) Technologies of the self, in I. Martin, H. Gutman and P. Hutton (eds) *Technologies of the Self: A Seminar with Michel Foucault*. London: Tavistock.

Fragner, B. (2000) Social reality and culinary fiction: the perspective of cookbooks from Iran and Central Asia, in S. Zubaida and R. Tapper (eds) *A Taste of Thyme: Culinary Cultures of the Middle East*. London: I.B. Tauris.

Franklin, A. and Crang, M. (2001) The trouble with tourism and travel theory?, *Tourist Studies*, 1(1): 5–22.

Franklin, B. (1986) *Benjamin Franklin's Autobiography*. New York: Norton.

Friedman, A. (1996) The evolution of science and technology museums, *Informal Science Review*, 17(1): 14–17.

Frith, S. (1981) *Sound Effects*. New York: Pantheon.

Frith, S. (1983) The pleasures of the hearth: the making of BBC light entertainment, in Formations Editorial Collective (eds) *Formations of Pleasure*. London: Routledge.

Fulton, M. (1968) *The Margaret Fulton Cookbook*. Sydney: Paul Hamlyn.

Fulton, M. (1973) *Italian Cookbook*. Sydney: Summit Books.

Furedi, F. (2003) *Therapy Culture*. London: Routledge.

Gallegos, D. and Newman, F. (1999) What about the women? Food, migration and mythology, *M/C: A Journal of Media and Culture*, 2(7): http://www.uq.edu.au/mc/9910/women.html.

Game, A. and Metcalf, A. (1996) *Passionate Sociology*. London: Sage.

Game, A. and Metcalf, A. (2002) *The Mystery of Everyday Life*. Annandale, NSW: Federation Press.

Gascoigne, T. and Metcalfe, J. (2001) Presentation to International Conference on the Public Communication of Science and Technology, Geneva, February. http://www.econnect.com.au/news_papers.htm#whydo (accessed 13 July 2004).

Gauntlett, D. and Hill, A. (1999) *TV Living: Television Culture and Everyday Life*. London: Routledge.

Geechoun, R. (1948) *Cooking the Chinese Way*. Melbourne: W. D. Joynt.

Geraghty, C. (1991) *Women and Soap Opera*. Cambridge: Polity Press.

Gibson, M. (2001) Myths of Oz cultural studies: the Australian beach and

'English' ordinariness, *Continuum: Journal of Media and Cultural Studies*, 15(3): 275–88.

Giddens, A. (1991*) Modernity and Self Identity: Self and Society in the Late Modern Age.* Cambridge: Polity Press.

Giddens, A. (1992) *The Transformation of Intimacy.* Cambridge: Polity Press.

Giles, D. (2002) Keeping the public in their place: audience participation in lifestyle television programming, *Discourse & Society*, 13(5): 603–28.

Gilling, T. (2003) Maestro on the Murray, *Weekend Australian Magazine*, 4 January.

Giroux, H. (1992) *Border Crossings: Cultural Workers and the Politics of Education.* New York: Routledge.

Gorham, M. (1952) *Broadcasting and Television since 1900.* London: Andrew Dakers.

Gough-Yates, A. (2003) *Understanding Women's Magazines: Publishing, Markets and Readerships.* London: Routledge.

Grace, D.J. and Tobin, J. (1997) Carnival in the classroom: elementary students making videos, in J. Tobin (ed.) *Making a Place for Pleasure in Early Childhood Education.* New Haven, CT: Yale University Press.

Gray, J. (1992) *Men are from Mars, Women are from Venus.* London: HarperCollins.

Green, B., Reid, J.A. and Bigum, C. (1998) Teaching the Nintendo generation?: children, computer culture and popular technologies, in S. Howard (ed.) *Wired-Up: Young People and the Electronic Media.* London: UCL Press.

Green, E. Hebron, S. and Woodward, D. (1990) *Women's Leisure, What Leisure?* New York: New York University Press.

Grigoriadis, V. (2005) The return of Martha Stewart, *New York*, 7 February.

Gronow, J. (1997) *The Sociology of Taste.* London: Routledge.

Grossberg, L. (1994) Introduction: bringin' it all back home – pedagogy and cultural studies, in H. Giroux and P. McLaren (eds) *Between Borders: Pedagogy and the Politics of Cultural Studies.* London: Routledge.

Guardian (2004) A helping hand, 31 May. www.mediaguardian/story/0,7558,128058,00.html (accessed 26 June 2004).

Gunew, S. (1993) Introduction, in S. Gunew and A. Yeatman (eds) *Feminism and the Politics of Difference.* Sydney: Allen & Unwin.

Hage, G. (2003) *Against Paranoid Nationalism: Searching for Hope in a Shrinking Society.* Annandale, NSW: Pluto Press.

Haldrup, M. and Larsen, J. (2003) The family gaze, *Tourist Studies*, 3(1): 23–45.

Hall, S. (1986) Popular culture and the state, in T. Bennett, C. Mercer and J. Woollacott (eds) *Popular Culture and Social Relations*. Milton Keynes: Open University Press.

Halligan, M. (1990) *Eat My Words*. Sydney: Collins/Angus & Robertson.

Hannerz, U. (1990) Cosmopolitans and locals in world culture, *Theory, Culture and Society*, 7(3): 237–51.

Harden, J., Scott, S., Backett-Milburn, K. and Jackson, S. (2000) Can't talk, won't talk? Methodological issues in researching children, *Sociological Research Online*, 5(2). http://www.socresonline.org.uk/5/2/harden.html.

Hardyment, C. (1995) *Slice of Life: The British Way of Eating Since 1945*. London: BBC Books.

Harper's Magazine (1994) On quitting, June.

Hartley, J. (1999) *Uses of Television*. London: Routledge.

Hartz, J. and Chappell, R. (1997) *Worlds Apart: How the Distance between Science and Journalism Threatens America's Future*. Nashville: First Amendment Center.

Harvey, D. (1989) *The Condition of Postmodernity*. Oxford: Blackwell.

Havinghurst, R. (1972) *Developmental Tasks and Education*. New York: McKay.

Hawkins, N., Davies, R. and Holmes, T. (1957) Evidence of psychosocial factors in the development of pulmonary tuberculosis, *American Review of Tuberculosis Pulmonary Disorder*, 75: 5.

Hays. C. (2004a) Martha Stewart Living Omnimedia is expanding into the worlds of health, fitness and self-healing, *New York Times*, 12 August.

Hays, C. (2004b) Martha Stewart Living replaces Chief Executive, *New York Times*, 12 November.

Hays, C. (2005) As Stewart does time, company rebounds, *New York Times*, 20 January.

Heaven, P. (2001) *The Social Psychology of Adolescence*. Basingstoke: Palgrave.

Hebdige, D. (1989a) After the masses, in S. Hall and M. Jacques (eds) *New Times: the Changing Face of Politics in the 1990s*. London: Lawrence and Wishart.

Hebdige, D. (1989b) *Hiding in the Light*. London: Routledge.

Heine, P. (2000) The revival of traditional cooking in modern Arab cookbooks, in S. Zubaida and R. Tapper (eds) *A Taste of Thyme: Culinary Cultures of the Middle East*. London: I.B. Tauris.

Hepburn, A. and Brown, S. (2001) Teacher stress and the management of accountability, *Human Relations*, 54(6): 691–715.

Hibbert, C. (1987) *The Grand Tour*. London: Weidenfeld and Nicolson.

Hobfoll, S. (1989) Conservation of resources: a new attempt at conceptualizing stress, *American Psychologist*, 44(3): 513–24.

Holland, P. and Spence, J. (1991) *Family Snaps: The Meanings of Domestic Photography*. London: Virago.

Hollows. J. (2000) *Feminism, Femininity and Popular Culture*. Manchester: Manchester University Press.

Hollows, J. (2003a) Feeling like a domestic goddess: postfeminism and cooking, *European Journal of Cultural Studies*, 6(2): 179–202.

Hollows, J. (2003b) Oliver's twist: leisure, labour and domestic masculinity in *The Naked Chef*, *International Journal of Cultural Studies*, 6(2): 229–48.

Holmes, S. and Jermyn, D. (2004) Introduction: understanding reality TV, in S. Holmes and D. Jermyn (eds) *Understanding Reality Television*. London: Routledge.

Holmes, T. and Rahe, R. (1967) The social readjustment rating scale, *Journal of Psychosomatic Research*, 11(2): 213–18.

Horwell, V. (2004) No worries mate, *Guardian Weekly*, 16 February, *Le Monde Diplomatique* section.

Hughes, P. (2001) When 'risk' is taboo: fun, spectacle and citizenship in science centres, *Open Museum Journal*, 4. http://amol.org.au/omj/volume4/hughes.pdf (accessed 13 July 2004).

Humble, N. (2002) Little swans with luxette and loved boy pudding: changing fashions in cookery books, *Women: A Cultural Review*, 13(3): 322–38.

Ireland, L. (1981) The compiled cookbook as foodways autobiography, in M.O. Jones, B. Giuliano and R. Krell (eds) *Western Folklore: Foodways and Eating Habits: Directions for Research*. California: California Folklore Society.

Jagose, A. (2003) The invention of lifestyle, in F. Martin (ed.) *Interpreting Everyday Culture*. London: Arnold.

James, A. and Prout, A. (1997) *Constructing and Reconstructing Childhood*, 2nd edn. London: Falmer Press.

Jameson, F. (1991) *Postmodernism: or the Cultural Logic of Late Capitalism*. London: Verso.

Jenks, C. (1996) *Childhood*. London: Routledge.

Jobling, P. (1999) *Fashion Spreads*. Oxford: Berg.

Johnson, H. (1992) Payback time, *Sabot Times* #1. Seattle, WA: fanzine.

Johnston-Woods, T. (2002) *Big Bother: Why Did that Reality-TV Show become such a Phenomenon?* Brisbane: University of Queensland Press.

Jupp, J. (1991) *Immigration*. Melbourne: Oxford University Press.

Kant, I. (1790/1952) *The Critique of Judgement*. Oxford: Oxford University Press.

Keffo (1994) *Temp Slave* #4. Madison, WI: fanzine.

Keffo (n.d.) *Welcome to the World of Insurance*. Bethlehem, PA: fanzine.

Kehily, M. (1999) More *Sugar*? Teenage magazines, gender displays and sexual learning, *European Journal of Cultural Studies*, 2(1): 65–89.

Kennedy, R. (2005) Stewart to star in spinoff, *New York Times*, 2 February.

Kenway, J. and Bullen, E. (2001) *Consuming Children: Entertainment, Advertising and Education*. Philadelphia, PA: Open University Press.

Kettle, P. (1999) Childish things, *Guardian*, 9 June.

Kingston, M. (1999) *Off the Rails: The Pauline Hanson Trip*. Sydney: Allen & Unwin.

Kroger, J. (1996) *Identity in Adolescence: The Balance between Self and Other*. London: Routledge.

Lafargue, P. (1989/1883) *The Right to be Lazy*. Chicago: Charles H. Kerr.

Laing, S. (1991) Raymond Williams and the cultural analysis of television, *Media, Culture and Society*, 13(2): 153–69.

Langer, J. (1981) Television's 'personality system', *Media, Culture and Society*, 4(3): 351–65.

Lash, S. (1990) *The Sociology of Post-Modernism*. London: Routledge.

Lash, S. and Urry, J. (1994) *Economies of Signs and Space*. London: Sage.

Leal, O. (1990) Popular taste and erudite repertoire: the place and space of TV in Brazil, *Cultural Studies*, 4(1): 19–29.

Lee, J. (2000) Teenage magazines suffer slide, *Campaign,* 18 February.

Lee, M. (1993) *Consumer Culture Reborn: The Cultural Politics of Consumption*. London: Routledge.

Leicester Mercury (1951) 29 August: 6.

Leiss, W., Kline, S. and Jhally, S. (1986) *Social Communication in Advertising: Persons, Products and Images of Well-being*. London: Methuen.

Leslie, D. and Reimer, S. (2003) Gender, modern design, and home consumption, *Environment and Planning D: Society and Space*, 21(3): 293–316.

Lief, A. (ed.) (1948) *The Commonsense Psychiatry of Dr. Adolf Meyer*. New York: McGraw Hill.

Little, J. (2003) Riding the rural love train: heterosexuality and the rural community, *Sociologia Ruralis*, 43(4): 400–417.

Livingstone, D. (2002) *Young People and New Media*. London: Sage.

Lloyd, C. (1984) *The Well Chosen Garden*. London: HarperCollins.

Low, A. (1985) *The Georgic Revolution*. Princeton, NJ: Princeton University Press.

Lowe, N. (2000) *The Classical Plot and the Invention of Western Narrative*.

Lull, J. (1988) *World Families Watch Television*. London: Sage.

Lumby, C. (2001) Watching them watching us: the trouble with teenage girls, *Continuum: Journal of Media and Cultural Studies*, 15(1): 49–55.

Lumsden, C. (1999) Sugar and spice, *Retail Week,* 25 June.

Lury, C. (1995) *Consumer Culture*. Cambridge: Polity Press.

MacCannell, D. (1976) *The Tourist: A New Theory of the Leisure Class*. New York: Shocken Books.

McCarthy, A. (2001) *Ambient Television: Visual Culture and Public Space*. Durham, NC: Duke University Press.

McCracken, G. (1988) *Culture and Consumption: New Approaches to the Symbolic Character of Consumer Goods and Activities*. Bloomington: Indiana University Press.

Macdonald, M. (1995) *Representing Women: Myths of Femininity in the Popular Media*. London: Arnold.

Macdonald, M. (2003) *Exploring Media Discourse*. London: Arnold.

Macdonald, S. (2004) Exhibitions and the public understanding of science paradox, *Pantaneto Forum*, 13. http://www.pantaneto.co.uk/issue13/macdonald.htm (accessed 13 July 2004).

McGuigan, J. (1998) Cultural populism revisited, in M. Ferguson and P. Golding (eds) *Cultural Studies in Question*. London: Sage.

McGuigan, J. (1999) *Modernity and Postmodern Culture*. Buckingham: Open University Press.

McKay, B. (1997) *Gay Phrase Book*. London: Freedom Editions.

McManus, P. (1992) Topics in museums and science education, *Studies in Science Education*, 20(2): 157–82.

McRobbie, A. (1982) *Jackie*: an ideology of adolescent femininity, in B. Waites, T. Bennett and G. Martin (eds) *Popular Culture: Past and Present*. London: Croom Helm.

McRobbie, A. (1991) *Feminism and Youth Culture*. Basingstoke: Macmillan.

McRobbie, A. (1994) *Postmodernism and Popular Culture*. London: Routledge.

McRobbie, A. (1996) *More!*: new sexualities in girls' and women's magazines, in J. Curran, D. Morley and V. Walkerdine (eds) *Cultural Studies and Communications*. London: Arnold.

Mackay, H. (1997) *Generations: Baby Boomers, their Parents and their Children*. Sydney: Pan Macmillan.

Maclean's (1999) How teens got the power: gen Y has the cash, the cool – and a burgeoning consumer culture: http://www.web4.infotrac.gale-group.com (accessed 1 July 2004).

Madigan, R. and Munro, M. (1996) House beautiful: style and consumption in the home, *Sociology*, 30(1): 41–57.

Malouf, D. (2003) *Made in England: Australia's British Inheritance*. Melbourne: Black.

Mamet, D. (1998) *Three Uses of the Knife: On the Nature and Purpose of Drama*. New York: Columbia University Press.

Marketing (1997) Young women's titles, 1 May.

Marling, K. (1994) *As Seen on TV: The Visual Culture of Everyday Life in the 1950s*. Cambridge, MA: Harvard University Press.

Marr, D. and Wilkinson, M. (2003) *Dark Victory.* Sydney: Allen & Unwin.

Marshall, P. (1997) *Celebrity and Power: Fame in Contemporary Culture.* Minneapolis: University of Minnesota Press.

Martin, B. (1994) Extraordinary homosexuals and the fear of being ordinary, *Differences,* 6(2–3): 100–125.

Marx, K. (1975/1844) Economic and political manuscripts, in *Early Writings.* New York: Vintage.

Medhurst, A. (1999) Day for night, *Sight & Sound,* 9(6): 26–7.

MediaWeek. (2001) The treasures in the attic, 1 March. www.media-week.co.uk (accessed 21 Jan. 2004).

Mennell, S. (1996) *All Manners of Food: Eating and Taste in England and France from the Middle Ages to the Present.* Oxford: Basil Blackwell.

Miles, S. (2000) *Youth Lifestyles in a Changing World.* Buckingham: Open University Press.

Miller, D. (1994) *Material Culture and Mass Consumption,* 2nd edn. Oxford: Blackwell.

Miller, D. (1998) *A Theory of Shopping.* Cambridge: Polity Press.

Miller, T. (1993) *The Well-Tempered Self: Citizenship, Culture and the Postmodern Subject.* Baltimore: Johns Hopkins University Press.

Milner, A. (1999) *Class.* London: Sage.

Mingay, G. (1989) *The Rural Idyll.* London: Routledge.

Mintel (1998) *Essentials Report.* London: Mintel.

Molloy, J. (1991) *Alligator Grundy Captions Wonder* #1, Shingletown, CA: fanzine.

Moloney, T. and Coleman, D. (1952) *Oh, For a French Wife!* Sydney: Shepherd Press.

Moore, S. and Rosenthal, D. (1993) *Sexuality in Adolescence.* London: Routledge.

Moores, S. (2000) *The Media and Everyday Life in Modern Society.* Edinburgh: Edinburgh University Press.

Moran, A. (1998) *Copycat TV: Globalisation, Program Formats and Cultural Identity.* Luton: University of Luton Press.

Morgan, N. and Pritchard, A. (1998) *Tourism Promotion and Power: Creating Images, Stealing Identities.* Chichester: Wiley.

Morley, D. (1995) Television: not so much a visual medium, more a visible object, in C. Jenks (ed.) *Visual Culture.* London: Routledge.

Morris, M. (1988) *The Pirate's Fiancée: Feminism Reading Postmodernism.* London: Verso.

Mort, F. (1988) Boy's own? Masculinity, style and popular culture, in R. Chapman and J. Rutherford (eds) *Male Order: Unwrapping Masculinity.* London: Lawrence and Wishart.

Moseley, R. (2000) Makeover takeover on British television, *Screen,* 41(3): 299–314.

Moseley, R. (2001) 'Real lads do cook . . . but some things are still hard to talk about': the gendering of 8–9, in C. Brunsdon, C. Johnson, R. Moseley and H. Wheatley, Factual entertainment on British television: the Midlands TV Research Group's '8–9 Project', *European Journal of Cultural Studies*, 4(1): 32–40.

Nash, C. (n.d.) Text, *Queer Magnolia* #40, Lansing, MI: fanzine.

Nash, D. (1996) *Anthropology of Tourism*. Oxford: Pergamon.

National Endowment for Science, Technology and the Arts (NESTA) (2004) http://www.nesta.org.uk/index.html (accessed 1 July 2004).

National Magazine Company (2003) Unpublished advertising and marketing plan.

National Multicultural Advisory Council (1997) *Multicultural Australia: The Way Forward: An Issues Paper*. Canberra: Dept Immigration and Multicultural Affairs.

Nava, M. (1992) *Changing Cultures: Feminism, Youth and Consumerism*. London: Sage.

Negus, K. (2002) The work of cultural intermediaries and the enduring distance between production and consumption, *Cultural Studies*, 16(4): 501–15.

Newton, J. (1996) *Wogfood: An Oral History with Recipes*. Sydney: Random House.

Newman, B. and Newman, P. (1987) *Development through Life: A Psychosocial Approach*. Homewood, IL: Dorsey Press.

Nixon, S. (1997) Exhibiting masculinity, in S. Hall (ed.) *Representation: Cultural Representation and Signifying Practices*. London: Sage.

Nixon, S. and Du Gay, P. (2002) Who needs cultural intermediaries? *Cultural Studies*, 16(4): 495–500.

NRS (2003) *National Readership Survey*. London: NRS.

O'Brien, K. (2000) Making science sexy, *7:30 Report*, 1 May.

Ofcom (2004) *The Communication Market 2004*. London: Ofcom.

O'Loughlin, M. (1978) *The Garlands of Repose*. Chicago: Chicago University Press.

O'Neill, H. (2001) The pudding proofer, *Weekend Australian Magazine*, 17–18 November.

O'Regan, M. (2000) Communicating science, *Radio National*, 4 May.

Organization for Economic Co-operation and Development (OECD) (1996) *The Knowledge-based Economy*. Paris: OECD.

Orwell, G. (1949) *Nineteen Eighty-four*. London: Secker & Warburg.

Osgerby, B. (1998) *Youth in Britain since 1945*. Oxford: Blackwell.

Ostermann, A. and Keller-Cohen, D. (1998) Good girls go to heaven, bad girls . . . learn to be good: quizzes in American and Brazilian teenage girls' magazines, *Discourse and Society*, 9(4): 531–58.

O'Sullivan, T. (1991) Television memories and cultures of viewing, 1950–65, in J. Corner (ed.) *Popular Television in Britain*. London: BFI.

Palmer, G. (2004) 'The New You': class and transformation in lifestyle television, in S. Holmes and D. Jermyn (eds) *Understanding Reality Television*. London: Routledge.

Papert, S. (1993) *The Children's Machine: Rethinking School in the Age of the Computer*. New York: Basic Books.

Peirce, C. (1878) How to make our ideas clear, in C. Hartshorne and P. Weiss (eds) *Collected Papers of Charles Sanders Peirce*, vol. 2. Cambridge, MA: Harvard University Press.

Peirce, C. (1902) Minute logic, in C. Hartshorne and P. Weiss (eds) *Collected Papers of Charles Sanders Peirce*, vol. 5. Cambridge, MA: Harvard University Press.

Peirce, C. (1905) What pragmatism is, in C. Hartshorne and P. Weiss (eds) *Collected Papers of Charles Sanders Peirce*, vol. 5. Cambridge, MA: Harvard University Press.

Phillips, M., Fish, R. and Agg, J. (2001) Putting together ruralities: towards a symbolic analysis of rurality in the British mass media, *Journal of Rural Studies*, 17(1): 1–27.

Pillsbury, R. (1998) *No Foreign Food: The American Diet in Time and Place*. Boulder, CO: Westview Press.

Pollack, K. (1988) On the nature of social stress: production of a modern mythology, *Social Science and Medicine*, 26(3): 381–92.

Pont, G., Santich, B. and Wilkins, P. (1988) *Landmarks of Australian Gastronomy: Catalogue of an Exhibition at the Senior Common Room Club, The University of New South Wales October 14–November 9, 1988*. Kensington: University of New South Wales.

Porter, D. (1991) *Haunted Journeys: Desire and Transgression in European Travel Writing*. Princeton, NJ: University of Princeton Press.

Poster, M. (ed.) (1988) *Jean Baudrillard: Selected Writings*. Stanford: Stanford University Press.

Postman, N. (1990) *Amusing Ourselves to Death*. London: Methuen.

Pountain, D. and Robins, D. (2000) *Cool Rules*. London: Reaktion.

PPA (2001) I'm no teenage dirtbag, baby, *Periodical Press Association*, 1 October. www.ppa.co.uk/features/ (accessed 21 Jan. 2004).

Private Eye (1997) Eye TV: Holiday (BBC1), The Real Holiday Show (Channel 4), 31 October.

Probyn, E. (1998) Mc-identities: food and the familial citizen, *Theory, Culture and Society*, 15(2): 155–73.

Probyn, E. (2000) *Carnal Appetites*. London: Routledge.

Probyn, E. (2005) *Blush: Faces of Shame*. Minneapolis: University of Minnesota Press.

Prout, A. (2000) Children's participation: control and self-realization in British late modernity, *Children and Society*, 14(4): 304–15.

Puar, J. (2002) Circuits of queer mobility: tourism, travel, and globalization, *GLQ*, 8(1–2): 101–37.

Quart, A. (2003) *Branded: The Buying and Selling of Teenagers*. London: Random House.

Rabinow, P. (ed.) (1991) *The Foucault Reader*. London: Penguin.

Rabkin, J. and Streuning, E. (1976) Life events, stress and illness, *Science*, 194: 1013–20.

Radner, H. (1989) 'This time's for me': making up and feminine practice, *Cultural Studies*, 3(3): 301–22.

Radner, H. (1995) *Shopping Around: Feminist Culture and the Pursuit of Pleasure*. London: Routledge.

Rahe, R. (1974) Life changes and subsequent illness reports, in E. Gunderson and R. Rahe (eds) *Life Stress and Illness*. Springfield, IL: Charles C. Thomas.

Rauch, R. et al. (eds) (1997) *Spartacus International Gay Guide*. Berlin: Bruno Gmünder.

Raymond, L. (1999) Our food culture, *Outrage*, 194: 29–33.

Ripe, C. (1993/1996) *Goodbye Culinary Cringe*. St Leonards, NSW: Allen & Unwin.

Ritchie, R. (2002a) News review, *Sydney Morning Herald*, 11 February.

Ritchie, R. (2002b) Hot woks aside, it's cooking sans zing, *Sydney Morning Herald*, 11 February.

Robb, G. (2003) *Strangers: Homosexual Love in the Nineteenth Century*. London: Picador.

Robb, S., Bullen, E. and Kenway, J. (2003) So young and enterprising: the knowledge economy in Australian schools, in A. Reid and P. Thomson (eds) *Rethinking Public Education: A Conversation*. Queensland: Redress Press and Australian Curriculum Studies Association.

Robins, J. and Robins, I. (1994) *Wild Lime: Cooking from the Bush Food Garden*. Sydney: Allen & Unwin.

Robinson, N. (2003) Behind the scenes at a TV makeover, *Guardian Weekend* magazine, 8 November.

Rojek, C. (1995) *Decentring Leisure: Rethinking Leisure Theory*. London: Sage.

Rojek, C. (2000) *Leisure and Culture*. London: Macmillan.

Rojek, C. (2001) *Celebrity*. London: Reaktion Books.

Rorty, R. (1989) *Contingency, Irony and Solidarity*. Cambridge: Cambridge University Press.

Rose, N. (1999) *Governing the Soul: The Shaping of the Private Self*, 2nd edn. London: Free Association Books.

Ross, J. (1995) *A Taste of Australia*. Melbourne: Five Mile Press.

Rushbrook, D. (2002) Cities, queer space, and the cosmopolitan tourist, *GLQ*, 8(1–2): 183–206.

Russell, R. and Tyler, M. (2002) Thank heaven for little girls: 'Girl Heaven' and the commercial context of feminine childhood, *Sociology*, 36(3): 619–37.

Sabot Times (1992) *Sabot Times* #1. Seattle, WA: fanzine.

Santich, B. (1996) *Looking for Flavour*. Adelaide: Wakefield Press.

Saunders, A. (2004) Pretentious, moi? *Sydney Morning Herald*, 17 July.

Savage, M., Barlow, J., Dickens, P. and Fielding, T. (1992) *Property, Bureaucracy and Culture: Middle-class Formation in Contemporary Britain*. London: Routledge.

Savage, M., Bagnall, G. and Longhurst, B. (2001) Ordinary, ambivalent and defensive: class identities in the Northwest of England, *Sociology*, 35(4): 875–92.

Scannell, P. (1996) *Radio, Television and Modern Life*. Oxford: Blackwell.

Scarry, E. (1985) *The Body in Pain: The Making and Unmaking of the World*. Oxford: Oxford University Press.

Schneiderman, I. (2000) Echo boomers: staggering spending power, *WWD*, 3 February. http://web4.infotrac.galegroup.com (accessed 13 July 2004).

Sefton-Green, J. (ed.) (1998) *Digital Diversions: Youth Culture in the Age of Multimedia*. London: UCL Press.

Shaw, N. (2003) Cloning scapegoats: Martha Stewart does insider trading, *Social Text*, 21(4): 51–67.

Shields, R. (1991) *Places on the Margin*. London: Routledge.

Shilling, C. (1997) The body and difference, in K. Woodward (ed.) *Identity and Difference*. London: Sage.

Silvey, R. (1974) *Who's Listening? The Story of BBC Audience Research*. London. Allen & Unwin.

Sinclair, E. (1970) *The Australian Women's Weekly Cookbook*. Sydney: Golden Press.

Skeggs, B. (1997) *Formations of Class and Gender*. London: Sage.

Skeggs, B. (2004) *Class, Self, Culture*. London: Routledge.

Slater, D. (1997) *Consumer Culture and Modernity*. Cambridge: Polity Press.

Smith, D. (1988) *The Everyday World as Problematic*. Milton Keynes: Open University Press.

Smith, G. and Wilson, P. (2004) Country cookin' and cross dressin': television, Southern white masculinities, and hierarchies of cultural taste, *Television and New Media*, 5(3): 175–95.

Smith, R. (2000) Order and disorder: the contradictions of childhood, *Children and Society*, 14(1): 3–10.

Solomon, C. (1973) *Chinese Cookbook*. Sydney: Paul Hamlyn.

Solomon, J. (1996) School science and the future of scientific culture, *Public Understanding of Science*, 5(2): 157–65.

South Australian Science and Technology Centre (2001) *A New Science and Technology Centre for South Australia: A Chance to Build the Future*, Press Release, January.

Sparke, P. (1995) *As Long as it's Pink: the Sexual Politics of Taste*. London: HarperCollins.

Spigel, L. (1992) *Make Room for TV: Television and the Family Ideal in Postwar America*. Chicago: University of Chicago Press.

Spigel, L. (2001) *Welcome to the Dreamhouse: Popular Media and Postwar Suburbs*. Durham, NC: Duke University Press.

Steele, J. and Brown, D. (1995) Adolescent room culture: studying media in the context of everyday life, *Journal of Youth and Adolescence*, 24(5): 551–76.

Stewart, M. (1982) *Entertaining*. New York: Clarkson N. Potter.

Stewart, M. (1998/9) A letter from Martha, *Martha Stewart Living*, December/January.

Stewart, M. (1999) A letter from Martha, *Martha Stewart Living*, June.

Stewart, S. (1993) *On Longing*. Durham, NC: Duke University Press.

Strange, N. (1998) Perform, educate, entertain: ingredients of the cooking programme genre, in C. Geraghty and D. Lusted (eds) *The Television Studies Book*. London: Arnold.

Stratton, J. (1998) *Race Daze: Australia in Identity Crisis*. Sydney: Pluto.

SubGenius Foundation (1981) *Subgenius Pamphlet #1*, Dallas, Texas: fanzine.

SubGenius Foundation (1987) *The Book of the SubGenius*. New York: Simon & Schuster.

Sugar (1997) *Media Information*. London: *Sugar*.

Symons, M. (1982) *One Continuous Picnic: a History of Eating in Australia*. Adelaide: Duck Press.

Talbot, M. (1992) The construction of gender in a teenage magazine, in N. Fairclough (ed.) *Critical Language Awareness*. London: Longman.

Taylor, B. (1987) *Modernism, Postmodernism, Realism: A Critical Perspective for Art*. Winchester: Winchester School of Art Press.

Taylor, E. (1989) *Prime Time Families: Television Culture in Post-war America*. Berkeley, CA: University of California Press.

Taylor, L. (2002) From ways of life to lifestyle: the 'ordinari-ization' of British gardening lifestyle television, *European Journal of Communication*, 17(4): 479–93.

Teenage Magazines Arbitration Panel (TMAP) (1996) *Guidelines on Sexual Content of Teenage Girls' Magazines*. London: Periodical Press Association.

Tesh, S. (1984) The politics of stress: the case of air traffic control, *International Journal of Health Services*, 14(4): 569–87.

Theatre of Science (2004) http://www.simonsingh.net/Theatre_of_Science.html. (accessed 1 July 2004).

Theophanous, A. (1995) *Understanding Multiculturalism and Australian Identity*. Melbourne: Elikia Books.

Thoits, P. (1983) Dimensions of life events that influence psychological distress: an evaluation and synthesis of the literature, in H. Kaplan (ed.) *Psychosocial Stress: Trends in Theory and Research*. London: Academic Press.

Thomson, A. (2004) Reality television ... Get me out of here, *Daily Telegraph*, 6 August.

Thornton, S. (1995) *Club Cultures: Music, Media and Subcultural Capital*. Cambridge: Polity Press.

Tinkler, P. (1995) *Constructing Girlhood: Popular Magazines for Girls Growing Up in England*. London: Taylor & Francis.

Townsend, H. (1988) *Serving the Country: The History of the Country Women's Association of New South Wales*. Sydney: Doubleday.

Triple J (2004) http://www.triplej.abc.net.au (accessed 13 July 2004).

Tufte, T. (2000) *Living with the Rubbish Queen: Telenovelas, Culture and Modernity in Brazil*. Luton: University of Luton Press.

Turner, B. and Featherstone, M. (eds) (1991) *The Body: Social Process and Cultural Theory*. London: Sage.

Turner, G. (1994) *Making it National: Nationalism and Australian Popular Culture*. Sydney: Allen & Unwin.

Turner, V. (1973) The center out there: pilgrim's goal, *History of Religions*, 12(2): 191–230.

Urry, J. (1990) *The Tourist Gaze*. London: Sage.

Usherwood, B. (1997) Trans-national publishing: the case of *Elle Decoration*, in M. Nava, A. Blake, I. MacRury and B. Richards (eds) *Buy This Book: Studies in Advertising and Consumption*. London: Routledge.

Van Gelder, L. and Brandt, P. (1992) *Are You Two ... Together? A Gay and Lesbian Guide to Europe*. London: Virago.

Villa, D. (1996) *Arendt and Heidegger: The Fate of the Political*. Princeton: Princeton University Press.

Virgil (1986) *Georgics*, trans. H.R. Fairclough. Cambridge, MA: Harvard University Press.

Walker, G. (2002) Seriously funny, *New Scientist*, 176(2365): 56–9.

Walton, J. (1992) *Fish and Chips and the British Working Class, 1870–1940*. Leicester: Leicester University Press.

Walton, R. (2000) Heidegger in the hands-on science and technology center: philosophical reflections on learning in informal settings, *Journal of Technology Education*, 12(1): 49–59.

Warde, A. (1997) *Consumption, Food and Taste: Culinary Antimonies and Commodity Culture*. London: Sage.

Warde, A. (2002) Setting the scene: changing conceptions of consumption, in S. Miles, A. Anderson and K. Meethan (eds) *The Changing Consumer: Markets and Meanings*. London: Routledge.

Warde, A. and Martens, L. (1998) A sociological approach to food choice: the case of eating out, in A. Murcott (ed.) *The Nation's Diet: The Social Science of Food Choice*. Harlow: Longman.

Weber, M. (1985) *The Protestant Ethic and the Spirit of Modern Capitalism*. London: Counterpoint.

Weiner, H. (1992) *Perturbing the Organism: The Biology of Stressful Experience*. Chicago: University of Chicago Press.

Wellings, K. (1996) *The Role of Teenage Magazines in the Sexual Health of Young People*. Department of Public Health and Policy, London School of Health and Tropical Medicine for Teenage Magazine Arbitration Panel. London: Periodical Press Association.

Welsch, W. (1996) Aestheticization processes: phenomena, distinctions and prospects, *Theory, Culture and Society*, 13(1): 1–24.

Werham, F. (1973) *The World of Fanzines*. Illinois: Southern Illinois Press.

Wilkinson, A. (1998) Magazine spin-offs proceed cautiously, *Marketing Week*, 15 October.

Williams, R. (1974) *Television: Technology and Cultural Form*. London: Fontana.

Williams, R. (1980) *Problems in Materialism and Culture*. London: Verso.

Williams, R. (1983) *Keywords*. London: Fontana.

Willis, P. (1978a) *Profane Culture*. London: Routledge & Kegan Paul.

Willis, P. (1978b) *Symbolism and Practice: A Theory for the Social Meaning of Pop Music*. Birmingham: University of Birmingham Centre for Contemporary Cultural Studies stencilled paper 13.

Wilson, J. (1991) *The Olecatronical Scatologica Chronicle*. Tucson, AZ: fanzine.

Winship, J. (1987) *Inside Women's Magazines*. London: Pandora Press.

Winship, J. (2000) New disciplines for women and the rise of the chain store in the 1930s, in M. Andrews and M. Talbot (eds) *All the World and Her Husband: Women in Twentieth-century Consumer Culture*. London: Cassell.

Winship, J. (2000) Women outdoors: advertising, controversy and disputing feminism in the 1990s, *International Journal of Cultural Studies*, 5(2): 131–56.

Wolff, H., Wolf, S. and Hare, C. (eds) (1950) *Life Stress and Bodily Disease*. Baltimore: Williams & Wilkins.

Wolff, J. (2000) The feminine in modern art: Benjamin, Simmel and the gender of modernity, *Theory, Culture and Society*, 17(1): 33–53.

Woods, G. (1995) Fantasy islands: popular topographies of marooned masculinity, in D. Bell and G. Valentine (eds) *Mapping Desire: Geographies of Sexualities*. London: Routledge.

Woodward, I. (2003) Divergent narratives in the imagining of the home amongst middle-class consumers: aesthetics, comfort and the symbolic boundaries of self and home, *Journal of Sociology*, 39(4): 391–412.

Young, A. (1980) The discourse on stress and the reproduction of conventional knowledge, *Social Science and Medicine*, 148(1): 133–46.

Young, I. (1990) *Throwing Like a Girl and Other Essays*. Bloomington: Indiana University Press.

Z, M. (1993) *The Reality Manifesto: A Look at Pseudo-life in the Post-modern Age*. Baltimore: Apathy Poets Press.

Index

ITV CULTURES
Independent Television Over Fifty Years

Catherine Johnson and Rob Turnock (eds).

"This exciting book goes to the heart of a creative commercial and public service culture – it shows why ITV matters and how it was made to work so well. A tremendous contribution."

Professor Jean Seaton, University of Westminster

"This is a valuable addition to studies of ITV's history and programming..."

Tom O'Malley, Professor of Media Studies, University of Wales, Aberyswyth, and Co-Editor of *Media History*.

Since breaking the BBC's monopoly in 1955, ITV has been at the centre of the British television landscape. To coincide with the fiftieth anniversary of the first ITV broadcast, this accessible book offers a range of perspectives on the complex and multifaceted history of Britain's first commercial broadcaster.

The book explores key tensions and conflicts which have influenced the ITV service. Chapters focus on particular institutions, including London Weekend Television and ITN, and programme forms, including *Who Wants to be a Millionaire?, Upstairs Downstairs* and *Trisha*. The contributors show that ITV has had to tread an uneasy line between public service and commercial imperatives, between a pluralistic regional structure and a national network, and between popular appeal and quality programming. A timeline of key events in the history of ITV is also included.

ITV Cultures provides a timely intervention in debates on broadcasting and cultural history for academics and researchers, and a lively introduction to the history of ITV for students and general readers.

Contents
*Introduction: Approaching the Histories of ITV – **Part 1: Histories** – From Start-up to Consolidation: Institutions, Regions and Regulation over the History of ITV-Importance, Significance, Cost and Value: Is an ITV Canon Possible? – And the rest is history: Lew Grade, creation narratives and television historiography – **Part 2: Institutions** – Transatlantic Ventures and Robin Hood – Mammon's Television? ITV in Wales, 1959-63 – LWT in the 1980s: Programmes, Public Service Obligations, Financial Incentives – From Newsreels to a Theatre of News: The Growth and Development of Independent Television News – **Part 3: Texts and Intertexts** – Rooms within Rooms: Upstairs Downstairs and the Studio Costume Drama of the 1970s – Real People with Real Problems? Public Service Broadcasting, Commercialism and Who Wants To Be A Fan of Who Wants To Be A Millionaire? Scholarly Television Criticism, 'Popular Aesthetics' and Academic Tastes – Conclusions: ITV a Hybrid Subject – Historical Timeline: The ITV Companies and the Broadcasting Acts*

Contributors
Rod Allen, Jonathan Bignell, John Ellis, Jackie Harrison, Catherine Johnson, Jamie Medhurst, Matt Hills, Steve Neale, Rob Turnock, Helen Wheatley, Sherryl Wilson

256pp   0 335 21727 X (Paperback)   0 335 21730 3 (Hardback)